wines of the PACIFIC NORTHWEST

wines of the PACIFIC NORTHWEST

a contemporary guide to the wines of Washington & Oregon

LISA SHARA HALL

MITCHELL BEAZLEY

Wine of the Pacific Northwest

by Lisa Shara Hall

First published in Great Britain in 2001 by Mitchell Beazley, an imprint
of Octopus Publishing Group Limited, 2–4 Heron Quays, London E14 4JP.

Copyright © Octopus Publishing Group Limited 2001

Text copyright © Lisa Shara Hall 2001

ISBN 1 84000 419 3

A CIP catalogue record for this book is available from the British Library.

Commissioning Editor **Rebecca Spry**
Executive Art Editor **Philip Ormerod**
Managing Editor **Jamie Grafton**
Design **Colin Goody**
Editor **Caroline Brooke**
Special Photography **Rueben Paris**
Cartography **Kenny Grant, Colin Goody**
Picture Research **Guilia Hetherington**
Production **Catherine Lay, Alex Wiltshire**
Index **Ann Barrett**

Typeset in Lino Letter and Helvetica Neue
Printed and bound by Toppan Printing Company in China

Contents

Foreword

Over the past fifteen years I've been able to follow many of the rising stars of the Pacific Northwest wine community. There are quite a few and one of my favourites is Lisa Shara Hall, who has been an advisor, tour guide, and hostess during my visits to the region.

I have great respect for the producers in the Northwest and I certainly can identify with their efforts. This book – written by an authority with international credentials – should take its place with the definitive volumes on the world's great wine regions.

We in California and around the wine world can learn much from Oregon's work with Pinot Noir and strong quality-value relationships

In my dozen or more visits to Oregon and Washington over the past decade I can see the focus on quality in both states and the sense of terroir in all the viticultural areas. While the players in the area are mostly small, personal wineries who have to fight for recognition in the world of wine, I feel that their efforts, like mine a generation ago, will achieve success. This should happen sooner rather than later as the wine consumer seeks new achievements, and media coverage like this book can point the way.

We in California and around the wine world can learn much from Oregon's work with Pinot Noir and strong quality-value relationships throughout the region. We at Robert Mondavi Winery may want to play a role in the area some day, as we are now doing in Italy, France, Chile, and throughout California.

When I began the Robert Mondavi Winery in 1966, I knew we had the soils, the climate, and the grape varieties to make wines that would certainly rank with the best wines in the world. Few people agreed, but we were committed to excellence and in a relatively short time began to get the recognition that we deserved. Because we were the first winery to do serious research in fine winemaking, we had great opportunities.

Some years ago I realized that all the fine wine regions could copy our format, and many have done so – some with our cooperation. Now we see this in the Northwest, as the pioneering efforts are a generation old and there are quite a few world-class wineries.

Through Lisa Shara Hall's book you will meet all of the players and get a sense of the exciting, "fermenting" times in the region. She has done a great job of research, analysis and forecasting – a breakthrough job in an important and emerging wine community.

Robert Mondavi, Napa Valley, 2001

The beauty of Oregon lies in the vineyards. Most wineries – such as Rex Hill, shown here – favour function over form.

Introduction

The wine industry of the Pacific Northwest and I have matured together.

I arrived in Oregon at about the same time as the pioneers of Oregon's then-nascent wine industry. I came to Portland as a college student, to learn, to sharpen my intellect, and to grow up. It took me a while to realize that I had settled in the land of good and plenty. And it took me even longer to develop an interest in wine and make it my passion and life's work.

I came to wine the way most people do, I think. I started my interest because of a friend's. I didn't grow up with wine, and it wasn't until my twenties that I started my pursuit of the grape. Classically, Bordeaux was my first lesson. When I could no longer afford those wines, I began a (still-continuing) gustatory exploration of other – mostly European – wine regions. I read. I tasted. I read more.

I came to writing a little differently. Food was my *entrée*. I have always been obsessed with delicious things to eat and I developed into a very fine cook by my teens. My family often dined in restaurants; my challenge was to recreate restaurant meals at home. I was successful more often than not. I worked my way through college, cooking. I catered. Then as now, I relax by cooking. I have always entertained.

About twenty-five years ago, I developed a friendship with a local food critic that would change my world. Through her, I began to write about food and restaurants for a local weekly paper. When she became an editor at Oregon's only statewide daily newspaper, I followed her there.

For ten years, I wrote about restaurants for *The Oregonian*. I co-authored a book on food in Oregon. And gradually, an amazing transition occurred: my growing fascination

with wine began to eclipse my prior focus on food.

By the late 1980s, I started to look around me, and pay attention to local wine. I realized how lucky I was to have a working "laboratory" within an hour from home, a growing industry on my doorstep. I was hungry to learn then (and I still am). I visited wineries and started to develop friendships with winemakers. I asked questions – constantly. I watched. I tasted. And wine became my passion.

More and more, I wrote about wine. And more and more, I wrote about the wines and people I had gotten to know in Oregon and Washington. By the mid-1990s, it dawned on me that no one had stepped up to specialize in the wines of the Northwest. No one wine writer paid much attention to the region. An occasional story would appear in print, but no one person had carved a niche writing about the Pacific Northwest.

Why not? Perhaps the wines weren't as universally wonderful as in other regions. Most of the wine writers who lived in the area seemed to be more interested in the proven European or California wines. Rightly so for them, as California, then as now, produced more wine than any other region of the United States. And European wines were of course the original models for all things vinous anyway.

For me, the silence presented a wonderful void to fill.

I love where I live and work. I choose to be here. I travel often, but always take pleasure in coming home to the Pacific Northwest. Its beauty, ruggedness, and charm still fascinate me. The native foods still tempt me. And the wines keep getting better and better.

I have a pride that I hope this book demonstrates. Oregon and Washington wines have been neglected too long.

Oregon

Oregon history

Oregon's wine history dates back to the early settlement of the state in the mid-nineteenth century. Accounts of grape growing activity in Oregon coincide with early winemaking in California, each following their annexation to the United States. However, grape growing in California dates back even earlier to 1779 when Franciscan missionaries planted the very first vines.

Henderson Luelling, a noted horticulturist who had crossed the Oregon Trail from the East, had planted grapes in the Willamette Valley by 1847. He and his son-in-law, William Meek, allegedly won a medal at the California State Fair in 1859 for a wine made from the Isabella grape, a Labrusca X vinifera – an American hybrid thought to have been developed in South Carolina in 1816.

By the 1850s, Peter Britt – now a well-known name in Oregon associated with a popular music festival which is held annually on the property of his former home in Jacksonville – is known to have grown wine grapes at his Valley View Vineyard. This was located in what is now the new Applegate Valley appellation of the Rogue Valley. The modern-day Valley View Winery was restored by the Wisnovsky family; they replanted grapes in 1972 and made their first wine in 1976.

A census of 1860 reveals the statistic that Oregon's wine production was some 11,800 litres (2,600 gallons), but certainly not all of it was *Vitis vinifera*.

By the 1880s, two German immigrants, brothers Edward and John Von Pessls, came north from California to plant Zinfandel, Riesling, and Sauvignon in southern Oregon. However, it is not known whether the Sauvignon was Cabernet or Blanc. Another German immigrant, Adam Doerner, visited his friends the Von Pessls in the 1890s. He obtained Riesling and Sauvignon (once again, no specification) from the Beringer Brothers in Napa and returned to the Umpqua region of southern Oregon to make wine.

Further north, in the Willamette Valley, Ernest Reuter had built a reputation by the 1880s for his Klevner wines; Reuter is purported to have won a gold medal at the St Louis World's Fair of 1904. (Klevner is a

Working ferries (such as this one near the Eola Hills) still cross the Willamette River, the waterway that defines the Willamette Valley.

12

OREGON

modern Alsatian or German term for Pinot Blanc, but has referred to various varieties, including Chardonnay.) Reuter's grapes were planted on Wine Hill, also known as David Hill, west of Forest Grove in Washington County, at the present site of the David Hill Winery.

The wine industry in Oregon fizzled out by 1919 due to the success of the Temperance Movement and the resultant Prohibition. It was also unable to compete with the growing California industry (with its larger scale and a climate that ripened grapes more easily).

Fruit wines dominated production in a post-Prohibition Oregon; "Farmer's Wineries" could be licensed by the late 1930s, and by 1938, there were twenty-eight bonded wineries, primarily producing fruit wines based on berries, Concord grapes, and other American hybrids. (Honeywood Winery near Salem, which has been in continuous operation since 1934, now produces both fruit- and vinifera-based wines.) There were only two notable vinifera-based exceptions from the 1930s: Louis Herbold – who had grown grapes in Europe and who had the first winery bonded in 1934 –cultivated sixty-five varieties of grape, and Adam Doerner's son, Adolph, who made a basic red wine that was sold only locally. His son Ray kept the winery going until 1965.

Oregon's modern era dates from 1961, when Richard Sommer established HillCrest Vineyard near Roseburg, in what is now the southern, Umpqua appellation. Sommer planted primarily Riesling, plus small amounts of Gewürztraminer, Pinot Noir, Chardonnay, and Cabernet Sauvignon. Like most of Oregon's first wine producers and winemakers, he was a refugee from the University of California at Davis, looking to find cooler viticultural sites. And like the other expatriates from Davis, he had been firmly advised that *Vitis vinifera* grapes could not be grown successfully in Oregon.

In 1965, Charles Coury left California for Oregon to plant a wide range of Alsatian varieties – including Pinot Noir – on the exact site on Wine Hill in Washington County as the nineteenth-century Ernest Reuter. Some of Coury's plant material was brought back to Oregon in his suitcase after he had spent a year in Colmar, Alsace at INRA (National Institute for Agronomic Research).

The **Pinot Noir era** dates from 1965. David Lett, of the Eyrie Vineyard, first rooted Pinot Noir cuttings near Corvallis, while researching a permanent vineyard site.

In 1966, he replanted them in the north end of the Willamette Valley in the Dundee hills – now the epicentre of Oregon's wine industry – convinced that Burgundian varieties could be grown better in Oregon than in California.

He approached the decision of what to plant by spending time in Europe studying what grew well, where, and by applying the priciples of a ripening date classification system first developed in 1888 in France by V. Pulliat. David Lett believed that Pulliat's Period I grapes – in particular Pinot Noir, Pinot Gris, Pinot Meunier, Muscat Ottonel, true Pinot Blanc, and Chardonnay – had the best chance of success in the climate of Western Oregon. This view of ripening contrasted with Amerine and Winkler's heat summation study and degree-days theory, a system as widely accepted in California then as now.

Lett focused on Period I varieties, but now allows that Riesling – which is a Period II grape – can also be viable because its flavours develop early and the grape can be picked slightly underripe, as is the practice at times in Germany. From the cuttings he brought up from Davis, Lett planted what he had been told was Pinot Blanc. It has subsequently turned out that most Davis-sourced Pinot Blanc should really have been labelled Melon. Lett, however, thinks the cuttings he brought up to Oregon believing them to be Pinot Blanc were, in fact, Chardonnay.

By the early 1970s, Oregon could make a claim to be a fledgling, and burgeoning, wine region. Other California immigrants included Dick Erath of Erath Vineyards Winery (then known as Knudsen-Erath, 1969) and Dick and Nancy Ponzi of their eponymous winery (1970); they were also joined by The Vuylsteke family (Oak Knoll, 1970), Susan and Bill Sokol-Blosser (Sokol-Blosser Winery, 1971), David and Ginny Adelsheim (Adelsheim Vineyard, 1972), Pat and Joe Campbell (Elk Cove Vineyards, 1973), Bill and Virginia Fuller (Tualatin Estate Vineyards, 1973), and Jerry and Ann Preston and Myron

> The Pinot Noir era dates from 1965. David Lett, of the Eyrie Vineyard, first rooted Pinot Noir cuttings near Corvallis, while researching a permanent vineyard site.

Redford (Amity Vineyards, 1974) in the Willamette Valley AVA.

But it was David Lett who was to ignite the flame that first cast light on Oregon wine. It was his 1975 Eyrie Vineyard's South Block Reserve Pinot Noir that put Oregon on the map. In 1979 in Paris, the French Gault Millau guide sponsored a grand tasting of wines from 330 countries to see how New World wines compared with the French. In the Pinot Noir category, David Lett's Eyrie was placed among the top ten. Beaune *négociant* Robert Drouhin staged a follow-up match in Beaune in early 1980; this time, the Eyrie came second, less than a point behind the Drouhin 1959 Chambolle-Musigny. The international press jumped on the story, and Oregon was placed on the world's wine map. This success continues to be a major component of "The Oregon Story" and is used as a benchmark against which to compare the achievements of Oregon wines today.

Robert Drouhin strongly endorsed the success of the 1980 Beaune tasting by purchasing land in 1987, and building a state-of-the-art, gravity-fed winery in 1989, within sight of Lett's own vineyards in the Red Hills of Dundee .

The **connection with France** has been strong from the beginning. Early pioneers Charles Coury and David Lett had both spent time in Alsace and Burgundy before founding their own wineries. As Oregon's early wine producers grew more confident in their belief that this was indeed a credible region for growing cool-weather, French varieties, they looked to refine their choice of plant material.

David Adelsheim took the lead, after a local 1974 tasting of Oregon Pinot Noirs by winemakers, which focused intense interest in the Pommard clone and, for the first time, brought clonal discussions to a community level. Adelsheim was concerned: if different clones were available, how could he know which ones would make the best wine? At the time, only the

University of California at Davis and the State University of New York in Geneva had importation licences and could bring in plant material from older, European wine-producing regions.

Adelsheim went to France in search of new plant material to bring back for cultivation at Oregon State University (OSU). The initial variety focus for imports was supposed to be Pinot Noir, but Adelsheim made a trip to Alsace in 1975 and arranged to send back to OSU samples of all of the region's grape varieties, including the then-never-seen true Pinot Blanc. In 1977, authentic Gamay and a few clones of French Pinot Noir and Chardonnay made their way to OSU as well.

By 1984 a relationship developed between clone expert Raymond Bernard (at ONIVINS in Dijon) and OSU, which resulted in the importation of the now-hot Pinot Noir and Chardonnay clones that are today widely planted in Oregon and which started to bear viable fruit by the 1995 vintage.

By the mid-1980s it became widely known in the United States that Oregon was bringing in clones from France to which no one else had access. As a result, California producers began purchasing plants from OSU, not Davis. When staff at Davis realized that, they forged a relationship with OSU that brought some of those clones to Davis. This was all a first – previously the flow of plant material had gone entirely in the other direction.

Oregon's important French link once came under strain when a French nurseryman figured out that the traditional French clones, which the French had paid to select, were being propagated in the US without the French receiving royalties. But the French connection is alive and well once more. In 1998, two commercial nurseries in California signed agreements with the French Ministry of Agriculture to pay royalties in exchange for a monopoly of select clonal material. Such clones are in quarantine in California, being evaluated for

By the mid-1980s, it became widely known in the United States that Oregon was bringing in clones from France to which no one else had access.

disease before propagation takes place.

Oregon's most exciting **new clonal material** – especially for Chardonnay – has started to bear fruit. The resultant wines are displaying more complexity, and almost more importantly, a ripeness not realized before, since California clonal selections were inappropriate for Oregon's cool climate. Oregon Chardonnay without the use of Dijon clones can taste very green and lean, unless the vintage achieves an unusual, extraordinary ripeness.

Oregon is finally beginning to reach its maturity as a wine region. The early pioneers are still at it, but the next generation has already joined them in the cellar. At Ponzi Vineyards, Dick Ponzi's daughter Luisa has assumed the role of winemaker; at Elk Cove, Joe Campbell's son Adam is now in charge. Even at Domaine Drouhin Oregon, it is Veronique Drouhin Boss – Robert's daughter – who makes the wine.

With only **forty years of modern experience**, Oregon is now starting to develop into a region of some standing, and its bountiful potential is being utilized enthusiatically by its talented and innovative winemakers. But with barely more than one generation of experience, there is still a lot of history to be written.

Oregon identity

The wine country of Oregon spans the state, rising up and falling over the rolling hills and gentle valleys that are home to more than 4,858 hectares (12,000 acres) – and growing – of *Vitis vinifera* plantings.

The largest wineries of Oregon seem small in comparison to those in California: the biggest producer only makes 125,000 cases per year. A great proportion of the nearly 170 wineries in Oregon (a number that increases each year) produce fewer than 35,000 cases of wine annually, and many wineries make only 2–5,000 cases each year. Most wine producers own and tend their own vineyards, some supplementing their needs with purchased grapes from contracted vineyards. Even those who buy grapes take an active role in overseeing the production of their contracted rows.

Production facilities range from small garage-based, simple operations to technologically advanced, modern gravity-fed wineries. With few exceptions, the wineries look purely functional: not the mega-châteaux of Bordeaux, or Napa in California, but more like the farms and utilitarian facilities of Burgundy, or Sonoma in California.

Oregon's vineyards lie primarily in the **temperate Willamette Valley**, between the Coast and Cascade Mountain Ranges; the smaller regions of the warmer southern Umpqua, Applegate, and Rogue Valleys lie in the river valleys bisecting a series of forested hills and mountains, just north of the Klamath Mountains. They are less sheltered by the Coast and Cascade Ranges, but offer their own moderated mesoclimates.

Warm days and cool nights make the Willamette Valley ideal for both Burgundian and Alsatian varieties. The weather pattern in the Willamette Valley, however, varies considerably from Alsace or Burgundy: Oregon's rainfall occurs most abundantly in the spring and autumn (and, of course, through the winter), with drier, drought conditions prevailing mid-July through August, sometimes causing fermentation and ageing problems for white wines in particular. In the warmer and considerably drier southern Valleys, as well as the eastern Columbia and Walla Walla Valleys of the state,

> **The largest wineries of Oregon seem small in comparison to those in California: the biggest producer only makes 125,000 cases per year.**

Ted Casteel knows well the rules of the road as viticulture director at Bethel Heights Vineyard in the Eola Hills.

smaller quantities of the Bordeaux (and now Rhône-style) thick skinned varieties can be grown with increasing success.

Rain in the Willamette Valley, where the greatest proportion of vines are planted, has given this region a false bad image. Indeed, rain in autumn is an annual threat, but no more than in many other cool-climate wine-producing regions around the world. The annual race begins at veraison (the intermediate stage of grape development when the grapes change from hard green berries to their softer, coloured state) to ripen the grapes before bad weather sets in. Oregon typically sees an average of 5–8cm (2–3in) of rain in the Willamette Valley in September to October, but the hope is that the fruit will ripen by early October and the deluge will commence after 15 October. Unfortunately for Oregon, three particularly wet autumns – 1995, 1996, and 1997 – compromised quality. And those years, sadly, were assumed to be the norm for the state; unfortunately it coincided with another wave of serious attention from the wine press.

Generally, the Willamette Valley can be viewed as the most marginal of the West Coast wine-producing regions. Some claim the weather patterns compromise quality, but others maintain that grapes that ripen in cool temperatures at the end of the growing season achieve greater complexity.

With only forty years of modern experience, there is no long-term, consistent record of weather or winemaking techniques. Nor are there many obvious differences in taste according to place; but an argument can still be made that it might be from the Northwest's cooler reaches that the best wines of the United States will ultimately emerge. And they are now emerging. With a trio of spectacular vintages – 1998, 1999, and 2000 – following a string of weather-compromised years, the state is finally poised for greater international attention. Oregon can be characterized as a young (but passionate) wine-producing region, one that is finally reaching a maturity promised by its early stellar achievements of the 1970s.

Pinot Noir continues as the state's signature varietal, representing thirty-six per cent of all wine produced and almost fifty per cent of all vineyard plantings. The discrepancy between grapes grown and wine produced is due in part to the increased vineyard plantings each year (and those vines not yet bearing viable fruit), and also to the lower yields that Oregon producers consider essential for quality production of Pinot Noir.

Oregon's first vines, of course, were self-rooted. The faster growing strain of **phylloxera** that wiped out California vineyards has not appeared further north. The shorter, cooler aspects of the growing season in Oregon lessens the generational growth of the louse, but does not prevent its occurrence. In Oregon, the affected sites – at least thirty-eight confirmed vineyards out of a total of 500 – are still isolated from each other, which also greatly slows the spread of phylloxera.

Phylloxera was first documented in Oregon in 1990, at four sites throughout the state. Until then, virtually all vineyards were planted with own-rooted vines, upon the belief that since Oregon hadn't yet seen any evidence of the problem, they could wait until it was discovered and only then replant. Most Oregon wineries before the 1990s faced financial constraints, and pulling or grafting productive plants would not have been financially feasible.

Robert Drouhin knew better. When the Burgundian purchased land in Oregon and planted his Dundee vineyards in 1988, his experience told him that phylloxera would come. Domaine Drouhin Oregon was the first large-scale vineyard to be planted with grafted vines. By 2000, more than thirty-seven per cent of all vines in Oregon were on grafted rootstocks.

Most of the rootstock-clonal plantings in Oregon were done after 1992, by newer, better-financed operations. Besides trying to prevent phylloxera, producers had been searching for a way to add depth and complexity to their wines. Their major focus has been concentrated on yields and clonal selections, with the resulting advantage of earlier ripening fruit. Oregon producers were the first champions in the United States of the imported French clones, working with the French government and Oregon State University in the mid-1980s to guarantee healthy propagation. The now abundantly planted Dijon clones promise potentially

International Pinot Noir Celebration

Oregon winemakers figured out that they could market Pinot Noir and Oregon together. They thought their passion for the potential magic of that grape should be shared. They sought to bring together a world of Pinot Noir producers and enthusiasts in a grand celebration of wine – located in Oregon, in the middle of wine country, of course.

The International Pinot Noir Celebration (IPNC) started in 1987 as a summer camp weekend of wine, food, and good spirit – a collegial, educational wine extravaganza showcasing the glory of the grape. Its intention all along was to bring together top producers from around the world to mingle with distributors, retailers, and regular folk. With no hierarchy of trade versus public, it was just a chance for everyone to get cosy with the best wine producers, taste glorious wines, and yes, of course, show off Oregon. Camp has become so successful that a lottery system now controls attendance. Size is limited by the facility at Linfield College in McMinnville. But also limited by design: camp would lose its charm if it became too big.

The fine-dining aspect has developed over the years. Food costs rise with quality, and the resultant ticket price for IPNC is now steep, at $795 in 2001. (IPNC breaks even each year, at best.) That's a lot of money for a three-day weekend, without lodging or transport. But amazingly, people clamber to attend.

more complex Pinot Noirs and Chardonnays. Even with Oregon's nationally recognized leadership in the area of **clonal development**, and the quality image and enthusiastic reception with which the wines have been met, Oregon has yet to produce a large attention-grabbing champion like those of Mondavi, Kendall-Jackson, or Gallo in California, or even a Chateau Ste Michelle in Washington. Oregon's demeanour and persona continue to lack true celebrity; the state's producers still regard themselves as farmers, reinforcing a cultivated image of rustic charm and simple hominess in contrast to the more glamorous marketeers of California. That image is given support by the nature of Oregon's growth in general. Land grants in the nineteenth century deeded properties to a maximum size of sixty-five hectares (160 acres). This has kept property scale in Oregon smaller than in its neighbouring states. The home-spun demeanour is certainly no act, it took little capital to create Oregon's early wineries and the properties here attracted a more self-sufficient, independent spirit. Most wineries lack fancy tasting rooms and showy visitor centres. A visitor is just as likely to meet the winemaker him or herself pouring wine in the tasting room as to have extreme difficulty locating the winery due to inadequate signage (occasionally by design).

But that modest, underfunded image has been changing: outside interests – from California, France, and Australia have brought money and sophistication to the region. With them have come higher prices for the better wines. This seems to have limited the region's ability to export its wines with the degree of success expected of such quality. In 2000, bottle pricing upwards of $40 retail means the wines could hardly stay competitive, with the added import taxes, international shipping, and VAT placed on top of that. Of course, the small number of bottles produced means that Oregon wines can never be exported in great quantities, anyway. But the pricing trend is problematic within the United States; as good as the wines can be, with prices exceeding those of *Premier Cru* Burgundy from top domaines, one has to wonder about value. If consumers are willing to pay the high prices, good for the producer. But where will they stop?

Styles also vary considerably, from simple unoaked whites to heavily extracted, oak-wrapped monsters. Lower yields, averaging between 28–42 hectolitres per hectare (2–3 tons per acre) are the norm for the top wines. Vintage certainly influences wine in Oregon, but more and more so does oak and concentration, consistent with the international trend.

As with most wine-producing regions around the world, **agricultural production** also plays a strong role within the appellations of Oregon. Throughout the wine-producing areas of the state, nut trees, apple and pear orchards, and berry vines can be seen on property that is not planted with grapes. Cows still graze lazily in pastoral settings. The rich availability of prized wild mushrooms has spurred an active mycological industry and a related culinary following marked by great enthusiasm. Salmon is as much a part of the Oregon identity as Pinot Noir. It seems natural that all these native foods marry well with wines, especially with the character of Pinot Noir.

A great interest in sustainable agriculture in this environmentally aware state has also exerted an influence on the grape-producing industry. Only a few vineyards can claim true organic certification (and Cooper Mountain Vineyard is currently trying in earnest for biodynamic status). However, the winemakers and viticulturists who founded a new program called LIVE (Low Impact Viticulture and Enology) have attempted to make earth-friendly grape growing and winemaking the standard practice in Oregon. They hope one day to see the concept and program succeed outside the state as well, as an overall standard and widely accepted mark of quality in wine and respect for our world.

It took less capital to create Oregon's early wineries and the properties here attracted a more self-sufficient, independent spirit.

Oregon regions and their wines

Oregon boasts a **diverse range of growing areas**, dramatically different in temperature, rainfall, elevation, and slope.

The largest region – both in geographic area and number of vineyards and wineries – is the Willamette Valley, stretching 193km (120 miles), from Portland south to Eugene, on either side of the north-flowing Willamette River. Nestled between the Coast and Cascade Mountain Ranges and about

97km (60 miles) east of the Pacific Ocean, this wide fertile valley – 97km (60 miles) at its broadest point – contains a number of significant rolling hills and ridges of prime sloping vineyard sites: Chehalem Mountains, the Red Hills of Dundee, the Eola Hills, the Amity Hills, and the South Salem Hills. Most vineyards are planted on south-facing slopes to the west of the Willamette River, where the soils are

The best vineyards in Oregon, such as this one in the Red Hills of Dundee, are well-sited on slopes to avoid spring frost as well as achieve speedy ripening.

primarily basaltic or sedimentary, alluvial, or volcanic in origin.

The climate carries a **maritime influence** from the west, with potentially overly wet weather mitigated by the 610–915 metre (2,000–3,000ft) Coastal Range which stops the flow of some precipitation. It is not atypical for parts of the Valley to see 3–8cm (1–3in) of rain in September and October (an average of 100cm (40in) of rain per annum throughout the Valley), with each harvest a nail biter to get grapes in before significant downpours. Weather patterns may be shifting, however; dry harvest periods have been the norm since 1998.

Temperatures in the Willamette Valley are moderate, rarely rising above 32°C (90°F) in July and August thanks to cloud cover flowing in from the Pacific; typically,

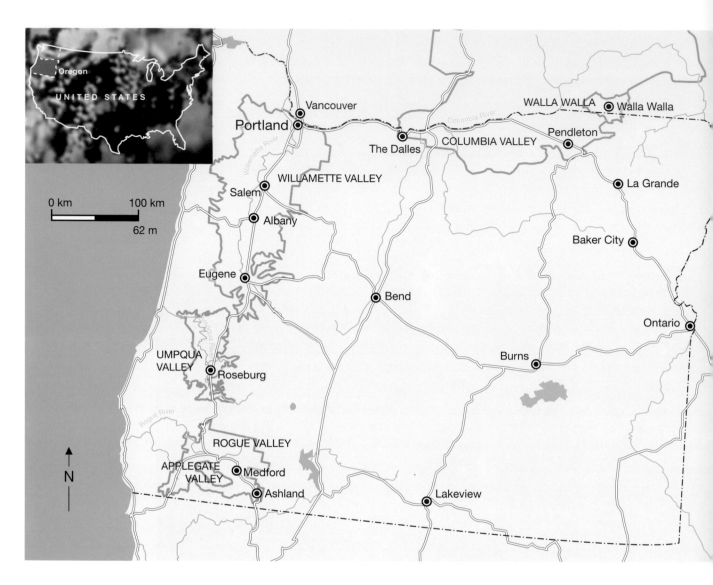

The fertile Willamette Valley also serves as Oregon's garden basket ... This valley was Oregon's first formal American Viticultural Area (AVA).

temperatures fall significantly in the evening hours. Using Amerine and Winkler's degree-days heat summation system, the Willamette Valley's range of 1,122–1,235 degree days Centigrade (2,052–2,255 degree days Fahrenheit) places the entire region in the coolest category, Region I. Amerine and Winkler devised a system to classify the climates of wine regions according to heat summation and expressed in "degree days". Based on a growing season from 1 April to 31 October, they calculated the number of degree days by multiplying the average monthly temperature in excess of 10°C (50°F) by the number of days in the month (10°C/50°F is the minimum temperature for

vine growth.) They divided California into five temperature categories from Region I, the coolest, to Region V, the hottest region.

The fertile Willamette Valley also serves as **Oregon's garden basket**, producing hazelnuts, walnuts, field crops, numerous fruits, and cane berries. This valley was Oregon's first formal American Viticultural Area (AVA); boundaries were established by drawing the lines up to elevations of 305 metres (1,000ft), the maximum height the grapes can thrive in the Valley's cool climate. Forest lands were left out of the designation, and no land outside the Willamette River basin was included (except for a few narrow valleys, which connect with the basin).

Pinot Noir is the most widely planted

variety within the AVA, and indeed, more Pinot Noir is produced in the Willamette Valley than anywhere else in Oregon. Chardonnay has had a historical presence, but in recent years has been eclipsed by Pinot Gris.

The **Umpqua Valley**, Oregon's second AVA, spans an area 113km (70 miles) long and 56km (35 miles) wide, southwest of Eugene. It is heavily forested, and the once-strong timber industry is now declining. The snaking Umpqua River weaves through this region, cutting its way from the Cascades, through the Coastal Range to the Pacific Ocean beyond. This allows cool marine air to reduce evening temperatures dramatically, even lower than in the Willamette Valley. In contrast, day temperatures are hotter than the Willamette Valley, but not as searing as parts of California.

This cluster of small hillsides – no higher than 152 metres (500ft) in elevation – and river drainages was historically known as the "hundred valleys of the Umpqua." The Umpqua region is slightly drier than the Willamette Valley, with an average rainfall of 81cm (32in) per annum. Degree days hover around 2,500, the lower range for the Region II grape-growing category. The higher heat allows thicker skinned grapes to ripen: Bordeaux varieties do well; Pinot Noir, Chardonnay, and the Alsatian varieties are also grown. Recent plantings of Tempranillo, Syrah, Grenache, and Dolcetto show promise.

The **Rogue Valley** was not created an AVA until 1991; it took until then to have enough producers to warrant a formal viticultural designation. The Rogue is a remote area, less developed than other areas along the Interstate 5 highway that travels north–south along the West Coast. Most of the Oregon wine industry lies just to the west of the highway. The Rogue Valley lies below the Umpqua Valley, stretching south to the California border. No major airport serves the region and the rugged geography makes access difficult for a visitor.

The Rogue Valley is defined by its many mesoclimates created in the three river valleys – the Illinois, Bear Creek, and Applegate – in the foothills of the Klamath and Siskiyou Mountains. Weather is very varied and defined by geography; annual rainfall can be as low as 48cm (19in) per annum in the Bear Creek Valley to a remarkable 152cm (60in) in the Illinois Valley. Degree days range from 2,300–2,500, generally increasing the further south towards Ashland you travel. The major varieties planted in the Illinois Valley – Pinot Noir, Pinot Gris, Gamay Noir, Chardonnay, and the Alsatian varieties – seem more similar to those of the Willamette Valley. In the neighbouring Bear Creek Valley – a much warmer mesoclimate – thicker skinned varieties such as Merlot, Cabernet Sauvignon, Syrah, Cabernet Franc, Viognier, Malbec, and Chardonnay are grown.

The **Applegate Valley** was designated an AVA in January 2001. Situated in the middle third of the Rogue appellation, along the Applegate River, the weather here is somewhere between that of the Illinois and Bear Creek Valleys, and the region is planted with Chardonnay, Cabernet Sauvignon, Merlot, Zinfandel, and a small amount of Syrah.

Both the **Columbia Valley** and the **Walla Walla Valley** regions share AVA designations with neighbouring Washington State. They straddle the Columbia River that separates Oregon and Washington; the Oregon side of each appellation is much smaller. Although both still have a large geographic area, there are few wineries in each region.

Oregon's piece of the Columbia Valley AVA stretches along the river, with vineyards planted on the south side of Interstate 84 highway, on rolling hills that also sport fruit trees. This northern border of the state – known generally as the Columbia Gorge, home of world-class windsurfing – forms a passable valley through the Cascade Range, thanks to the mighty Columbia River. This

More Pinot Noir is produced in the Willamette Valley than anywhere else in Oregon. Chardonnay has ... in recent years ... been eclipsed by Pinot Gris.

region was classified an AVA late in 1984.

The arid **climate** of eastern Oregon collides with the more maritime patterns of the western part of the state, creating very changeable mesoclimates in the region. Since the wind can be high, vines must be low to the ground to fare well. Rainfall is low. Grape varieties grown include a little bit of everything: Chardonnay, Riesling, Pinot Noir, Cabernet Sauvignon, Merlot, Zinfandel, Petite Syrah, and Nebbiolo.

The Walla Walla region has little Oregon identity, although this high desert plateau technically reaches south into the state across the Columbia River, to the Oregon town of Milton-Freewater and beyond. Only one winery – Seven Hills – once produced here; they moved their winery operation to the town of Walla Walla in Washington, feeling they were more closely aligned with the Washington producers who annually purchased some of their fruit than their own Oregon label suggested. A number of other vineyards have been planted in the last six years, but no production facility – and therefore no Oregon winery – exists in the Walla Walla region.

Geography influences the character of wine in Oregon, as anywhere else in the world. These influences on the wines are potentially huge; and there is a developing sense of *terroir* now apparent in the wines. Style, though, can be affected by the varieties chosen, rootstocks, clones, oak, and cellar techniques. However, the most important style issue, perhaps, is yield – which is controllably influenced by spacing, trellising, and green harvesting, and uncontrollably influenced by the soil, and the weather at bud break, bloom, and during the vine growing season.

In the following pages, regions are discussed by geographic definitions, not strictly by AVAs or true appellations. Oregon's vineyards are established enough to start to develop a sense of the place – a locally definable character.

Oregon varieties

Pinot Noir is the grape most identified with Oregon. The character of the top varietals lies somewhere between the fruity, lush style of California-grown fruit and the earthy structured elegance of quality Burgundies. The demand for grapes at harvest is high and the price has risen steeply. The blending of clones – including older California selections, Wadenswil, Pommard, and the new Dijon clones – is creating a greater range of complexity in the wines. While most Oregon Pinot Noir is consumed young, the wines can and do age well. Indeed, some vintages like 1997 and 1999 need time in bottle for the full expression of the wine.
Statistics: 1,958 hectares (4,835 acres) planted; 1,396 hectares (3,447 acres) bearing.

> **Pinot Noir is the grape most identified with Oregon. ... While most Oregon Pinot Noir is consumed young, the wines can and do age well.**

Pinot Gris, by 2000, had eclipsed Chardonnay as the number one white grape variety grown and produced. In style, the wines may be closer to the full-bodied Alsatian wines than the lean crisp Italian versions, but the (too) frequent use of oak, and a sometimes malolactic, leesy character make them uniquely Oregon wines.
Statistics: 583 hectares (1,442 acres) planted; 514 hectares (1,269 acres) bearing.

Chardonnay vines have been pulled out by many growers in recent years. California clones account for most of the early planting of the variety; the Oregon weather rarely co-operates to fully ripen those grapes before the cooler temperatures and the rain arrive in the autumn. The resultant wines are often lean and green. The Dijon clones have made

a tremendous difference for Chardonnay, bringing earlier ripening fruit and a fuller, broader range of flavours and textures.
Statistics: 529 hectares (1,306 acres) planted; 456 hectares (1,125 acres) bearing.

Merlot grows well in the warmer reaches of the state, not the Willamette Valley. Good varietal expression is emerging from the Walla Walla, Umpqua, Rogue, and Applegate appellations, where there is enough heat to ripen thick-skinned varieties. The wines – both varietal and blended – try to be good quality and value to stand apart from the sea of Merlot coming from Washington and California.
Statistics: 253 hectares (624 acres) planted; 175 hectares (433 acres) bearing.

White Riesling was one of the original grape varieties in the state, usually produced then, as now, as off-dry wine. Plantings in Riesling, unfortunately, have decreased steadily since the early 1990s because of competition from the value driven Washington wines, and also due to a lack of popularity in the state.
Statistics: 249 hectares (604 acres) planted; 223 hectares (550 acres) bearing.

Cabernet Sauvignon, like Merlot, needs the heat of the warmer areas of the state to ripen. Producers generally find it tough to compete with the better known and marketed Washington and California Cabernets and blends.
Statistics: 191 hectares (472 acres) planted; 151 hectares (373 acres) bearing.

Gewürztraminer, like Riesling, has probably been grown in Oregon since the early days of wine production. Since it's hard wine to sell, plantings have been decreasing for some time. However, some very credible ice wines have been produced.
Statistics: 74 hectares (182 acres) planted; 64 hectares (159 acres) bearing.

Syrah is the newcomer grape in southern Oregon, with vines just starting to bear fruit. Although the quality has been uneven, but

beginning with the 1999 vintage, the wines are showing some promise.
Statistics: 67 hectares (165 acres) planted; 32 hectares (80 acres) bearing.

Pinot Blanc in Oregon is the real thing, not a mislabelled Melon as in California. Only twenty producers make this varietal, and they have banded together to market the wines as it can be hard to sell. One hurdle is to distinguish the wine from Pinot Noir labelled "Pinot Noir Blanc" (a blush wine). The lack of consistent style of Oregon Pinot Blanc is somewhat of an issue: some have been processed with oak, some with malolactic

Pinot Noir. Oregon's pride and joy, also known as the heartbreak grape for its difficulty in ripening well.

fermentation, and some even with lees contact. Retail pricing comes in at over $10 per bottle, elevating the grape's status above its role in Alsace, where it has always been an inexpensive wine. And Oregon Pinot Blancs are priced at the same level or higher than their Alsatian equivalents in the US market.
Statistics: 48 hectares (119 acres) planted; 39 hectares (97 acres) bearing.

Müller-Thurgau is the flagship of Chateau Benoit. Fewer than a dozen other producers make this often-maligned cross variety (controversially either *Riesling* X *sylvaner* or two strains of Riesling). In most years, the wines are lean, low-acid and anonymous. Every now and again, in unusually ripe vintages, such as 1998 and 1999, the wines can be very pleasant. Most Müller-Thurgau wines are made off-dry.
Statistics: 36 hectares (88 acres) planted; 33 hectares (80 acres) bearing.

Sauvignon Blanc is another vine whose numbers are diminishing. Like Merlot and Cabernet, this variety faces tough quality and value competition from Oregon's neighbouring states.
Statistics: 34 hectares (85 acres) planted; 32 hectares (78 acres) bearing.

Sémillon, **Zinfandel**, **Cabernet Franc**, **Tempranillo**, **Viognier**, **Grenache**, **Dolcetto**, **Arneis**, and **Nebbiolo** are also being planted around the state.

Legal restrictions

Wine **labelling regulations** in Oregon can boast the strictest requirements in the United States. In the 1970s, Oregon's grape growers sought to protect the integrity of their small industry by setting up laws stricter than the United States' standards, as set out in the Bureau of Alcohol, Firearms, and Tobacco (BATF) regulations.

Enacted by the **Oregon Liquor Control Commission** (OLCC) in 1977, the rules require a varietal wine contain 90 per cent of the labelled variety, with the exception of Cabernet Sauvignon (and subsequently, all Bordelais varieties). At the time these regulations were enacted, the BATF standard was only 51 per cent; in 1983, the Federal standard was raised to 75 per cent. Appellations are mandatory for all wines in Oregon; varietal-labelled wines must be made entirely from fruit grown in the region of origin. Wines labelled "Estate" must be made from grapes grown in vineyards owned or have been long-term managed within 8km (5 miles) of the bottling facility.

Oregon was also ahead of the curve on restricting the use of European appellation

names. It has been illegal since 1977 to use such European-named places as Burgundy and Chablis on labels unless the grapes are actually grown in the appellation listed.

Formal American Viticultural Areas (AVAs) came into existence with the 1983 Federal regulations; the first American Viticultural Areas in Oregon, the Willamette Valley followed by the Umpqua Valley, were created in 1984; the Rogue Valley didn't receive AVA status until 1991. Shared jointly between Washington and Oregon, Columbia Valley became an AVA late in 1984, while Walla Walla became an AVA in 1987. The newest Oregon appellation, the Applegate Valley, was approved by the BATF in January 2001.

Oregon, though, had developed its own appellation system before the Federal AVAs were implemented: then, as now, a producer can use county names (for example, Yamhill) to designate appellation.

The OLCC administratively handles all licensing of wineries and implements all rules and regulations. All wine sales in the state must be paid cash on delivery through a licensed wholesaler, without any provision for credit or quantity purchasing. Wholesalers may sell wine directly to consumers as well, at the same price as to retailers and restaurants, but in minimum two-case lot purchases through a not-very-often used provision known as dock sales.

Oregon's wine commission, the **Oregon Wine Advisory Board** (OWAB), was set up in 1983 by the state's winemakers and legislators to co-ordinate the research, marketing, and promotion of Oregon's wines. (OWAB was preceded by the Table Wine Research Advisory Board, founded in 1977.) The effectiveness, though, of representing such a diverse state can often be compromised. The wineries in the southern part of the state feel slighted that the Willamette Valley and Pinot Noir claim all the attention. They tend not to understand that if top-quality wines – like Abacela's Tempranillo – attract broad attention that will reach to the south.

The lack of big cities in southern Oregon and its remoter location mean that people visiting the state's winery-packed Willamette Valley – especially the Yamhill County area – are less likely to venture down to the Umpqua, Rogue, or Applegate Valleys. They are about three to five hours driving distance away from Portland.

Ironically, the wineries of the Willamette Valley feel the OWAB doesn't promote Pinot Noir and their interests enough. It's a lose-lose situation for the staff of the OWAB, made even more acute by their lack of funds and lean-staffing structure. Funding is a delicate issue indeed, and is the reason why the wine community hasn't pushed to move the OWAB out from under state government to become a more accountable, less bureaucratic structure.

Grape taxes are assessed at $25 per ton of Oregon-grown grapes; the fee is shared between growers and wineries. Additionally, funding comes from a $.02 per 4.5 litres (1 gallon) tax on finished wines; wineries producing under 378,500 litres (100,000 gallons) per year may sell up to 151,400 litres (40,000 gallons) tax free. All monies are collected by the OLCC and distributed to OWAB within the State Department of Agriculture. An out-of-state tonnage assessment of $12.50 per ton is levied on grapes grown outside Oregon, and this is collected by the Department of Agriculture.

The first American Viticultural Areas in Oregon, the Willamette Valley followed by the Umpqua Valley, were created in 1984.

The OWAB Board of Directors – made up of eleven members representing the three major wine-producing regions, commercial wineries and vineyards, wine-grape producers without commercial winery interests, and winemakers of fruit or berry wines – allocates the funds. This is subject to a statutory requirement that at least one-third goes to research and one-third to promotion, with the balance available for other programme and administrative needs. Historically, the OWAB has devoted 40 per cent of the funds to research, 40 per cent to promotion and 20 per cent to administration.

Yamhill County

Within the Willamette Valley, **Yamhill County** should be viewed as the epicentre of Oregon's wines country: this area has the greatest concentration of wineries – especially quality wineries – in the state. More a political boundary than an appellation or single geographic division of land, Yamhill County as a region is a useful artificial boundary to incorporate two of the most important geographic vineyard areas of Oregon – the Red Hills of Dundee and Chehalem Mountains – with other significant vineyards nearby.

The county stretches down from Newberg south to Amity, through sleepy Dundee to just beyond McMinnville, the commercial centre of

the area. On the western edges of the region, you'll find the small towns of Carlton, Yamhill, and Gaston.

Connecting these small communities, which are now well defined by the wine industry, Yamhill County presents itself as an interlocking series of hills, created by volcanic eruptions millions of years ago: the northern-most Chehalem Mountains – an east–west running ridge; the central Dundee Hills; and the northern edge of the more southern Eola Hills. These generally south- and southwest-facing slopes are made up of numerous significantly different soil types, creating a diverse landscape suitable for

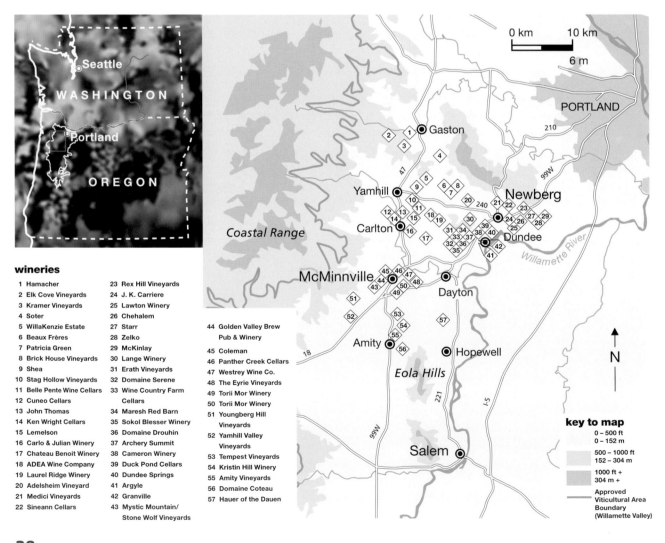

wineries

1 Hamacher
2 Elk Cove Vineyards
3 Kramer Vineyards
4 Soter
5 WillaKenzie Estate
6 Beaux Frères
7 Patricia Green
8 Brick House Vineyards
9 Shea
10 Stag Hollow Vineyards
11 Belle Pente Wine Cellars
12 Cuneo Cellars
13 John Thomas
14 Ken Wright Cellars
15 Lemelson
16 Carlo & Julian Winery
17 Chateau Benoit Winery
18 ADEA Wine Company
19 Laurel Ridge Winery
20 Adelsheim Vineyard
21 Medici Vineyards
22 Sineann Cellars

23 Rex Hill Vineyards
24 J. K. Carriere
25 Lawton Winery
26 Chehalem
27 Starr
28 Zelko
29 McKinlay
30 Lange Winery
31 Erath Vineyards
32 Domaine Serene
33 Wine Country Farm
   Cellars
34 Maresh Red Barn
35 Sokol Blesser Winery
36 Domaine Drouhin
37 Archery Summit
38 Cameron Winery
39 Duck Pond Cellars
40 Dundee Springs
41 Argyle
42 Granville
43 Mystic Mountain/
   Stone Wolf Vineyards

44 Golden Valley Brew
   Pub & Winery
45 Coleman
46 Panther Creek Cellars
47 Westrey Wine Co.
48 The Eyrie Vineyards
49 Torii Mor Winery
50 Torii Mor Winery
51 Youngberg Hill
   Vineyards
52 Yamhill Valley
   Vineyards
53 Tempest Vineyards
54 Kristin Hill Winery
55 Amity Vineyards
56 Domaine Coteau
57 Hauer of the Dauen

a multitude of different ways of expressing a now-emerging *terroir*.

In contrast to many growing regions – particularly Burgundy – you could drive through Yamhill County on Highway 99W and not see a vineyard from the road. Yamhill County's vines are grown on the south, east, and occasionally west-facing slopes, at elevations of 76–305 metres (250–1,000ft) – the former number being the necessary height for winter frost protection, and the latter elevation is not ideal but the highest point at which Pinot Noir can ripen consistently.

Soils vary within Yamhill county, each contributing a different set of flavours to the grapes grown in them. Desirable Willakenzie soil – shallow clay loam over sedimentary rock – dominates the Chehalem Mountains, home to top wineries including Brick House Vineyards, Adelsheim Vineyard, Patricia Green Cellars, Beaux Frères, Soter Wines, Medici Vineyards, and WillaKenzie Estate. This area can also claim such noted vineyards as Guadeloupe (leased by Ken Wright Cellars), Lemelson Winery, John Thomas Wines, Shea Wine Cellars (whose grapes are sold to Panther Creek, Ken Wright, Beaux Frères, St Innocent, Patricia Green Cellars, Sine Qua Non in California, and its own, newly commercial Shea label), and Ridgecrest (owned by Chehalem). Willakenzie soils are a bit sandy and produce slightly earlier-ripening fruit than other soils; consistent elements in the Pinot Noir wines produced on this soil have a strong earthy note, chocolate, and a definite flavour of anise and spice.

In the Dundee Hills (also known as the Red Hills of Dundee), Jory soil predominates, and the "red" name of the Hills reflects the high iron content of the soil: a deep (up to 3 metres/10ft in places), silty clay loam over a basaltic-volcanic rock base, with a high water-holding capability.

Vines on Jory soil keep their vegetation longer and have delayed fruit ripening. The Eyrie Vineyard is located here, as are Domaine Drouhin Oregon, Argyle, Erath Vineyards Winery, Cameron, Sokol Blosser, Archery Summit, and Lange Winery, among others; notable vineyards without a winery affiliation include the Maresh Red Barn, Goldschmidt, Niederberger, and Webber. On the lower elevations – and at such well-known properties as Rex Hill – combinations of many different soil types can be found.

In the more southern reaches of Yamhill County, just north of the Eola Hills, Yamhill soil predominates: a clay loam over cobbled basalt, without the iron of the Jory found in the Red Hills of Dundee. Ripening at Amity Vineyards, for example, comes about a week

Outside investment

David Lett's dramatic Paris tasting victory in 1979 – and its restaging in Beaune by Robert Drouhin – was the catalyst that attracted Oregon's most illustrious foreign investor. Drouhin's instincts have been a model for Oregon producers. When the Burgundian planted his Dundee Hills Vineyards in 1988, since his experience told him that phylloxera would come, he initiated the first large-scale rootstock planting in the state.

Drouhin also built Oregon's first gravity-fed winery, completed in 1989. It was built into a hillside to take advantage of nature. Drouhin saw Oregon as his opportunity to break from the rigidity of Burgundy. Gravity flow was not an option in his cellars under the city of Beaune; all the hillsides along the Côte d'Or are planted with grapes. Drouhin knew that handling the grapes gently was paramount for fine wine and preserving the fruit's integrity.

Oregon's (and Yamhill County's) other major international player hails from Australia. Davis-trained winemaker Rollin Soles was working at Petaluma Winery in South Australia when he and Petaluma owner Brian Croser cooked up an off-beat notion: they wanted to make sparkling wine in the United States, and the two chose Yamhill County's cool climate as the prime spot. At Argyle, the Dundee Wine Company owned by Petaluma and its stockholders, Soles makes Oregon's finest premium sparkling wine, *méthode traditionelle*, and claims to be the only producer anywhere crafting a Blanc de Blancs from 100 per cent Dijon clone Chardonnay. Soles also produces balanced, firmly structured Pinot Noir, Chardonnay, and dry Riesling table wines.

Winemakers from older California regions have begun to drift up to Yamhill County to make wine as well.

after the eastern Eola Hills just south, closer to Amity than either the Dundee Hills or the Chehalem Mountains. That later harvest time may be influenced – as the Eola Hills are – by the cooling effect of the Van Duzer Corridor, which allows marine air to reach through, rather than over, the Coastal Range. Heavy soils, where Yamhill Valley Vineyards lie, can produce coarse, tannic Pinot Noir. Dauenhauer Vineyard, east of Amity near the Willamette River, sits on valley soil, but produces low tannin, light wines.

Soils are a hot topic in Yamhill County. Most of the annual research funded by the Oregon Wine Advisory Board and conducted by the Agricultural Experiment Station of Oregon State University focuses on soils – looking at identity, characteristics, nutrient deficiencies and soil management of specific vineyards. Yamhill County soil has even caught the attention of Burgundian soil experts.

In the mid 1990s, Cyrille Bongiraud revitalized **GEST**, a study group for monitoring Burgundian soil and *terroir*. Bongiraud brought his soil obsession to Oregon in the spring of 1998. He and geologist-agricultural scientist Yves Hérody (of the *Bureau de Recherches sur le Development Agricole* in Charency) came to the Willamette Valley in order to analyze and evaluate the soils at a number of Oregon's top wineries: Adelsheim, Archery Summit, Bethel Heights, Brick House, Chehalem, Cristom, Domaine Drouhin Oregon, Ponzi, Ken Wright, Rex Hill, and WillaKenzie Estate. With one complex (and unfortunately poorly translated) initial report completed, both Bongiraud and the Oregon winemakers are eager for the French "soil guys" to return for further, more illuminating studies.

The **grapes** grown on Yamhill Valley soils tend to reflect the standard variety selections of the Valley: Pinot Noir, Chardonnay, Pinot Gris, Pinot Blanc, and small amounts of Riesling, Gewürztraminer, Gamay Noir, and Müller-Thurgau. The early Pinot Noir clones that

Production facilities range from small, garage-based operations to modern, gravity-fed, technologically-advanced wineries.

Protective tubes keep recently planted vines in a controlled and protected environment, and maintain their growth upright.

were first planted in the area are still bearing fruit: Wadensville, Pommard and the upright clone known as Pinot Droit. Some older Chardonnay vines still bear fruit. The newer Dijon clones of Pinot Noir and Chardonnay have been introduced at almost every vineyard, with many now either incorporated into blends or bottled and identified as Dijon clone selections.

Surprisingly, a few other varieties are grown in small quantities in Yamhill County. At Erath Vineyards Winery, Dick Erath grows Arneis and Dolcetto, bottling only the Dolcetto and selling his Arneis fruit to Ponzi Vineyards. At Deux Vert Vineyard on Chehalem Mountain, just below WillaKenzie Estate, 5 hectares (2 acres) of Syrah and 7.4 hectares (3 acres) of Viognier are grown and have actually managed to ripen; Elemental Cellars (in the Eola Hills) and Eugene-based Eugene Wine Cellars buys the grapes.

Most producers in Yamhill County closely follow **Burgundian models of viticulture**. Vertical shoot positioning (VSP) is the norm, but you can find split-canopy systems, including Scott Henry and Geneva Double Curtain, in places to increase production and improve canopy management in some more marginal sites.

Vine spacing has narrowed and tightened over the years, with earlier plantings set wider, typically at 1.8 x 3 metres or 3.6 metres (6 x 10ft or 12ft), and bearing more fruit. Newer vineyard plantings are more densely planted to produce more competitively achieved, lower yields. The spacings are set anywhere from 1.5 x 2.1 metres (5 x 7ft) to the tightly planted Stoller Vineyards at 0.9 x 1.5 metres (3 x 5ft), and the Drouhin vineyards set at a very French 1 x 1.3 metres (3 x 4ft). Tractor widths, in part, have dictated planting schemes. Drouhin's spacing is too narrow for American-style tractors, so it brought from France a narrow over-the-rows tractor. In three blocks of Archery Summit's Estate Vineyard, hillside planting is so narrow (0.85 x 1 metre/2ft 8in x 3ft) that no tractor is able to get through, necessitating that all work is done by hand.

In terms of plants per hectare, 1,730 or fewer

(per acre, 700 or fewer) would have been standard through the 1980s; newer vineyards from 1990 can be anywhere from 3,088–9,259 plants per hectare (1,250–3,747 per acre), with 4,942–7,431 per hectare (2,000–3,000 per acre) plants being the average. The higher density plantings began with the John Thomas Vineyard, just before the larger scale plantings of Drouhin in the late 1980s.

The range of **yields** can vary from 70–84 hectolitres per hectare (5–6 tons per acre) for the more commercial efforts to as low as 14 hectolitres per hectare (1 ton per acre) for the most concentrated, extracted styles of boutique wines. Between 25.2–28 hectolitres per hectare (1.8–2 tons per acre) is the goal most top producers set for Pinot Noir. Yields for white varieties such as Chardonnay and Pinot Gris vary widely (as do the wines), from 14 hectolitres to more than 56 hectolitres per hectare (1 ton to more than 4 tons per acre), depending on intent: for example, Chehalem got less than 14 hectolitres per hectare (1 ton

per acre) at Ridgecrest Vineyard in 1999 because it was experimenting with radical crop dropping in order to do a *Vendange Tardive*-style (late-harvest-style) Pinot Gris. Mother Nature also controls yields: 1994 and 1998 were both down by more than 30 per cent in weight.

The higher yields are generally associated with the more commercial sites. However, in 2000, the much in-demand Stoller Vineyards produced 56 hectolitres per hectare (4 tons per acre) from some of the high-density vineyards, where there were 6,622 plants per hectare (2,680 plants per acre), despite crop dropping to one cluster per shoot in Chardonnay. This raised the issues of too much irrigation and too high a yield.

When Yamhill County was first planted with grapes, producers believed they were at the mercy of the weather, without the experience or understanding of vineyard techniques that would best accommodate the weather patterns, especially rain. Now, in order to accelerate ripeness and beat the late autumn rain, most vineyard managers will do crop thinning as well as the canopy management that is best suited for both the specific micro- and broader mesoclimates.

Approximately 60 per cent of Oregon's vines are **still self-rooted**, even though phylloxera was documented in Yamhill County as early as 1990. Most of the rootstock-clonal plantings in Yamhill County were done after 1992 by newer, better financed operations including Domaine Drouhin Oregon, Archery Summit, Brick House, Willakenzie Estate, Argyle/The Dundee Wine Company, Shea Vineyard and the Stoller Vineyards. A number of older wineries such as Erath and Adelsheim have also planted new vineyards or replanted existing ones. But pioneers including David Lett of The Eyrie Vineyard still have self-rooted plants.

Besides the obvious issue of cost, another argument for keeping the self-rooted vines relates to the natural life cycle for a grapevine. Most vines are likely to be pulled up before anyone really ever knows their true life cycle because of a producer's desire to change spacing, clone selection, or even variety choice as the producer seeks to refine fruit production and the quality of the wines.

Organic viticulture is a much-discussed topic, but only five vineyards in the state have qualified for the Oregon Tilth Certification (the local authority that certifies to US standards). Three of the vineyards are in Yamhill County; two are owned by the Cattrel brothers, who sell grapes to Amity Vineyards (the first producer of organic wine, in 1990), and the other is Brick House Vineyards on Ribbon Ridge. The Low Impact Viticulture and Enology (LIVE) programme has a strong showing in Yamhill County (see page 63).

Irrigation is a controversial topic that is ironic given the region's reputation for dampness. The most savvy (and well-financed) producers – including Domaine Drouhin Oregon, Argyle, Domaine Serene, parts of Shea Vineyard, Stoller Vineyards, and WillaKenzie Estate – have installed drip irrigation to help control the amount and timing of water delivered to each plant. This is most important for young, developing vines. Oregon faces an unusual problem for such a wet growing region: in contrast to Burgundy (where rain can be abundant over the summer months), Yamhill County's rainfall is heaviest, and most frequent, in the early spring and late autumn. This leaves late July and August – and the critical *veraison* period – in a drought situation. Without adequate water at the time when the grapes change colour, nutrient uptake can be compromised, resulting in some white wines developing maturity too early and limiting the longevity of the finished wine. More and more properties are devising solutions to the water-timing issues, which is difficult in an area where the riparian rights can be contested. The drier summer months, however, also mean that the downy mildew and other humidity-dependent diseases that plague Burgundy are less prevalent in Yamhill County, the most densely planted area of the state.

In the cellar, Burgundian practices again have been the model for most Yamhill County producers. Many of them have done *stages* in the Cote d'Or. Generally, Pinot producers bring in cool grapes at harvest. They either inoculate them with yeast and then wait two to three days for fermentation to begin, or they let the native yeasts commence at their own speed; two to seven days is the norm for pre-fermentation maceration, with varying degrees of cold, depending on the weather and the cellar. More and more, producers are opting for native-yeast fermentations – long and hot for Pinot Noir – with a period of pre-fermentation maceration. A few producers occasionally do a post-fermentation soak

Approximately 60 per cent of Oregon's vines are still self-rooted, even though phylloxera was documented in Yamhill County as early as 1990.

The Maresh red barn sits smack in the heart of the Dundee Hills; Maresh grapes are vinified by Rex Hill Vineyards.

before pressing to get even more tannin and extraction, including Harry Peterson-Nedry (Chehalem), who learned this from his work with Burgundian Patrice Rion.

The trend in Yamhill County is towards barrel-ageing in new French *barriques*, with the same sometimes over-oaky (and sometimes tannic) results seen increasingly in Burgundy and elsewhere. Tannin, in fact, is the major style issue, with little agreement on how much is appropriate for Pinot Noir, whether it is grape tannin (not unusual in drought-stressed vineyards), stem tannin, or oak tannin.

Style is also an issue for the Alsatian varietals. There are producers who craft dry, crisp wines. Others introduce malolactic fermentation, *sur lies* ageing, and even oak Alsatian varieties may have a long history in Oregon, but winemakers are still learning how to make and market them.

One innovative technique has seen great success. Cryoextraction – making ice wine via the freezer – has been applied to Gewürztraminer, Riesling, and Pinot Gris by a number of Yamhill County producers, with some very fine results. Elk Cove was the first producer to consistently use this technique, beginning in 1989 with the release of its Ultima, made from Riesling. In some years, small quantities of Gewürztraminer are also treated this way. Other producers making ice wines worth noting include Ponzi (in Washington County), Erath, and Andrew Rich. In the 1999 vintage, Chehalem produced its first *Vendange Tardive*-style Pinot Gris.

For new wineries coming into Yamhill County – especially those that are well-financed – **gravity-fed cellars** have been the trend. Domaine Drouhin, Adelsheim, Archery Summit, WillaKenzie Estate, Lemelson Vineyards, and the just-completed Domaine Serene boast state-of-the-art, gravity-fed wineries. Though the concept of gravity-fed production is one of simplicity and working with, rather than against, the laws of science, it takes a commitment to gentle processes and a pocketful of money to create a true gravity-flow winery, engineered into a slope.

Most winemakers around the world acknowledge that Pinot Noir requires far gentler treatment than most other red varieties. This delicate grape has a thinner skin than most other red varieties and requires as little handling as possible in order to preserve the integrity of its fruit. Roughing up Pinot Noir can drive flavours and aromas out of the wine and creates the risk of introducing harsh, astringent tannins from the skin and seed fragments. But it certainly doesn't require gravity to make excellent Pinot Noir. There are a million things more important than just gravity flow, among them fruit site and selection, spacing, yields, and fermentation techniques. Such highly regarded wineries as Beaux Frères, Brick House, Panther Creek, and Ken Wright Cellars don't make wine in gravity-fed facilities. But gravity flow is certainly a piece of this complicated puzzle.

Archery Summit rises up on a crest surrounded by its impeccably well-manicured vineyards. Estate fruit produces well-focused rich wine.

But it doesn't require gravity to make excellent Pinot Noir. There are a million things more important than just gravity flow...

Must concentrators appear in Oregon

Concentration is certainly a key to quality wine, and more and more the better wineries around the world are indeed focusing on the vineyard as the most important element to assure wine quality.

But grapes – mostly red varieties – lacking a desired concentration can be manipulated in the cellar in a number of ways to improve its quality. Modern technology has made its way to cool-climate Oregon, where the issues relate more to phenolic ripening than dilution, but where rain at harvest – and potential dilution – is always a threat. Entropy evaporators – first introduced in Bordeaux in 1989 – use low heat and a vacuum system to remove excess weather-created water from must; the reverse osmosis machine employs pressure and a filter-like membrane to achieve the same results: concentrating must and the resultant wine. These processes only have conditional appellation approval in France. It's still too early to know whether these expensive ($30,000–$100,000) machines will be a smart investment, as this equipment only became available in Oregon in the late 1990s, and the last three vintages of the century were ripe and dry. Wineries that have purchased entropy evaporators include Archery Summit in Dundee, Cristom in the Eola Hills, Domaine Serene in Dundee, Ken Wright in Carlton, and WillaKenzie Estate in Yamhill.

No one intends to use the machines as a matter of course each harvest. Many say they bought the equipment as an insurance policy, to have it available if it is needed. The prevailing thought is if the Willamette Valley sees another rain-diluted vintage as in 1995, the machines will be very useful indeed. The risk of this concentration technique, though, is the potential for creating unnaturally changed flavours.

Harvest time is usually cool in the Willamette Valley, in which lies Yamhill County, allowing fermentation tanks to live outside without risk of overheating, thanks to the ambient temperatures. Think of it as natural tank temperature control.

Notable producers

ADEA Wine Company

☎ 503-662-4509 ℻ 503-662-3259
✉ info@adeawine.com
🌐 www.adeawine.com
26423 NW Highway 47, Gaston, Oregon 97119
Acreage in production 0.4ha (1 acre) Pinot Noir (planted in 1990)
New plantings 0.6ha (1.5 acres) Pinot Noir
Production capacity 3,000 cases
2000 production 1,200 cases
Established 1995
First wines released 1995 vintage
Formerly known as Fisher Family Cellars, the name ADEA (the initials of each member of the Fisher family) applies to the 1998 vintage onwards. Production is limited to Pinot Noir, Pinot Gris and Chardonnay, from their own fruit, and vines leased by the acre from local vineyards.

Adelsheim Vineyard

☎ 503-538-3652 ℻ 503-538-2248
✉ mail@adelsheimvineyard.com
🌐 www.adelsheimvineyard.com
PO Box 909, 16800 NE Calkins Lane, Newberg, Oregon 97132
Acreage in production 32.2ha (79.6 acres) Pinot Noir, 12.7 ha (31.4 acres) Pinot Gris, 3ha (7.5 acres) Chardonnay, 1.4ha (3.5 acres) Pinot Blanc, 1.3ha (3.3 acres) Tocai Friulano
New plantings 14.9ha (36.7 acres) Pinot Noir, 1ha (2.5 acres) Pinot Gris, 1ha (2.5 acres Auxerrois)
Production capacity 35,000 cases
2000 production 17,000 cases
Established 1971
First wines released 1978 vintage
David Adelsheim is the Dean of the Oregon wine industry, taking a leading role on most of the issues over the last 30 years. His wines have been inconsistent over the years; quality is now much improved with Adelsheim directly overseeing wine production again at his new gravity-fed facility.

Amity Vineyards

☎ 503-835-2362, 888-264-8966
℻ 503-835-6451
✉ amity@amityvineyards.com
🌐 www.amityvineyards.com
18150 Amity Vineyards Road, Amity, Oregon 97101
Acreage in production 3ha (7.5 acres) Pinot Noir, 1.2ha (3 acres) Riesling, 1.8ha (4.5 acres) Pinot Blanc**Production capacity** 14,200 cases

2000 production 11,400 cases
Established 1976
First wines released 1976 vintage
Located at the base of the Eola Hills, just within Yamhill County. Owner and winemaker Myron Redford does not use any new oak on his Pinot Noir, leaving his wines light and fruity; his white wines can be lively and fresh.

Archery Summit Winery

☎ 503-864-4300 ℻ 503-864-4038
✉ info@archerysummit.com
🌐 www.archerysummit.com
18599 Archery Summit Road, Dayton, Oregon 97114
Acreage in production 33.7ha (83.1 acres) Pinot Noir, 1.1ha (2.8 acres) Chardonnay, 4.6ha (11.4 acres) Pinot Gris, 0.7ha (1.7 acres) Pinot Blanc
New plantings 3.2ha (8 acres) Pinot Noir
Production capacity 13,500 cases
2000 production 12,000 cases

Established and first vintage produced:1993
Until its impressive gravity-fed winery was constructed in 1995, grapes were trucked to its sibling Pine Ridge Winery in the Napa Valley (both operated by Gary Andrus). Pinot Noir is the focus, and the wines are huge, concentrated beauties, aged in close to 100 per cent new oak. Many consider these wines to be Oregon's finest (with a release price of $100 per bottle for one of the cuvées), and they would be if the oak were a little less prominent feature. The vineyards – the Estate, Arcus (the former Archibald Vineyard) and the Red Hills Vineyard (former Fuqua Vineyard) – produce some of the most focused, well-structured fruit in the state. Viriton, a white wine blend, is the property's only white wine.

David Adelsheim of Adelsheim Vineyard

Rollin Soles of Argyle Winery

Argyle Winery/The Dundee Wine Company

☎ 503-538-8520, 888-4 ARGYLE
ⓕ 503-538-2055
ⓔ buywine@argylewinery.com
ⓦ www.argylewinery.com
P.O. Box 280, 691 Highway 99W, Dundee, Oregon 97115
Acreage in production 39.7ha (98 acres) Pinot Noir, 23.5ha (58 acres) Chardonnay, 1.2ha (3 acres) Pinot Meunier
New plantings 11.7ha (29 acres) Pinot Noir, 2.8ha (7 acres) Chardonnay
Production capacity 50,000 cases
2000 production 40,000 cases
Established 1987
First wines released 1987 vintage
Oregon's top sparkling wine producer (*méthode traditionelle*), owned by Petaluma Wines of Australia. Winemaker Rollin Soles crafts very fine Pinot Noir and Chardonnay, as well. Dijon clones are a specialty, in use for sparkling wines as well as still. A tiny amount of Riesling is still grown, producing one of the best dry Rieslings in Oregon.

Beaux Frères

☎ 503-537-1137 ⓕ 503-537-2613
ⓔ info@beauxfreres.com
ⓦ www.beauxfreres.com
15155 NE North Valley Road, Newberg, Oregon 97132
Acreage in production 9.7ha (24 acres) Pinot Noir
New plantings 3.2ha (8 acres) Pinot Noir
Production capacity 5,000 cases
2000 production 3,700 cases
Established 1988
First wines released 1991 vintage
One of Oregon's best-known labels, due to the ownership: brothers-in-law (*beaux frères*) Mike Etzel and wine writer Robert Parker. Etzel crafts very smooth, powerful Pinot Noir, changing his style from the early years' (the first commercial release was 1992) tannic, muscular personality to a sleeker, more refined wine with softer tannins. Wines produced from the estate vineyards are labelled Beaux Frères; wines made from purchased fruit and/or barrel selections are labelled the Belle Soeurs (sisters-in-law).

Belle Pente Vineyard & Winery

☎ 503-852-9500 ⓕ 503-852-6977
ⓔ wine@bellepente.com
ⓦ www.bellepente.com
12470 NE Rowland Road, Carlton, Oregon 97011
Acreage in production 3.2ha (8 acres) Pinot Noir, 0.2ha (0.5 acre) Chardonnay, 0.2ha (0.5 acre) Pinot Gris
New plantings 1.2ha (3 acres) Pinot Noir, 0.8ha (2 acres) Pinot Gris, 0.8ha (2 acres) Chardonnay
Production capacity 4,000 cases
2000 production 3,500 cases
Established 1994
First wines released 1996 vintage
Excellent, well-focused wines produced by Brian O'Donnell, a home winemaker since 1986.

Brick House Vineyards

☎ 503-538-5136 ⓕ 503-538-5136
ⓔ info@brickhousewines.com
ⓦ www.brickhousewines.com
18200 Lewis Rogers Lane, Newberg, Oregon 97132
Acreage in production 7.3ha (18 acres) Pinot Noir, 1.2ha (3 acres) Chardonnay, 1.8ha (4.5 acres) Gamay Noir
New plantings 0.2ha (0.4 acre) Chardonnay
Production capacity 2,000 cases
2000 production 1,650 cases
Established 1990; certified organic 1990
First wines released 1993 vintage
Doug Tunnell is a former CBS foreign correspondent who returned to his native Oregon to plant grapes. He has become one of the best producers in Oregon, known for small quantities of earthy, well-structured, polished wines, especially his 1999 Pinot Noir 50 per cent whole-cluster *cuvée* called Cinquante. (All *cuvées* for 2000 were also vinified that way; as long as stems get ripe enough to begin to lignify, Tunnell prefers to use whole clusters.) Gamay Noir is treated like Pinot Noir and resembles a fine Cru Beaujolais. The low-yielding, organic vineyards focus on French clones (Dijon and Pommard Pinot Noir).

Cameron Winery

☎ 503-538-0336 ⓕ 503-538-0336
PO Box 27, 8200 Worden Hill Road, Dundee, Oregon 97115
Acreage in production Clos Electrique (estate) vineyard – 0.8ha (2 acres) Pinot Noir, 0.7ha (1.75 acres) Chardonnay; Abbey Ridge

Mike Etzel of Beaux Frères

Vineyard – 1.8ha (4.5 acres) Chardonnay, 0.8ha (2 acres) Pinot Bianco, 2.6ha (6.5 acres) Pinot Noir
Production capacity 4,000 cases
2000 production 4,000 cases
Established 1984
First wines released 1984 vintage
Fine, balanced wines crafted by the quirky Jon Paul, a talented winemaker who has worked in Burgundy, California, and New Zealand. Labels communicate an Italian influence and clever design. Paul's occasional newsletters make delightful, humorous reading.

Carlo & Julian
☎ 503-852-7432 ℻ 503-852-7432
✉ carlojulwine@aol.com
1000 Main Street, Carleton,
Oregon 97111
Acreage in production 0.8ha (2 acres) Pinot Noir
New plantings 1.2ha (3 acres) Pinot Noir
Production capacity 1,000 cases
2000 production 600 cases
Established 1991
First wines released 1996 vintage

Former Erath Vineyards Winery and Rex Hill Vineyards enologist Felix Madrid now produces his own low yielding, well-structured Pinot Noir, as well as an occasional estate Nebbiolo, but the Nebbiolo gets frost damage easily. He also makes a "field blend" of the Nebbiolo with some estate Tempranillo and Merlot. His plan is to eventually include some Carmenère . Madrid also produces a barrel-fermented Sauvignon Blanc with fruit from the Croft Vineyard.

Chateau Benoit Winery
☎ 503-864-2991 ℻ 503-864-2203
✉ info@chateaubenoit.com
🌐 www.chateaubenoit.com
6580 N.E. Mineral Springs Road, Carlton,
Oregon 97111
Acreage in production Estate vineyard: 4.1ha (10 acres) White Riesling, 5.7ha (14 acres) Müller-Thurgau; Other vineyards: 2ha (5 acres) Pinot Gris, 2ha (5 acres) Chardonnay, 2ha (5 acres) Pinot Noir
New plantings 2ha (5 acres) Pinot Noir
Production capacity 18,000 cases
2000 production 14,500 cases

Established 1979
First wines released 1979 vintage
Columbia Empire Farms, a large berry and hazelnut producer in Dundee (owned by Yamhill County investor and media mogul Dr Robert B Pamplin Jr), purchased Chateau Benoit and its food and wine factory-outlet store in Lincoln City (on the Oregon coast) in 2000. Since then, the quality has risen, even for its flagship Müller-Thurgau, an often undistinguished varietal that in the 1998 and 1999 vintages has shown promise.

Chehalem
☎ 503-538-4700 ℻ 503-537-0850
✉ harrypn@chehalemwines.com
🌐 www.chehalemwines.com
31190 NE Veritas Lane, Newberg,
Oregon 97132
Acreage in production Three estate vineyards (Ridgecrest, Stoller, and Corral Creek): 47.8ha (118 acres) Pinot Noir, 13.8ha (34 acres) Chardonnay, 7.3ha (18 acres) Pinot Gris, 0.4ha (1 acre) Pinot Blanc, 0.4ha (1 acre) Riesling, 0.8ha (2 acres) Gamay Noir
Production capacity 12,000 cases
2000 production 12,000 cases
Vineyards **established** 1980
First wines released 1990 vintage
Former chemical engineer Harry Peterson-Nedry and co-winemaker Cheryl Francis produce well-balanced, very focused wines. Top *cuvée* is the Rion Reserve, which uses the best fruit from Chehalem's oldest vineyard (Ridgecrest) and is named in honour of Burgundian Patrice Rion, who consulted with Chehalem in its early years. New Stoller Vineyard is very impressive.

Coleman Vineyard
☎ 503-843-2707 ℻ 503-843-3845
✉ colemanvineyard@msn.com
🌐 www.colemanvineyard.com
22734 Latham Road, McMinnville,
Oregon 97128
Acreage in production 5.7ha (14 acres) Pinot Noir, 3.6ha (9 acres) Pinot Gris
Production capacity 5,000 cases
2000 production 1,000 cases
Established 1991
First wines released 1999 vintage
New label, formerly selling all its fruit to area wineries.

Cuneo Cellars

☎ 503-835-2782 📠 503-835-6106
📧 gino@cuneocellars.com
🌐 www.cuneocellars.com
**750 Lincoln Street, Carlton,
Oregon 97111**
Acreage in production 4.5ha (11 acres)
Cabernet Sauvignon, 2.4ha (6 acres) Cabernet
Franc, 2.8ha (7 acres) Merlot, 0.2ha (0.5 acre)
Malbec, 0.4ha (1 acre) Petit Verdot, 8.1ha
(20 acres) Pinot Noir, 0.8ha (2 acres) Syrah, 4.5ha
(11 acres) Sangiovese, 0.8ha (2 acres) Nebbiolo
New plantings 0.8ha (2 acres) Cabernet
Sauvignon, 0.4ha (1 acre) Cabernet Franc, 0.4ha
(1 acre) Merlot, 0.2ha (0.5 acre) Malbec, 0.4ha
(1 acre) Petit Verdot, 0.4ha (1 acre) Pinot Noir,
4.9ha (12 acres) Sangiovese, 0.4ha (1 acre)
Barbera, 0.4ha (1 acre) Montepulciano
Production capacity 8,000 cases
2000 production 4,000 cases
Established 1993
First wines released 1989 vintage
Previously located near the vineyards in the
former Hidden Springs Winery near Amity,
Gino Cuneo relocated his winery in 2001.

Doug Tunnell of Brick House Vineyards

While certainly a Pinot Noir producer, Cuneo
takes pride in small lots of Italian varietals and
wines from the warm weather grapes.

Domaine Coteau

☎ 503-697-7319 **8849 Three Trees Lane,
Amity, Oregon 97101**
Acreage in production 6.9ha (17 acres)
Production capacity 3,000 cases
2000 production 729 cases
Established 1995
First wines released 1998 vintage
New producer with very limited distribution.

Domaine Drouhin Oregon

☎ 503-864-2700 📠 503-864-3377
P.O. Box 700, Dundee, Oregon 97115
Acreage in production 32.4ha (80 acres)
Pinot Noir, 2.4ha (6 acres) Chardonnay
Production capacity 18,000 cases
2000 production 15,000 cases
Established 1988
First wines released 1988 vintage
Oregon's premier Burgundy connection,
producing an amazingly similarly styled wine in
Oregon as it does at Maison Joseph Drouhin in
Burgundy, a silky, complex Pinot Noir with good
ageing ability. No wonder, as Veronique Drouhin
travels back and forth from Beaune to make the
Oregon wine in the family's signature style. The
Chardonnay, released since the 1997 vintage,
shows the same restraint and elegance.

Domaine Serene Vineyards and Winery

☎ 503-852-7777 📠 503-852-7776
📧 rob@viclink.com
🌐 www.domaineserene.com
**6555 NE Hilltop Lane, Dayton,
Oregon 97114**
Acreage in production 47.8ha (117.5 acres)
Pinot Noir, 4.6ha (11.5 acres) Chardonnay
New plantings 10.7ha (26.4 acres) Pinot Noir
Production capacity 15,000 cases
2000 production 8,500 cases
Established 1989
First wines released 1990 vintage
Tony Rynders, with experience at Hogue in
Washington and Argyle in Oregon, took over
Domaine Serene winemaking responsibilities
from Ken Wright beginning with the 1998 vintage.
Rynders' great strength is in blending, although
the raw material Domaine Serene produces
stands very well on its own; the Evenstad Reserve
is a stunning example of Oregon Pinot Noir.
A new, glamorous, gravity-fed winery debuts
with the 2001 harvest.

Duck Pond Cellars

☎ 503-538-3199 📠 503-538-3190
📧 duckpond@duckpondcellars.com
🌐 www.duckpondcellars.com
**PO Box 429, 23145 Highway 99W,
Dundee, Oregon 97115**
Acreage in production In Oregon – 60.8ha
(150 acres) Pinot Noir, 46.6ha (115 acres) Pinot
Gris, 14.2ha (35 acres) Chardonnay. In
Washington – 74.9ha (185 acres) Merlot, 40.1ha
(99 acres) Chardonnay, 27.5ha (68 acres)
Cabernet Sauvignon, 8.9ha (21.9 acres) Cabernet
Franc, 3.5ha (8.7 acres) Sauvignon Blanc, 5.3ha
(13 acres) Semillon, 7.3ha (18 acres) Syrah, 0.8ha
(2 acres) Gewürztraminer, 2.3ha (5.7 acres)
Viognier
New plantings In Washington – 2.2ha (30
acres) Syrah, 10.1ha (25 acres) Cabernet
Sauvignon, 2ha (5 acres) Riesling
2000 production 75,000 cases

Dick Erath of Erath Vineyards Winery

Established 1993
First wines released 1989 vintage
The Duck Pond winery sits in 99W, the main road through Dundee; its nicely landscaped front gardens make it an often-visited attraction. This is one of the Northwest's most commercial operations, with a growing vineyard inventory and ever-increasing production. Quality tends to be good, but commercial.

Dundee Springs Winery

☎ 503-538-8000 📠 503-538-6032
📧 sales@dundeesprings.com
🌐 www.dundeesprings.com
P O Box 9, 9605 Fox Farm Rd. Dundee,
Oregon 97115
Acreage in production 16.2ha (40 acres)
Pinot Noir, 6.1ha (15 acres) Pinot Gris, 2ha (5 acres) Pinot Blanc
Production capacity 23,000 cases
2000 production 3 ,000 cases
Established 1990
First wines released 1992 vintage
The first vintage, a 1992 Pinot Noir (with fruit from their Perry Bower Vineyard, planted in 1989) won a gold medal at the San Diego International Wine Competition. The bulk of their high quality grapes are sold to Dundee-area winemakers.

Elk Cove Vineyards

☎ 503-985-7760 📠 503-985-3525
📧 elkcove@teleport.com
🌐 www.elkcove.com
27751 NW Olson Road, Gaston,
Oregon 97119
Acreage in production 26.7ha (66 acres
Pinot Noir, 8.1ha (20 acres) Pinot Gris, 3.2ha (8 acres) Riesling, 0.8ha (2 acres) Pinot Blanc, 1.2ha (3 acres) Gewürztraminer, 0.4ha (1 acre) Viognier
Production capacity 25,000 cases
2000 production 15,000 cases
Established 1974
First wines released 1977 vintage
One of the pioneering wine families, son Adam Campbell is now in charge. Quality dessert wines called Ultima since 1989; Pinot Noirs keep getting better and better, with the 1998 and 1999 wines very lovely indeed.

Erath Vineyards Winery

☎ 503-538-3318 📠 503-538-1074
📧 info@erath.com 🌐 www.erath.com
94009 NE Worden Hill Road, Dundee,
Oregon 97115
Acreage in production 25.2ha (62.2 acres)
Pinot Noir, 12 acres Pinot Gris, 9.1 acres

Chardonnay, 4.3 acres Pinot Blanc, 4 acres of miscellaneous grapes including Dolcetto
Production capacity 42,000 cases
2000 production 41,400 cases
Established 1967
First wines released 1972 vintage
Pioneer Dick Erath began his winery with colleague Cal Knudsen, hence the labels bearing an Erath-Knudsen name, still seen until the early 1990s when the two parted ways. Erath's wines from the late 1970s continue to show well, especially the Rieslings, which have developed that classic diesel nuance. His best Pinot Noirs are vineyard designated, and reveal lovely fruit with strong acid backing. His Vintage Select series offers good value. Erath was one of the first wineries to plant and bottle Dijon-clone Chardonnay. He grafts his own plant material and provides grafted vines to colleagues, important especially in the early years of clonal diversity in the Yamhill County area. Rob Stuart now serves as winemaker with Erath. Erath Vineyards Winery was an early proponent of synthetic corks.

The Eyrie Vineyards

☎ 503-472-6315 📠 503-472-5124
PO Box 697, Dundee, Oregon 97115
Acreage in production 9.7ha (24 acres)
Pinot Gris, 7.3ha (18 acres) Pinot Noir, 1.6ha (4 acres) Chardonnay, 0.6ha (1.4 acres) Pinot meunier, 0.7ha (1.6 acres) Pinot Blanc, 0.5ha (1.3 acres) Muscat Ottonel
Production capacity 10,000
2000 production 8,000
Established 1966
First wines released 1970 vintage
Oregon's Pinot pioneer, Papa Pinot (as David Lett is affectionately known), produces balanced, lighter-styled Pinot Noirs that mature with age to become lovely, elegant, and somewhat earthy examples of what Oregon can offer. Even his white wines age well. Surprisingly, Pinot Gris is his primary product, as Lett claims, it allows him to dabble in his true passion, Pinot Noir.

Granville Wine

☎ 503-554-1861 📠 503-554-1861
📧 info@granvillewine.com
🌐 www.Granville.com
POB 566, Dundee, Oregon 97115
Acreage in production 1.2ha (3 acres)
Pinot Noir, 0.4ha (1 acre) Pinot Gris
New plantings 1.6ha (4 acres) Pinot Noir
Production capacity 500 cases

2000 production 500 cases
Established 2000
First wines released 2000 vintage
Viticulturist Allen Holstein manages some of the finest vineyards in Yamhill County: Domaine Drouhin Oregon, Argyle Winery, and Stoller Vineyards. His first efforts at winemaking show off the fruit quality for which he has become known, from Dundee vineyards planted in 1972.

Hamacher Wines

☎ 503-985-0120 ⊕ 503-985-3300
ⓔ eric@hamacherwines.com
ⓦ www.hamacherwines.com
40845 SW Burgarsky Road, Gaston, Oregon 97119
Production capacity 2,500 cases
2000 production 2,000 cases
Established 1995
First wines released 1995 vintage
Talented winemaker Eric Hamacher formerly served as winemaker at Tony Soter's well-regarded Étude Winery in California. Hamacher purchases fruit from small vineyards, and supervises all the work on those vines. He produces only Pinot Noir and Chardonnay, and very fine examples of each. Hamacher helped design the Lemelson Vineyard's gravity-fed winery, where he served as Lemelson's first winemaker and where he makes his own wine.

Hauer of the Dauen Winery

☎ 503-868-7359 ⊕ 503-868-7216
ⓔ jadauen@attglobal.net
16425 SE Webfoot Road, Dayton, Oregon 97114
Acreage in production 13ha (32 acres) Pinot Noir, 10.5ha (26 acres) Pinot Gris, 7.7ha (19 acres) Riesling, 5.7ha (14 acres) Chardonnay, 4.1ha (10 acres) Gewürztraminer, 1.2ha (3 acres) Lemberger, 1.2ha (3 acres) Gamay Noir
Production capacity 10,000 cases
2000 production 4,000 cases
Established 1999
First wines released 1998 vintage
The vineyards were planted in 1980, east of Amity and south of the town of Dayton. Wine styles at this family-operated winery tend to be fruity. Most of their grapes are sold to other wineries.

J K Carriere Wines

☎ 503-781-1150
ⓔ jim@jkcarriere.com
ⓦ www.jkcarriere.com

PO Box 662, 30295 Highway 99W, Newberg, Oregon 97132
Production capacity 2,000 cases
2000 production 750 cases
Established 1999
First wines released 1999 vintage
Jim Prosserhas served as a cellar assistant at Chehalem and Brick House, where hehas learned well. His Pinot Noir is among the top wines in the Valley, although in small production.

Ken Wright Cellars

☎ 503-852-7070 ⊕ 503-852-7111
ⓔ kwcellar@viclink.com
ⓦ www.kenwrightcellars.com
PO Box 190, 236 N. Kutch Street, Carlton, Oregon 97111
Production capacity 12,000 cases
2000 production 7,000 cases
Established 1994
First wines released 1994 vintage
One of Oregon's top winemakers, with a cult following for very pretty (verging on floral), elegant wines from low yielding vines. Wright manages all the vines from which he sources the grapes; remarkable given he owns none of them.

Most of his wines sell in advance of release, as "futures". Wright was the founder and winemaker of Panther Creek Cellars, which he sold in 1994. He also made the wines for Domaine Serene its fist few vintages.

Kramer Vineyards

☎ 503-662-4545 ⊕ 503-662-4033
ⓔ kramer@oregonwine.org
ⓦ www./kramerwine.com 26830 NW Olson Road, Gaston, Oregon 97119
Acreage In production 2.6ha (6.5 acres) Pinot Noir, 1.7ha (4.3 acres) Pinot Gris, 1.2ha (3 acres) Müller-Thurgau, 1.3 hecares (3.3 acres Chardonnay, 0.4ha (1 acre) Carmina
New plantings 0.8ha (2 acres) Pinot Noir, 0.4ha (1 acre) Chardonnay, 0.2ha (0.5 acres) Müller-Thurgau
Production capacity 7,000 cases
2000 production 2,600 cases
Established 1984
First wines released 1989 vintage
First **established** as a berry-wine producer. Trudy Kramer crafts very bright and pleasing varietal wines, as well as a number of seasonal fruit wines. Dijon clones account for the new plantings of Pinot Noir and all of the Chardonnay.

Ken Wright of Ken Wright Cellars

Kristin Hill Winery

☎ 503-835-0850 🖷 503-835-4012
✉ kristinhill@msn.com
🌐 www.kristinhill.com
3330 SW Amity Dayton Highway, Amity, Oregon 97101
Acreage in production 6.9ha (17 acres) in total planted to Gewürztraminer, Pinot Noir, Chardonnay, and Pinot Gris
New plantings 1.2ha (3 acres) Chardonnay
Production capacity 2,000 cases
2000 production 1,000 cases
Established 1990
First wines released 1990 vintage
The Aberg family first planted the vineyards in 1985. Wines produced include a *méthode traditionelle* sparkling wine, Pinot Noir, Chardonnay, Gewürztraminer, Riesling, Pinot Gris, and Müller-Thurgau.

Lange Estate Winery and Vineyards

☎ 503-538-6476 🖷 503-538-1938
✉ donlange@europa.com
🌐 www.langewinery.com
18380 NE Buena Vista Drive, Dundee, Oregon 97115
Acreage in production 2.4ha (6 acres) Pinot Noir
New plantings 3.2ha (8 acres) Pinot Noir
Production capacity 12,000 cases
2000 production 7,000 cases
Established 1987
First wines released 1988 vintage
These are high-quality wines. The Willamette Valley series blends from vineyards located in the north end of the valley; these wines are released earlier, see less oak, if any, and are more immediately drinkable. The reserve wines are a bit more complex and age-worthy. An Estate Pinot Noir from the Dundee property is a lovely, velvety wine. Willamette Valley Pinot Gris can be lively and crisp; the Reserve Pinot Gris, however, is fermented in 500-litre (11-gallon) oak puncheons and aged *sur lie*, making it rich and creamy.

Laurel Ridge Winery

☎ 503-852-7050 🖷 503-852-7404
13301 NE Kuehne Road, Carlton, Oregon 97111
Acreage in production 5.7ha (14 acres) Pinot Noir, 8.9ha (22 acres) Riesling, 4.1ha (10 acres) Sauvignon Blanc
New plantings 8.1ha (20 acres) Pinot Noir.

56.7ha (140 acres) to be planted.
Production capacity 20,000 cases
2000 production 9,000 cases
Established 1986
First wines released 1988 vintage
The Teppola family formerly operated its winery at the site that is now David Hill Winery in Washington County. The Laurel Ridge production facility was relocated to be closer to its premier vineyards in the Dundee Hills.

Lawton Winery, Ltd.

☎ 503-538-6509 🖷 503-538-7854
✉ keith@lawtonwinery.com
🌐 www.lawtonwinery.com
20990 NE Kings Grade, Newberg, Oregon 97132
Acreage in production 2ha (5 acres) Pinot Noir, 0.4 hecatare (1 acre) Riesling
New plantings 0.4ha (1 acre) Pinot Noir
Production capacity 2,400 cases
2000 production 650 cases
First wines released 1998 vintage

Lemelson Vineyards

☎ 503-852-6619 🖷 503-852-6119
✉ info@lemelsonvineyards.com
🌐 www.lemelsonvineyards.com

12020 NE Stag Hollow Road, Carlton, Oregon 97111
Acreage in production 14.2ha (35 acres) Pinot Noir, 2ha (5 acres) Chardonnay, 2ha (5 acres) Pinot Gris, 0.2ha (0.5 acre) Gamay Noir
New plantings 18.2ha (45 acres) Pinot Noir, 1.2ha (3 acres) Chardonnay
Production capacity 12,000 cases
2000 production 3,500 cases
Established 1998
First wines released 1999 vintage
Gravity-fed principles dominate this impressive new winery owned by Eric Lemelson. Winemaker Thomas Batchelderhas made a number of stunning wines in his inaugural (1999) vintage.

McKinlay Vineyards

☎ 503-625-2534 ✉ mckwine@aol.com
7120 Earlwood Road, Newberg, Oregon 97132
Acreage in production 4.9ha (12 acres) Pinot Noir
New plantings 4.1ha (10 acres) Pinot Noir
Production capacity 2,000 cases
2000 production 1,000 cases
Established 1987
First wines released 1987 vintage
UC Davis-trained winemaker Matt Kinne

Mike Stevenson and Ron Kaplan of Panther Creek Cellars

purchased grapes before his vineyard began, in 1994, to bear enough quality fruit. The McKinlay wines – Pinot Noir, Pinot Gris, and barrel-fermented Chardonnay – are well-made and offer complex layers of flavour.

Medici Vineyards and Winery

☎ 503-538-9668 ⓕ h.medici@juno.com
28005 NE Bell Road, Newberg,
Oregon 97132
Acreage in production 9.3ha (23 acres) Pinot Noir, 6.9ha (17 acres) Riesling
New plantings 4.1ha (10 acres) Pinot Noir
Production capacity 3,500 cases
2000 production 3,500 cases
Established 1970 (vineyards), 1995 (winery)
First wines released 1995 vintage
Peter Rosback (of the Sineann label) serves as winemaker, crafting good-quality Pinot Noir, Late Harvest Riesling, and a Riesling ice wine.

Mystic Mountain Vineyards

☎ 503-434-9025 ⓕ 503-474-9463
ⓔ mystic@mysticmountainvineyard.com
22470 SW Bennette Road, McMinnville,
Oregon 97128
Acreage in production 2ha (5 acres) Pinot Noir, 1.2ha (3 acres) Chardonnay
Production capacity 2,500 cases
2000 production 1,000 cases
Established 1997
First wines released 1997 vintage
First wine released was a youthful Chardonnay, with Pinot Noir not available until the 1998 vintage.

Panther Creek Cellars

☎ 503-472-8080 ⓕ 503-472-5667
ⓔ info@panthercreekcellars.com
ⓦ www.panthercreekcellars.com
455 N Irvine Street, McMinnville,
Oregon 97128
Production capacity 7,500 cases
2000 production 7,500 cases
Established 1985
First wines released 1986 vintage
Very high quality wine, now made by Michael Stevenson. Owner Ron Kaplan purchases grapes from some of the top vineyards of the state: Freedom Hill, Shea, Bednarik, Nysa, Arcus, Red Hills, DePonte, Colilo, Youngberg Hill, and Melrose, with long-term contracts for specific

rows of vines; Panther Creek controls the crop thinning, pruning, canopy management, and harvesting of the grapes. Yields are kept at two tons or less. The Pinot Noir is both cold pre-fermentation macerated and post-fermentation macerated, in each case for 2–3 days. The wines are deeply coloured, with concentrated fruit flavours and complexity. A new Pinot Gris shows great finesse.

Patricia Green Cellars

☎ 503-554-0821 ⓕ 503-538-3681
ⓔ pgc@viclink.com
15225 NE North Valley Road, Newberg,
Oregon 97132
Acreage in production 9.1ha (22.5 acres) Pinot Noir, 0.6ha (1.5 acres) Pinot Gris, 0.4ha (1 acre) Sauvignon Blanc
New plantings 1ha (2.5 acres) Pinot Noir
Production capacity 7,500 cases
2000 production 5,000 cases
Established 2000
Patricia Green was the celebrated winemaker at Torii Mor, leaving there in 1999 to purchase the former Autumn Wind Vineyard and create her own label. Her signature is a well-structured style; deeply coloured wines with great pizzazz.

Rex Hill Vineyards

☎ 503-538-0666 ⓕ 503-538-1409
ⓔ info@rexhill.com ⓦ www.rexhill.com
30835 N. Highway 99W, Newberg,
Oregon 97132
Acreage in production 44.1ha (109 acres) Pinot Noir, 14.2ha (35 acres) Pinot Gris, 9.3ha (23 acres) Chardonnay. Developing acres: 19.4ha (48 acres) Pinot Noir, 1.2ha (3 acres) Pinot Gris
New plantings 14.2ha (35 acres) Pinot Noir
Production capacity 32,000 cases
2000 production 31,000 cases
Established 1982
First wines released 1985 vintage
Winemaker Lynn Penner-Ash crafts a wide range of wines, with her top reserve and vineyard-designated wines showing great depth and elegance. Unusual wines included a barrel-fermented Pinot Gris, a pleasant rosé made in wet years (from the *saignée* process), and a sparkling wine. The winery operates a tasting room on its attractive property, and also maintains the tasting room at the Maresh Vineyard Red Barn (located in Dundee), whose wines Rex Hill produces.

Shea Wine Cellars

☎ 503-241-6527 ⓕ 503-241-6527
ⓔ Rshea007@aol.com
12321 Highway 240, Yamhill,
Oregon 97221
Acreage in production 25.5ha (63 acres) Pinot Noir, 6.5ha (16 acres) Chardonnay, 1ha (2.5 acres) Pinot Gris
New plantings 24.3ha (60 acres) Pinot Noir
2000 production 1,100 cases
First wines released 1996 vintage
Shea is one of Oregon's premier vineyard sites, selling grapes to many top winemakers. Dick Shea's own-label Pinot Noir is produced by Michael Stevenson at Panther Creek Cellars, typically a well-structured and concentrated wine.

Sineann

☎ 503-538-5894
ⓔ sineann@earthlink.net
PO Box 10, Newberg, Oregon 97132
2000 production 2,500 cases
Established 1994
First wines released 1994 vintage
Peter Rosback makes a range of small lot, big, intense (sometimes too much so) wines from purchased fruit from both Oregon and Washington, including old-vine Zinfandel (a specialty), Cabernet Sauvignon, Pinot Noir, Merlot, Sauvignon Blanc, Gewürztraminer, Pinot Gris, and even a Zinfandel ice wine! He also consults for a number of newer Oregon wineries.

Soter Vineyards

☎ 707-257-5300
PO Box 400, Yamhill, OR 97148; 22050
N.E. Ridge Road, Yamhill, Oregon 97148
Acreage in production 6.5ha (16 acres) Pinot Noir, 2.4ha (6 acres) Dijon clone Chardonnay
Production capacity 4,000 cases
2000 production 1,000 cases
Established 2000
First wines released 1997 vintage
Étude Winery (California) founder/owner and long-time respected winery consultant Tony Soter purchased the Beacon Hill vineyard, located above WillaKenzie on the Chehalem Mountains. The vineyard was first planted in 1988, and later expanded with grafted, clonal plants in 1988–1989. The first wines Soter released (in 2001) were the lovely 1998 Beacon Hill Pinot Noir and a sparkling wine, 1997 Brut Rosé (Beacon Hill Vineyard). Soter and his family currently divide their time between Oregon and California.

Sokol Blosser Winery

☎ 503-864-2282 📠 503-864-2710
📧 info@sokolblosser.com
🌐 www.sokolblosser.com
PO Box 399, 5000 NE Sokol Blosser Lane,
Dundee, Oregon 97115
Acreage in production 6.8ha (16.8 acres)
Pinot Noir, 2.7ha (6.6 acres) Pinot Gris, 2.1ha
(5.3 acres) Chardonnay, 0.9ha (2.3 acres) White
Riesling, 0.4ha (1 acre) Müller-Thurgau
New plantings 13ha (32 acres) Pinot Noir,
0.2ha (0.4 acre) Pinot Gris, 1ha (2.5 acres)
Müller-Thurgau
Production capacity 30,000 cases
2000 production 23,000 cases
Established 1971
First wines released 1977 vintage
Pioneer Susan Sokol Blosser's winery has always
produced consistently good wines; with the hiring
of skilled winemaker Russ Rosner in the late
1990s, the quality of the wines leapt forward.
The winery has seen great success with a non-
vintage white called Evolution, a mouthfilling,
slightly sweet blend of Müller-Thurgau,
Sémillon, Sylvaner, Riesling, Pinot Gris, Muscat,
Gewürztraminer, Chardonnay, and Pinot Blanc.

Stag Hollow Wines

☎ 503-662-4022 📠 503-662-4581
📧 stag.hollow-vineyards@staghollow.com
🌐 www. staghollow.com
7930 Blackburn Road, Yamhill,
Oregon 97148
Acreage in production 2ha (5 acres)
Pinot Noir, 0.4ha (1 acre) Chardonnay, 0.4ha
(1 acre) Early Muscat and Muscat Ottonel,
0.4ha (1 acre) Dolcetto
New plantings 0.4ha (1 acre) Pinot Noir
Production capacity 1,000 cases
2000 production 400 cases
Established 1994
First wines released 1994
Mark Huff and Jill Zarnowitz planted the vineyard
in 1990 and produced a lovely debut Pinot Noir
in 1994. Two estate reserve-style Pinot Noirs
are made, Celebré and the more structured
Vendange Sélection. In 1997, Stag Hollow began
producing a white dessert wine, a sweet blend of
Muscat Ottonel, Early Muscat, and Chardonnay.

Starr Winery

☎ 503-538-3467 📠 503-642-5989
📧 starrwinery@teleport.com
31590 NE Schaad Road, Newberg,
Oregon 97132
New plantings 3.2ha (8 acres) Pinot Noir
Production capacity 3,000 cases
2000 production 1,850 cases
Established 1989
First wines released 1989
Former Portland retail merchant Rachel Starr and
her partner Bob Hanson purchase fruit to make
both their Pinot Noir and Chardonnay.

Stone Wolf Vineyards

☎ 503-434-9025 📠 503-474-9463
📧 stone@stonewolfvineyards.com
PO Box 1232, McMinnville, Oregon 97128
Acreage in production 6.5ha (16 acres) Pinot
Noir, 6.1ha (15 acres) Chardonnay, 3.6ha (9 acres)
Müller-Thurgau
Production capacity 15,000 cases
2000 production 5,000 cases
Established 1997
First wines released 1997
Owned and operated by the same people who
own Mystic Mountain Vineyards, Stone Wolf is
entered in numerous state fair competitions and
has won many awards for its estate-grown
Chardonnay and Pinot Noir, as well as for a very
nice Pinot Gris it produces.

Thomas

☎ 503-852-6969
PO Box 48, Carlton, Oregon 97111
Acreage in production 1.6ha (4 acres)
Pinot Noir
New plantings replanting due to phylloxera
ongoing at the rate of 0.2ha (0.5 acre) per year
Production capacity 500 cases
2000 production 450 cases
Established 1984
First wines released 1988
John Thomas is a high-quality producer, releasing
wines from less-than-optimal vintages under the
ACME Wineworks label, a non-vintage wine.

Tempest Vineyards

☎ 503-252-1383 or 503-835-2600
📠 503-252-7059 📧 keithorr@jps.net
PO Box 370, 6000 Karla's Road, Amity,
Oregon 97101
Acreage in production 2ha (5 acres) Pinot
Noir, 1.2ha (3 acres) Chardonnay, 0.6ha (1.5 acres)
Pinot Gris, 0.6ha (0.5 acre) Muscat
Production capacity 4,000 cases
2000 production 1,500 cases
Established 1988

First wines released 1988
Keith Orr treats his wines to long barrel-ageing:
the Chardonnay sees four years in barrel, Pinot 24
to 30 months, while the Willamette Valley
Cabernet Sauvignon and Zinfandel spend four
to five years in barrel. Other specialties include
two *apéritif* wines, a fortified Cabernet Sauvignon-
based wine flavoured with walnuts and orange
peel, and a fortified Pinot Noir flavoured with
citrus and vanilla.

Torii Mor Winery

☎ 503-434-1439 📠 503-434-5733
📧 kelvin@toriimorwinery.com
🌐 www.toriimorwinery.com
905 East 10th St., McMinnville, Oregon
97128
Acreage in production 2.1ha (5.1 acres)
Pinot Noir, 0.7ha (1.7 acres) Chardonnay, 0.4ha
(0.9 acres) Pinot Gris
Production capacity 8,000 cases
2000 production 5,460 cases
Established 1993
First wines released 1993
A consistently strong producer of concentrated
vineyard-designated Pinot Noir, Chardonnay, and
Pinot Gris. Originally under talented Patty Green's
winemaking direction, now with Willamette Valley
Vineyards' skilled winemaker Joe Dobbes.
Owned by Dr Don Olson and his wife Margie, Torii
Mor was initially a small project that was intended
to showcase the fruit from their vineyard.

Westrey Wine Company

☎ 503-434-6357 📠 503-474-9487
📧 info@Westrey.com
PO Box 386, Dundee, Oregon 97115,
1065 NE Alpine Street, McMinnville,
Oregon 97128
New plantings 2.6ha (6.5 acres) Pinot Noir,
1.2ha (3 acres) Chardonnay, 0.8ha (2 acres)
Pinot Gris
Production capacity 5,000 cases
2000 production 3,200 cases
Established 1993
First wines released 1993
David Autrey and Amy Wesselman scout for good
fruit each year and produce good wines with
clean varietal character. In 2000, they purchased
an old abandoned vineyard site in the Dundee
Hills and have started to plant it. Wesselman is
currently line managing director of the annual
International Pinot Noir celebration.

WillaKenzie Estate Winery

☎ 503-662-3280 or 888-WKE -WINE
℻ 503-662-4829
🄴 winery@willakenzie.com
🅦 www.willakenzie.com
19143 NE Laughlin Road, Yamhill, Oregon 97148
Acreage in production 48.6ha (120 acres) in total of Pinot Noir, Pinot Meunier, Pinot Blanc, Pinot Gris, and Chardonnay
Production capacity 20,000
2000 production 15,000 cases
Established 1995
First wines released 1995 vintage
Sun Microsystems executive Bernie Lacroute and his wife Ronni "retired" to this 170ha (420 acre) property on the Chehalem Mountains. The vineyards were first planted in 1992, with strong clonal diversification. Winemaker Laurent Montalieu produces a range of Pinot-family wines in an impressive gravity-fed winery, including two very different Pinot Noirs named after Bernie Lacroute's parents: the Pierre Léon, a robust, structured wine, and the Aliette, a softer, silkier wine.

Wine Country Farm

☎ 503-864-3446 ℻ 503-864-3109
🄴 winecountryfarm@webtv.net
🅦 www.winecountryfarm.com
6855 Breyman Orchards Road, Dayton, Oregon 97114
Acreage in production 0.2ha (0.5 acre) Pinot Noir, 0.2ha (0.5 acre) Gamay Noir, 0.4ha (1 acre) Chardonnay, 0.4ha (1 acre) Riesling, 0.8ha (2 acres) Müller-Thurgau
2000 production 800 cases
Established 1975
First wines released 1993 vintage
A bed and breakfast inn located across the street from Domaine Drouhin Oregon, with its small vineyards adjacent to David Lett's. Small production served and sold at the B & B.

Winter's Hill Vineyard

☎ 503-864-4610 ℻ 503-864-3992
🄴 info@wintershillwine.com
🅦 www.wintershillwine.com
P O Box 160, Lafayette, Oregon 97127
Acreage in production 5.3ha (13 acres) Pinot Noir, 5.3ha (13 acres) Pinot Gris
New plantings 3.2ha (8 acres) Pinot Noir, 0.5ha (1.3 acres) Pinot Blanc, 0.5ha (1.3 acres) Pinot Gris

David Lett of The Eyrie Vineyards

Production capacity 2,000 cases
2000 production 725 cases
Established 1990
First wines released 1998 vintage
Planted on the fruit and grain farm site of owner Emily Gladhart's parents on a south-facing slope of the Dundee Hills, the winery is run by the family.

Youngberg Hill Vineyards

☎ 503-472-2727 ℻ 503-472-1313
🅦 www.youngberghill.com
10660 SW Youngberg Hill Road, McMinnville, Oregon 97128
Acreage in production 4.9ha (12 acres) Pinot Noir
Production capacity 1,200 cases
2000 production 310 cases
Established 1989
First wines released 1996 vintage
A charming country inn, surrounded by 4.9ha (12 acres) of vineyard. The Pinot Noir is low yielding, the wines very pleasant and slightly herbal. Very limited distribution.

Yamhill Valley Vineyards

☎ 503-843-3100 or 800-825-4845
℻ 503-843-2450 🄴 info@yamhill.com
🅦 www.yamhill.com
16250 SW Oldsville Road, McMinnville, Oregon 97128
Acreage in production 27.9ha (69 acres) Pinot Noir, 6.5ha (16 acres) Pinot Blanc, 1.2ha (3 acres) Pinot Gris, 1.2ha (3 acres) Riesling
Production capacity 17,000 cases
2000 production 15,000 cases
Established 1983
First wines released 1983 vintage
Solid producer, with fresh crisp whites and pleasant, bright Pinot Noir. Good success with the 1998 and 1999 vintages.

Zelko

☎ 503-528-0704 ℻ 503-528-0708
🄴 jrz-kmz@worldnet.att.net
31590 NE Schadd Road, Newberg, Oregon 97312
Acreage in production 6.1ha (15 acres) Pinot Noir
New plantings 1.2ha (3 acres) Pinot Noir
Production capacity 3,000 cases
2000 production 3,000 cases
Established 2000
First wines released 2000 vintage
Brand new winery with no wine on the market yet.

Northern Willamette Valley

Few grapevines are in evidence around **Portland** – Oregon's largest city and certainly the commercial and cultural hub of the northern Willamette Valley.

This is the most urban part of Oregon; any available land possibly suited for grapes gets gobbled up for housing and development. In fact, most of Portland is within what is called an Urban Growth Boundary (UGB), a government-established "zone" inside of which are housing goals, density standards, and development curbs. The UGB exists to define and control the growth of a city, and encourage compact and efficient development within the UGB, farm activity is intentionally limited. At the same time, Oregon's very rigid

and protective land use laws—legislated in 1972 with some assistance from the young Oregon wine growing community—were designed to keep farm land and forest land outside the UGB protected area.

Not all of the northern Willamette Valley lies within the UGB. Multnomah County, Clackamas County, and part of Washington County constitute the political divisions of the area; some protected farm and forest land lie within each. But encroaching development in unregulated pockets outside the UGB also means sprawl and haphazard growth.

Beyond the obvious choices of vineyard **site selection** (including climate, air movement,

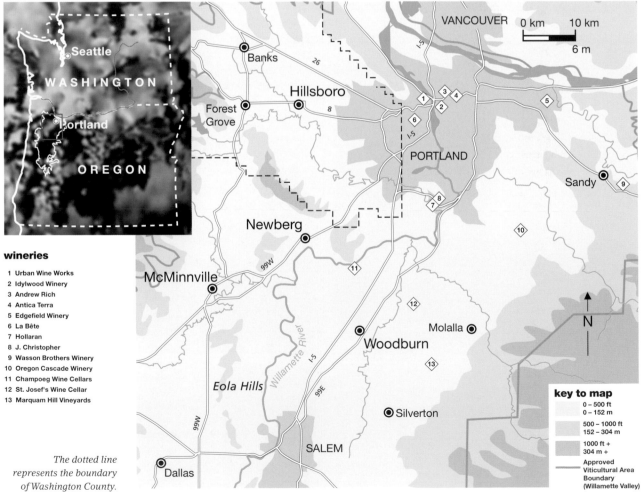

wineries

1 Urban Wine Works
2 Idylwood Winery
3 Andrew Rich
4 Antica Terra
5 Edgefield Winery
6 La Bête
7 Hollaran
8 J. Christopher
9 Wasson Brothers Winery
10 Oregon Cascade Winery
11 Champoeg Wine Cellars
12 St. Josef's Wine Cellar
13 Marquam Hill Vineyards

The dotted line represents the boundary of Washington County.

key to map

0 – 500 ft
0 – 152 m

500 – 1000 ft
152 – 304 m

1000 ft +
304 m +

Approved Viticultural Area Boundary (Willamette Valley)

elevation, slope, wind, soil, aspect, wind, and water), considerations about choosing sites anywhere include the cost of the land, local-zoning restrictions, and proximity to an established wine industry. The cost of land in the northern Willamette Valley is high. There are large operations cultivating produce such as berries, corn, vegetables, flowers and nursery stock, and nuts. But that land is mostly flat and not suited to growing grapes.

You can find grapes even in these areas: ornamental grapevines and table grapes grow in public and private gardens – and a few commercial operations produce them as well. However, the growing of vinifera has been limited in modern times. The concentration of Oregon wineries lies further south and west, situated on the well-sloped hills of Yamhill, Washington, Polk, and Marion Counties. The only two producing vineyards close to Portland are located in Troutdale, on the eastern edge of Multnomah County, and Sandy in nearby Clackamas County.

Edgefield Winery in Troutdale began life as the Multnomah County Poor Farm, growing potatoes, raspberries, corn, and table grapes. The soils are deep alluvial, from an ancient riverbed. The McMenamin family – local beer brewers – purchased the by-then idle property from the County in 1990 and planted 1.2 hectares (3 acres) of Pinot Gris, rightfully thinking that variety had the best chance of ripening: the property lies on a north-facing gentle slope, not far south from the Columbia River – winter winds from the east can be problematic. Planting was done in 1.2 x 1.8 metres (4 x 6ft) spacing, with vertical shoot positioning. A small amount of Syrah – 1 hectare (2.5 acres) – was planted in 1995 and manages to ripen, although flavours are not profound. Most grapes used by the winery (Pinot Noir, Chardonnay, Cabernet Sauvignon, Merlot, and Zinfandel) are purchased from sites around the state.

The Wasson brothers near Sandy, on the

road to Mt Hood – a major, snowy recreation area – had been part-time farmers since the 1960s. In 1978, they planted wine grapes, and not long after devoted themselves to the wine business. Current production is split evenly between vinifera-based wines (Riesling, Chardonnay, Gewürztraminer, and Pinot Noir), and fruit wines (rhubarb, loganberry, and blackberry) and each has won medals at the Oregon State Fair. All wines from the Wasson Brothers Winery are fruity and accessible.

Historically, though, it was in the Milwaukie area of Clackamas County – further south than Wasson Brothers and in a town next to Portland – where horticulturist Henderson Luelling first planted grapes by 1847.

There certainly has not been continuous wine-grape growing in the now more urban Clackamas County since that first effort. But in the southern end of the county, undeveloped, mostly forested land lies across the Willamette River from the grape-producing epicentres of

The only two producing vineyards close to Portland are located in Troutdale, on the eastern edge of Multnomah County, and Sandy in nearby Clackamas County.

Newberg and Yamhill County. These few wineries in southern Clackamas County – Marquam Hill Vineyards outside of Molalla, St Josef's Wine Cellar in Canby, and Saga Vineyards near Colton – are included in this chapter because their designation as part of a wooded Clackamas County makes them a closer fit to the wineries of the greater Portland area than to the more quality-driven, winery-rich Yamhill County.

But Portland itself is not devoid of wineries. Yamhill County Vineyard's owner Reuel Fish (of Bishop Creek Farms, Gaston) created a **Portland winery** within the city limits in 2001, named Urban Wineworks. While Fish holds a winery licence (registered at Erath Vineyards Winery in Dundee, where he vinifies his wine), he now barrel ages and blends his wines in a northwest Portland building, open daily to the public for tastings, and sales of everything from one bottle up.

This could not have happened before 1999. Before then, while anyone could grow or buy grapes and hire a licensed winery as a facility to make the wine, only those producers with winery licences could sell wine in quantities less than 20 litres (5 gallons), the equivalent of about 25 bottles. Having a distributor for wine sales helped, but it could be tough for new and/or small wineries to find a distributor.

In 1999, members of the wine industry lobbied the Oregon Legislature to change the law. Led by Yamhill County winemaker Eric Hamacher, they secured a change in the law that now accommodates several producers who register at the same winery address in order to share space, equipment, and costs. They are then permitted to sell wine directly to the public in small quantities.

Some of the following wineries listed purchase grapes from diverse and varied sources around the state and make their wines at one of the wineries further south in the Willamette Valley. The lack of their own production facilities – they are nomad wineries of a sort – place them here in this geographic chapter.

> **A change in the law ... now accommodates several producers who register at the same winery address in order to share space, equipment, and costs.**

Notable producers

Andrew Rich Wines

☎ 503-284-6622 🖷 503-284-6622
✉ tabras@teleport.com
3287 NE Alameda Street, Portland, Oregon 97212
Production capacity 5,000 cases
2000 production 4,000 cases
Established 1995
First wines released 1995 vintage
Andrew Rich produces several wines under his two labels Tabula Rasa and Andrew Rich at Adelsheim Vineyard, some with grapes from the Willamette Valley (Pinot Noir, Sauvignon Blanc, Chenin Blanc-Sauvignon Blanc blend, Gewürztraminer ice wine) and others with grapes from Washington's Yakima and Columbia Valleys (a Bordeaux blend, Cabernet Franc, and Syrah). His white (and occasional rosé) wines are especially impressive.

Antica Terra

☎ 503-281-7696
6120 NE 22nd Avenue, Portland, Oregon 97211
Acreage in production 1ha (2.5 acres) Pinot Noir
New plantings 1.6ha (4 acres) Pinot Noir
Production capacity 350 cases
Established 1996
Marc Peters and Marty Weber purchased land in the Amity Hills and began to plant it (very densely) in the early 1990s. Yields are kept low and the wines show that focused concentration.

Carabella Vineyard

☎ 303-423-3272
✉ pinot@carabellawine.com
🌐 www.carabellawine.com
6671 Secrest Circle, Arvada, Colorado 80007
Acreage in production 4.3ha (10.5 acres) Pinot Gris, 4.7ha (11.5 acres) Chardonnay, 10.7ha (26.5 acres) Pinot Noir
2000 production 1,200
First wines released 1998 vintage
Owner Cara Hallock lives in Colorado, but her vineyards are located in Wilsonville. Mike Hallock produces the wine in rented space.

J Christopher Wines

☎ 503-231-5094 🖷 503-231-5094
✉ jchristopherwines@msn.com
3823 SE Washington, Portland, Oregon 97214
Production capacity 2,000 cases
2000 production 1,200 cases
Established 1996
First wines released 1998 vintage
Jay Somers, a former assistant winemaker at Cameron Winery, produces Pinot Noir, Pinot Gris,

Chardonnay, Sauvignon Blanc, and Cristo Misto, blend of Sauvignon Blanc, Pinot Grigio, and Riesling. Somers purchases fruit from Dundee and Salem-area vineyards

Edgefield Winery

☎ 503-665-2992 ℻ 503-661-1968
Ⓦ www.mcmenamins.com
2126 SW Halsey Street, Troutdale, Oregon 97060
Acreage in production 12 hectares (3 acres) Pinot Gris, 1.2 hectares (3 acres) Pinot Noir
Production capacity 25,000 cases
2000 production 25,000 cases
Established 1990
First wines released 1990 vintage
Part of the mammoth McMenamin's brewpub enterprise, the winery produces commercial quality wines, sold primarily at the ubiquitous brewpubs and restaurants within the McMenamin's empire. Varietals produced include Pinot Noir, Merlot, Cabernet Sauvignon, Zinfandel, Grenache, Syrah, Chardonnay, Riesling, Viognier, Muscat, a Port-style wine, and sparkling wine, all made from purchased fruit. Only a Pinot Gris is produced from grapes grown at the Edgefield site east of Portland

Holloran Vineyard Wines

☎ 503-638-6224 ℻ 503-638-3680
Ⓔ bill@holloranvineyardwines.com
2636 SW Schaeffer Road, West Linn, Oregon 97068
Acreage in production 2ha (5 acres) Pinot Noir, 0.6ha (1.5 acres) Riesling, 0.6ha (1.5 acres) Chardonnay, 0.6ha (0.5 acre) Pinot Gris
New plantings 2.2ha (5.5 acres) Pinot Noir
Production capacity 2,000 cases
2000 production 650 cases
Established 1999
First wines released 1999 vintage
New winery, showing good promise.

Idylwood Winery

☎ 503-236-3890 ℻ 503-631-7188
Ⓔ vintner@idylwoodwines.com
Ⓦ www.idylwoodwines.com
917 SE Yamhill Street, Portland, Oregon 97214
Production capacity 5,000 cases
2000 production 1,500 cases
Established 1998
First wines released 1998 vintage
The only working winery within Portland's city limits, owner Tony Nemeth uses grapes from both Oregon and Washington: Muscat Ottonel, Chardonnay, Pinot Gris, Marechal Foch, Merlot, Cabernet Sauvignon, Pinot Noir, and a semi-sweet, ice wine-style, white blend of grapes.

La Bete Wines

☎ 503-977-1493 ℻ 503-977-1493
Ⓔ labete@teleport.com
8026 SW 10th Avenue, Portland, Oregon 97219
Production capacity 2,500 cases
2000 production 1,200 cases
Established 1998
First wines released 1998 vintage
John and Kay Eliassen source grapes from all over, producing Burgundian varietals in a traditional way, de-emphasizing the use of oak: Dijon clone Chardonnay, Pinot Gris, Aligote (sourced from the only commercially producing vineyard with this variety, Newhouse vineyard in the Yakima Valley), Gamay Noir, and Pinot Noir.

Marquam Hill Vineyards

☎ 503-829-6677 ℻ 503-829-8810
Ⓔ jandmd@iglide.net
35803 S. Highway 213, Molalla, Oregon 97038
Acreage in production 2.4ha (6 acres) Chardonnay, 1.8ha (4.5 acres) Pinot Noir, 1ha (2.5 acres) Müller-Thurgau, 2.4ha (6 acres) Riesling, 1ha (2.5 acres) Gewürztraminer
Production capacity 6,000 cases
2000 production 2,000 cases
Established 1988
First wines released 1989 vintage
Joe and Marylee Dobbes (parents of Willamette Valley Vineyards and Torii Mor winemaker Joe Dobbes, Jr) produce wines from estate grapes planted in 1983, plus a small amount of Pinot Gris and Pinot Blanc that they purchase. They have a tasting room in the central Oregon recreational area in Sisters at the Sisters Drugstore.

St Josef's Wine Cellar

☎ 503-651-3190 ℻ 503-651-3190
28836 ☎ Barlow Road, Canby, Oregon 97013
Acreage in production 2,4ha (6 acres) Pinot Noir, 2.2ha (5.5 acres) White Riesling, 1ha (2.5 acres) Chardonnay, 1ha (2.5 acres) Gewürztraminer, 0.8ha (2 acres) Cabernet Sauvignon, 0.8ha (2 acres) Merlot, 2ha (5 acres) Pinot Gris
New plantings 0.6ha (1.5 acres) Syrah, 0.6ha (1.5 acres) Gewürztraminer, 0.8ha (2 acres) Sauvignon Blanc
Production capacity 15,000 cases
2000 production 7,000 cases
Established 1983
First wines released 1985 vintage
Joe Fleischmann crafts Zinfandel from Columbia Valley fruit; in ripe years it 's a big zesty wine while, in less good vintages, Joe produces a white Zin.

Andrew Rich of Andrew Rich Wines

Urban Wineworks/ Bishop Creek Cellars

☎ 503-226-9797 or 1-888-GOPINOT
℻ 503-226-9799
Ⓔ info@urbanwineworks.com
407 NW 16th, Portland, Oregon 97209
Acreage in production 4.1ha (10 acres) Pinot Noir, 1.2ha (3 acres) Pinot Gris, 0.4ha (1 acre) Chardonnay
New plantings 2ha (5 acres) Pinot Noir, 0.8ha (2 acres) Pinot Gris
2000 production 1,800 cases
Established 1999
First wines released 1999 vintage
Until the 1999 vintage, owner Reuel Fish sold his Bishop Creek Farms grapes – planted in 1988 – to Erath, where Fish now produces his own wine under two labels: a premium line, Bishop Creek Cellars, and a more value-driven product under the Urban Wineworks label, available for custom blending at the Urban Wineworks Portland facility.

Wasson Brothers Winery

☎ 503-668-3124 ℻ 503-668-3124
Ⓔ WassonBW@teleport.com
Ⓦ www.wassonbrotherswinery.com
41901 Highway 26, Sandy, Oregon 97055
Acreage in production 0.6ha (2 acres) Pinot Noir, 0.8ha (2 acres) Chardonnay, 1.6ha (4 acres) Gewürztraminer, 1.6ha (4 acres) Muscat, 0.8ha (2 acres) White Riesling
Production capacity 4,170 cases
2000 production 3,750 cases
Established 1981
Jim Wasson and his twin John had been part-time farmers since the 1960s; they planted wine grapes in 1978. In the early 1980s, Jim opened the winery. Production is split between fruit and berry wines, varietal grape wines, and carbonated offerings.

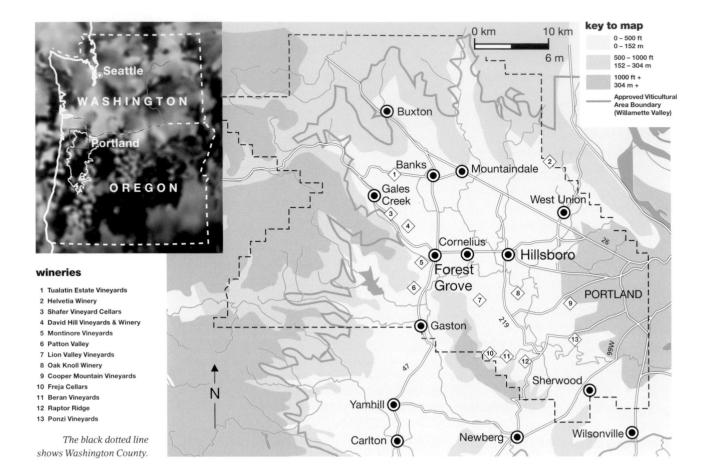

key to map

0 – 500 ft
0 – 152 m

500 – 1000 ft
152 – 304 m

1000 ft +
304 m +

Approved Viticultural
Area Boundary
(Willamette Valley)

wineries

1   Tualatin Estate Vineyards
2   Helvetia Winery
3   Shafer Vineyard Cellars
4   David Hill Vineyards & Winery
5   Montinore Vineyards
6   Patton Valley
7   Lion Valley Vineyards
8   Oak Knoll Winery
9   Cooper Mountain Vineyards
10 Freja Cellars
11 Beran Vineyards
12 Raptor Ridge
13 Ponzi Vineyards

*The black dotted line
shows Washington County.*

Washington County

Washington County lies due west of Portland, snuggled against the foothills of the Coastal Range to the west, reaching up toward the Chehalem Mountains to the south, and within the Tualatin River basin. Historically, this was farm and orchard land, and that agricultural activity still continues to this day.

The south end of Washington County, in fact, can be seen as an extension of northern Yamhill County, with a few vineyards scattered across the hilly north side of the Chehalem Mountains; vineyards such as Ponzi's Abetina and Aurora are sited there with a southeast exposure, on elevations between 122–183 metres (400–600ft). The town of Gaston sits on the southwestern line between Washington and Yamhill Counties, and is the gateway into Willakenzie soil and a greater density of vineyards.

Portland's metropolitan growth has been creeping west into Washington County since the early 1990s; housing and commercial development fans out from the city – most of it within the Urban Growth Boundary – encroaching on what was once vacant land. High-tech industries have located here, and brought with them a demand for urban services and resources, making the Beaverton area a successful suburb of Portland. The cities to the west in a line towards the Coastal Range (Hillsboro, Cornelius, and Forest Grove) still seem rural, but are steadily developing and gaining population.

The **wineries and vineyards** located in Washington County are more spread out than in Yamhill County, with greater distances between producers. This area developed early, but never grew into the wine hub that the Dundee Hills and the Yamhill County just south of here did. It's ironic that many of the wineries in Washington county are located closer to Portland but see fewer visitors. Perhaps this is because of the greater concentration of wineries in Dundee and the fact there is no central highway that brings a visitor directly to the area from Portland. More wending and weaving is necessary to reach the scattered Washington County properties.

What brought Ernest Reuter in the 1800s to the Forest Grove area – specifically to an area of gentle slopes named David Hill – is not known. But his effort brought Charles Coury to the same site in 1965. Coury's property was purchased in 1986 by David and Susan Teppola, who renamed it Laurel Ridge Winery. The Teppolas sold the winery in 2000 to Milan' and Jean Stoyanov (who had bought the vineyards in 1992), and the Stoyanovs re-named the property to reflect its location, David Hill Vineyard. The Teppolas have recently re-established Laurel Ridge Winery nearer to their own vineyards in the Dundee Hills.

Coury's presence in Washington County brought to the area fellow University of California-at-Davis student Bill Fuller, who founded the nearby Tualatin Estate in 1973. For a time, Fuller considered the Dundee Hills for his vineyard, as his friend David Lett had done, but eventually found a property near Forest Grove – a former tree nursery – that was a warmer site than any other he had seen. Tualatin Estate is situated in a geographic cul-de-sac, where heat accumulates at the base of the foothills; the vineyards are only 53–137 metres (175–450ft) in elevation, but, somehow, the fruit reaches a maturity earlier than in the Dundee Hills, more like the early ripening near Monroe in the southern Willamette Valley.

Charles Coury, though, wasn't really an influence for Dick Ponzi. He and his wife Nancy came up to Oregon in 1970, from California (where he had been an engineer for Disneyland), having grown grapes and made wine at their home there. Nancy Ponzi's parents lived in Gaston, and the nearby area of Scholls appeared attractive to the Ponzis, offering appealing hillside vineyard possibilities. They also liked the proximity to Portland being close to their desired market. Then as now, land prices were extremely high, because of the closeness to the city. Plus, Ponzi knew Coury was close by in Forest Grove, which was a validation in making a Washington County decision.

Laurelwood soil predominates in Washington County, a well-drained soil that makes it harder to establish a vineyard in some lower elevations because it has less clay and less water-retaining capability than other soils such as Jory; in higher elevations the soil can be more moisture-retentive. These soils are not very deep, 1–1.2 metres (3–4ft), and have a high iron content (but not as great as that of red Jory soil).

The early trends in grape growing in Washington County followed the same lines as in Yamhill County, with vine spacing being limited by tractor tire widths. Ponzi's early spacing was 1.8 x 2.4 metres (6 x 8ft), with Tualatin Estate's being 2 x 3 metres, (7 x 10ft). New plantings at Ponzi are spaced at 1 x 2 metres (3 x 7ft), with 5,486 plants per hectare (2,220 plants per acre). Area newcomer Patton Valley Vineyards near Gaston is planted 1.5 x 1.8 metres (5 x 6ft), with 3,652 plants per hectare (1,478 plants per acre); small Lion Valley Vineyard near Cornelius is planted on a very gentle slope with unusually tight spacing – 1 x 1 metre (3 x 3ft). Bill Fuller of Tualatin is still convinced, however, that his early plantings of 1,645 plants per hectare (600 plants per acre) was not far off the ideal number, and that high-density plantings do not necessarily produce better wines. On new plantings (before Fuller sold Tualatin Estate to Willamette Valley Vineyards in 1997), he didn't follow the pack to high-density planting.

After the sale of Tualatin, Fuller went to manage Cooper Mountain Vineyards in Beaverton, a property founded in 1988, and largely modelled on Fuller's Tualatin Estate.

This area developed early, but never grew into the wine hub that the Dundee Hills and Yamhill County just south of here did.

Cooper Mountain is organically certified and is the only Oregon winery currently aiming for biodynamic certification.

A number of Washington County vineyards are terraced, on the crowns of hills, especially those near Cornelius. The terracing exposes the vines to plenty of sunlight and good air circulation, but weed control is an issue, as all work must be done by hand, without tractors.

Irrigation is an issue in this area, as it is in Yamhill County. Ponzi installed **drip irrigation** in 2001; the newer Patton Valley Vineyard chose to irrigate 4 hectares (10 acres) of Pinot Noir at its 8 hectare (20 acres) vineyard, in order to establish part of their fruit more quickly to bring about an earlier production of wine. Many Washington County vineyards (and vineyards in other areas around the state of Oregon as well) are located in state-designated "red zones" limiting groundwater access, and their owners would need to apply for water rights if they wish to dig any new wells. But generally, it is only the better-financed operations that have the means to install irrigation (either in new vineyards, or through retro-fitting established vineyards), and Washington County just doesn't boast the same large influx of money that Yamhill County has seen over the years.

> **The terracing exposes the vines to a lot of sunlight and good air circulation, but weed control is an issue, as all work must be done by hand.**

While most of the properties in Washington County – Beran Vineyards, Oak Knoll Winery, Montinore Vineyards, Ponzi, Tualatin Estate, Patton Valley Vineyards, Lion Valley Vineyard, David Hill Vineyards and Winery, and Shafer Vineyards Cellars – focus on estate plantings, some also purchase fruit from Yamhill County vineyards. The mix of varieties planted is more often than not the same as what is grown in Yamhill County. The exceptions include Arneis and Dolcetto that are found at Ponzi (a commitment to their Italian heritage; most of the Arneis grapes are their own, although some have been purchased from Erath in Dundee). David Hill produces a "Port" that is made from Pinot Noir – perhaps not the best

use of Pinot Noir grapes. For Pinot Noir, clonal material is generally Pommard and Wadensville; new plantings such as Patton Valley's 8 hectares (20 acres) focus on the Dijon clones.

Washington County perpetually struggles to be **seen as equal** to or included with the more well-known, better reviewed, and more

visited Yamhill County. The Ponzi family, with its focused and assured marketing finesse – they founded Oregon's first micro-brewery and successfully fought a battle with the licnsing authorities to change the law to allow direct sales of beer at the place of brewing – even opened a wine bar and bistro smack in the middle of Yamhill County, in Dundee on the main thoroughfare, Highway 99W. Ponzi is the exception to the perennial Washington County identity problem; it has discovered an excellent way to ensure that its name is associated with its more illustrious Yamhill County peers. Ponzi's intention was to create one central location that offered the opportunity to taste a wide range of area wines which include, of course, its own.

A well-established typical Willamette Valley (in which lies Washington County) vineyard, with its age denoted by the wide-spacing and thick vine trunks.

Notable producers

Beran Vineyards

☎ 503-628-1298 📠 503-628-0228
✉ beran@teleport.com
30088 SW Egger Road, Hillsboro,
Oregon 97123
Acreage in production 2.8ha (7 acres)
Pinot Noir
Production capacity 1,000 cases
2000 production 800 cases
Established 1979
First wines released 1997 vintage
Small producer with a commitment to Pinot Noir
only, using estate fruit planted in 1972 and 1979.

Cooper Mountain Vineyards

☎ 503-649-0027 📠 503-649-0702
✉ sales@coopermountainwine.com
Ⓦ www.coopermountainwine.com
9480 SW Grabhorn Road, Beaverton,
Oregon 97007
Acreage in production 14.6ha (36 acres)
Pinot Noir, 6.8ha (17 acres) Pinot Gris, 1.6ha
(4 acres) Chardonnay, 0.8ha (2 acres) Pinot Blanc
Production capacity 10,000
2000 production 10,000 cases
Established 1978
First wines released 1987 vintage
Physician Bob Gross has made a commitment
to sustainable agriculture; Cooper Mountain is
Oregon's largest certified organic vineyard and
has applied for biodynamic certification. Quality
has been rising, with the 1999 vintage of Pinot
Noir being particularly fine.

Dr Robert Gross of Cooper Mountain

Freja Cellars

☎ 503-628-7843 📠 503-628-7843
✉ Willy@frejacellars.com
Ⓦ www.frejacellars.com
16691 SW McFee Place, Hillsboro,
Oregon 97123
Acreage in production 3.6ha (9 acres)
Pinot Noir
Production capacity 2,000 cases
2000 production 600 cases
Established 1988
First wines released 1998 vintage
Until the winery was constructed in 1998, owner
Willy Gianopulos sold all his fruit to other wineries.

Helvetia Winery

☎ 503-647-5169 📠 503-647-5169
✉ Jplatt@helvetiawinery.com
Ⓦ www.helvetiawinery.com
22485 NW Yungen Road, Hillsboro,
Oregon 97124
Acreage in production 1.6ha (4 acres) Pinot

David Hill Vineyards & Winery

☎ 503-992-85245 📠 503-992-8586
Ⓦ www.davidhillwinery.com
PO Box 366, 46350 NW David Hill Road,
Forest Grove, Oregon 97116
Acreage in production 5.7ha (14 acres)
Pinot Noir, 0.8ha (2 acres) Pinot Gris, 1ha (2.5
acres) Pinot Blanc, 0.6ha (1.5 acres) Chardonnay,
3.6ha (9 acres) Riesling, 1ha (2.5 acres)
Gewürztraminer, 1ha (2.5 acres) miscellaneous
(including Sylvaner and Sémillon)
New plantings 1.4ha (3.5 acres) Pinot Noir,
0.8ha (2 acres) Pinot Gris, 0.2ha (0.5 acres)
Chardonnay
Production capacity 7,500 cases
2000 production 3,700 cases
Established 2000
First wines released 1998 vintage
Formerly the Laurel Ridge Winery, Milan and Jean
Stoyanov have owned this Forest Grove estate
since 1991. Laurel Ridge relocated to Yamhill
County in 2000; the Stoyanovs renamed this
estate David Hill Winery, after a local geographic
name. The estate vineyards contain one of the
first vineyard plantings in Oregon; pioneer Charles
Coury planted Alsatian varieties here in the late
1960s. David Hill has begun a vineyard expansion
and replanting programme, but will keep most
of the Coury early plantings of Gewürztraminer,
Riesling, and Pinot Noir. Sparkling wines and
a Port-style wine are also produced.

Noir, 2.4ha (6 acres) Chardonnay
Production capacity 3,000 cases
2000 production 3,000 cases
Established 1992
First wines released 1996 vintage
Jon Platt and Elizabeth Furse first planted their
vineyard – located in the northern end of the
Tualatin Valley, in the foothills of the Tualatin
Mountains – in 1982. They produce pleasant,
food-friendly wines.

Lion Valley Vineyards

☎ 503-628-5458 ✉ levinth@jf.intel.com
Ⓦ www.lionvalley.com
35040 SW Unger Road, Cornelius,
Oregon 97113
Acreage in production 1.2ha (3 acres)
Pinot Noir, 1ha (2.5 acres) Chardonnay, 0.4ha
(1 acre) Pinot Gris
Production capacity 4,000 cases
2000 production 2,200 cases
Established 1994
First wines released 1994 vintage
David Leventhal's vineyards boast the highest
plant density in Oregon, at over 9,660 vines per
ha (4,000 per acre); he blends the Pinot Noir and
Chardonnay from his vineyard with purchased
fruit from Shea Vineyard for his best wines, which
show great complexity. Leventhal spent two years
in Burgundy, and follows the classic Burgundian
mantra of minimal handling. His new winery is
gravity-fed.

Montinore Vineyards

☎ 503-359-5012 📠 503-357-4313
PO Box 490, 3663 SW Dilley Road, Forest
Grove, Oregon 97116
Acreage in production 49.8ha (123 acres)
Pinot Noir, 12.6ha (31 acres) Chardonnay,
11.7ha (29 acres) Pinot Gris, 11.7ha (29 acres)
White Riesling, 9.7ha (24 acres) Müller-Thurgau,
15.7ha (4 acres) Gewürztraminer
New plantings 4.1ha (10 acres) Dijon-clone
Pinot Noir
Production capacity 70,000 cases
2000 production 38,000 cases
Established 1981
First wines released 1987 vintage
Leo and Jane Graham purchased a 146-ha (361-
acre) ranch in 1965 and later purchased additional
bordering land. They hired consultants to evaluate
the land for vineyards and planted grapes in 1981.
Burgundian Jacques Tardy serves as winemaker.
The wines are pleasant, but lacking some depth.

Michel, Maria, Dick, and Nancy Ponzi of Ponzi Vineyards

Oak Knoll Winery

☎ 503-648-8198 📠 503-648-3377
✉ oakknoll@ipinc.net
🌐 oakknollwinery.com
29700 SW Burkhalter Road, Hillsboro,
Oregon 97123
Production capacity 35,000 cases
2000 production 25,000 cases
Established 1970
First wines released 1971 vintage
Until the early 1980s, this pioneering family winery
mainly produced fruit and berry wines. The switch
to vinifera rewarded them with a number of quality
awards including one the Oregon State Fair for
their 1980 Pinot Noir. A dessert wine from
raspberries is still produced, as is a Niagra wine.

Patton Valley Vineyard

☎ 503-985-3445 📠 503-985-0425
✉ monte@pattonvalley.com
🌐 www.pattonvalley.com
PO Box 328, Gaston, Oregon 97119
Acreage in production 6.1ha (15 acres)
Pinot Noir
Production capacity 2,500 cases
2000 production 1,200 cases
Established 1995
First wines released 1999 vintage
Investment banker Monte Pitt and venture
capitalist Dave Chen had talked about opening a
winery since graduate school; and started this
one (with vineyards) after years of research. Pitt is
winemaker and manager; Chen kept his day job.

Ponzi Vineyards

☎ 503-628-1227 📠 503-628-0354
✉ info@ponziwines.com
🌐 www.ponziwines.com
14665 SW Winery Lane, Beaverton,
Oregon 97007
Acreage in production 16.2ha (40 acres)
Pinot Noir, 8.1ha (20 acres) Pinot Gris, 2ha (5
acres) Chardonnay, 1.6ha (4 acres) Arneis, 1.6ha
(4 acres) Pinot Blanc, 0.8ha (2 acres) Dolcetto,
0.4ha (1 acre) White Riesling.
Production capacity 15,000 cases
2000 production 10,000 cases
Established 1970
First wines released 1974 vintage
Pioneer Dick Ponzi's daughter Luisa now makes
the wine here, maintaining Ponzi's reputation for
high quality and finesse. All family members are
involved with the winery: wife Nancy and
daughter Maria handle marketing and son Michel
serves as business manager. Ponzi, while in
Washington County, is more often a name
associated with the quality leaders in Yamhill
County; the Ponzis have opened a prominent
tasting room and bistro in the heart of Dundee.

Raptor Ridge Winery

☎ 503-887-5595 📠 503-628-6255
✉ wineman@raptoridge.com
🌐 www.raptoridge.com
29090 SW Wildhaven Lane, Scholls,
Oregon 97123
Acreage in production 3.2ha (8 acres)

Pinot Noir, 1.2ha (3 acres) Pinot Gris, 0.4ha
(1 acre) Chardonnay
New plantings 1.8ha (4.5 acres) Pinot Noir,
0.8ha (2 acres) Pinot Gris
Production capacity 2,000 cases
2000 production 1,200 cases
Established 1992
First wines released 1995 vintage
Scott Shull crafts focused, quality wines (notably
the Pinot Gris); his vineyards are planted on
Willakenzie soils. Most of Raptor Ridge's wines
are sold through its mailing list and website.

Shafer Vineyard Cellars

☎ 503-357-6604 📠 503-357-6604
6200 SW Gales Creek Road, Forest
Grove, Oregon 97116
Acreage in production 3.8ha (9.3 acres)
Pinot Noir, 3.7ha (9.1 acres) Chardonnay, 2ha
4.9 acres) White Riesling, 2.5ha (6.2 acres) Pinot
Gris, 0.6ha (1.6 acres) Gewürztraminer, 0.4ha
(1.1 acres) Sauvignon Blanc, 0.6ha (1.6 acres)
Müller-Thurgau
Production capacity 12,000 cases
2000 production 10,000 cases
Established 1974
First wines released 1978 vintage
Harvey Shafer makes full-bodied wines from
the vineyards he planted in 1973. A *méthode
traditionelle* wine is also produced.

Tualatin Estate Vineyards

☎ 503-357-5005 📠 503-362-0062
✉ lauraannekirk@aol.com
🌐 www.wvv.com
10850 NW Seavey Road, Forest Grove,
Oregon 97116
Acreage in production 7.3ha (18 acres)
Pinot Noir, 2.8ha (7 acres) Pinot Blanc, 6.7ha
(16.5 acres) Chardonnay, 13ha (32 acres) Riesling,
4.1ha (10 acres) Muscat, 2.4ha (6 acres)
Gewürztraminer, 0.4ha (1 acre) Ehrenfelser
New plantings 19.8ha (49 acres) Pinot Noir,
1.6ha (4 acres) Pinot Blanc
Production capacity 22,000 cases
2000 production 10,000 cases
Established 1973
First wines released 1975 vintage
Purchased by Willamette Valley Vineyards (WVV)
in 1997. All brands of WVV are produced by
winemaker Joe Dobbes at the Turner location.
White wines in particular shine under this label,
including a semi-sparkling Muscat.

Eola Hills

The **Eola Hills** form the southernmost cluster of hills that make up the holy triumvirate of prime vineyard sites in the Willamette Valley, along with the Chehalem Mountains and the Red Hills of Dundee. (See pages 000)

The Eola Hills really begin their rise in Yamhill County and stretch into their mass in Polk County, where their higher elevations – and hence more desirable slopes – can be found. This cluster of hills – about 61–274 metres (200-–900ft) high – is located 24km (15 miles) south of Dundee, bordered on the east by the Willamette River, southeast by Oregon's state capital, Salem, and extends south to a westward jog of the Willamette River. There is some valley land between the Eola Hills and the Coastal Range, but without any grape-growing activity.

The **coolest areas** of the Willamette Valley appear near the Van Duzer Corridor, about 64km (40 miles) west and slightly north of the Eola Hills, where a break in the Coastal Range brings in cooler marine air, most noticeably in the northern reaches of this region.

The northern foothills of the Eola Hills within Yamhill County – in an area sometimes called the Amity Hills – are home to properties such as Amity Vineyards and Cuneo Vineyards (nearer McMinnville), and could be classified as the upper end of the Eola Hills. These wineries were discussed in the previous chapter because they are more commonly grouped with the Yamhill County cluster of producers, in large part because of similar elevation and soil composition.

It is a possibility that the Eola Hills were formed from a discrete volcanic event that was different from the formation of the other ridges in the Willamette Valley; in some places more aluminium can be found in the Eola Hills' soils, in other areas, there is more basaltic material. This stark contrast of soil types can sometimes be found on individual properties, as well, such as Bethel Heights and Cristom, resulting in isolated pockets – vineyard blocks – that ripen at different times.

Nekia soil prevails in the Eola Hills, a volcanic, sandy clay loam in the same series as Jory soil. Nekia is shallower than the deep Jory, to a depth of only 61–92cm (2–3ft). This well-draining soil can be found primarily on the hillside uplands 122–213 metres (400–700ft) of such winery vineyards as Bethel Heights, Witness Tree, and the higher elevation soils of Cristom and Evesham Wood, as well as such notable vineyards as Temperance Hill (with elevations of 189–244 metres/620ft–800ft), which sells grapes to a number of top wineries throughout the Willamette Valley. Fruit on Nekia soil tends to ripen a little earlier than fruit in the Dundee Hills, even with the Eola Hills' slightly cooler weather, creating fruit with greater acidity and more colour. (Interestingly, Nekia spelled

The three-vineyard experiment

What started as an intriguing one-time programme for the annual International Pinot Noir Celebration has evolved into a major, annual learning experiment for three leading wineries.

In 1995, the IPNC was searching for a programme to tackle the timeless, Old World question of t*erroir*-versus-human intervention. Bill Fuller (founder of Tualatin Vineyards) proposed an experiment: to trade small lots of grapes among three vineyards and wineries, with each lot to be vinified by each participating winemaker.

In 1996, Tualatin, Rex Hill, and Bethel Heights each traded 1.3 tons of "reserve quality" Pommard clone Pinot Noir; each lot was harvested simultaneously. Each winery used "Oregon fermenters". But little consistency emerged from their efforts. The slopes, exposures, trellising systems and yields for each lot were substantially different. And, of course, each winemaker handled the fruit differently in the winery.

Three distinctly different vineyard sites are now used in what has become an annual experiment: Rex Hill's Jacob-Hart Vineyard on Yamhill soil, Bethel Heights' Southeast Block on Nekia soil, and Chehalem's Ridgecrest Vineyard on Willakenzie soil. As a result of the experiement, all three have learnt from each other and changed their preexisting winemaking practices.

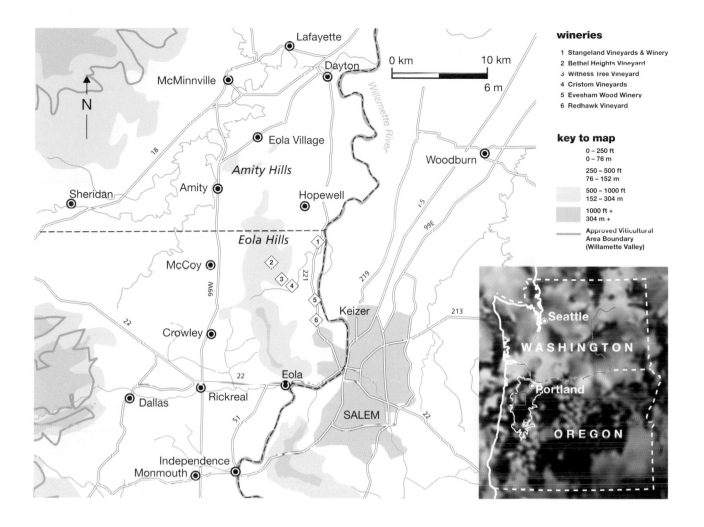

backwards is the same soil type, Aiken, found in the Sierra Foothills of California.)

In contrast, parts of the Eola Hills at lower elevations tend to have Jory, Yamhill, or combination soils, more consistent with the soils of the Valley floor. At Evesham Wood, at the lower elevations of its vineyard at 92 metres (300ft), Jory soil is found. Argyle Winery and Domaine Serene – both based in the Dundee Hills – have new vineyards in the Eola Hills, each on Jory and/or Yamhill soils. The respected Seven Springs Vineyards – which sells fruit to a wide range of wineries from Yamhill County and the Eola Hills – contains a mix of Jory and Nekia soils.

On the east side of the Eola Hills, vineyards have a more protected aspect and a warmer exposure; the few west-oriented vineyards are cooler, more influenced by the Van Duzer Corridor. For the few vineyards over 183 metres (600ft) in elevation – such as Temperance Hill – the winds are stronger and the grapes more exposed and cooler, with ripening later than the lower sites.

Irrigation is just beginning to appear in the Eola Hills, although Bethel Heights used irrigation in its early years for new plant material that was then self-rooted (as most plants were in Oregon before 1990). Now, many new vineyards in the area are seriously looking at irrigation, not just to establish new plants, but also to provide hydration to established vines during the critical *veraison* period, typically the drought season in Oregon. Temperance Hill has installed drip irrigation in its new plantings; Argyle has installed the same in its new vineyards near Seven Springs Vineyard. Water access and water rights are an issue in the Eola Hills, too, making irrigation not just dependent on the money to fund it.

59

EOLA HILLS

The **first vineyards** in the broader Eola Hills were planted in the early 1970s, at Hidden Springs Vineyard in Yamhill County, which was subsequently purchased by Gino Cuneo (Cuneo Cellars) in 1989. On the east side of the Eola Hills within Polk County, Jim Feltz planted his eponymous vineyard in 1973. (It is now leased to Cristom and 100 per cent grafted over to Pinot Noir.) The Casteel and Dudley families purchased an already-planted vineyard in 1978; they planted additional grapes and opened Bethel Heights winery in 1984. Today they own 125 south- and southeast-facing vineyards at 152–183 metres (500–600ft) of elevation. Evesham Wood and Witness Tree settled in the Eola Hills in the late 1980s. Stangeland Vineyard and Winery was first planted in 1978, although it was not until 1991 that Stangeland began its own production.

In 1991, Pennsylvanian Paul Gerrie – who had had no previous ties to a winery – attended the International Pinot Noir Celebration and fell in love with Oregon. After searching around for possible vineyard locations in California, he came back to Oregon and enlisted the help of Beaux Frères' Mike Etzel in an attempt to identify possible vineyard property. Etzel managed to uncover an available vineyard in the Eola Hills, an under-performing winery called Pellier, that was owned and operated by a member of the family that operates Mirassou Vineyards in California. While Etzel himself wasn't excited about the property – it had been seriously neglected, and was rife with blackberries and poison oak – Gerrie could see its potential; he purchased it in 1992 and hired Jim Feltz's son Mark to serve as vineyard manager. Thus Gerrie created what became known asCristom Vineyards.

Gerrie then hired Steve Doerner as winemaker. Doerner's arrival marks a first in Oregon's history as a wine region: a seasoned California Pinot Noir producer – from the respected Calera Winery in California – who chose to move north. Doerner was the first winemaker to make his way to

Doerner's arrival marks a first in Oregon's history; a seasoned California Pinot Noir producer – from the respected Calera Winery in California – who chose to move north.

Quercus garryana, Oregon white oak, here called the Witness Tree based on Native American tales, standing tall above its eponymous vineyard in the Eola Hills.

the state with in-depth experience at a renowned Pinot Noir label. Doerner had just left Calera in 1992 after fourteen years at the brand.

Cristom now boasts 52 hectares (130 acres) – of which 18 hectares (45 acres) are currently planted – on the east slope of the Eola Hills. Elevations range from a low of 76 metres (250ft) near the winery and the original vineyard, which is now called the Marjorie Vineyard, to a high of 229 metres (750ft), just below Temperance Hill. The winery's 2000 production used estate-planted fruit for 60 per cent of its wines; the remaining grapes were purchased from other established vineyards in the Yamhill County area – Arcus (owned by Archery Summit), Brick House, and Beaux Frères – as well as from the Eola Hills – Temperance Hill, Seven Springs, and Canary Hill.

The vineyards of the Eola Hills outnumber the wineries, and produce highly prized grapes. Eola Hills wineries, as well as some of the top Yamhill County and south Salem wineries, purchase grapes from such named vineyards as Temperance Hill, Seven Springs, O'Connor, Madrona, Brunker Hall, Carter, and Canary Hill. All of these vineyards produce the same range of grape varieties as in Yamhill County: Pinot Noir, Chardonnay, Pinot Gris, Pinot Blanc, and small amounts of Gewürztraminer. Newer vineyards in the region have planted the same successful array of Dijon clones as well. And at Cristom, about a hundred cases of barrel-fermented Viognier are produced annually from estate-grown fruit.

Vine training systems are more diverse in the Eola Hills than in the more northern regions. Double and single Guyot is found, as well as some Scott Henry (see box, page 83), single wire hanging canopy, and Lyre systems.

Sustainable viticulture also takes centre stage in the Eola Hills. While Evesham Wood Winery was the first vineyard in this region to be certified organic (in 2000), much of Oregon's well-known sustainable agriculture efforts originated in the Eola Hills.

Ted Casteel of Bethel Heights Vineyards had been searching for a way to formalize an earth-friendly approach to growing grapes, without the need of going all the way to organic certification, a process that is too difficult for many growers. In 1996, with the assistance of Oregon State University, he applied the standards of a Swiss sustainable agriculture programme to Oregon vineyards and formed a committee called the Integrated Production Programme to carry out a two-year sustainable agriculture trial. Thirty-two vineyards within Oregon participated, a little more than ten per cent of the total number of vineyards in the state. The trial proved to be successful and had evolved into the still on-going Low Input Viticulture and Enology (LIVE) programme by March 1999. Seven Springs Vineyard owner MacDonald now chairs the state-wide LIVE programme

there are frequent discussions of merging the Yamhill County Wine Association with its Eola Hills equivalent, to create one ... promotional effort.

(see page 63). In 1999, MacDonald and Casteel were responsible for the creation of a vineyard training programme that is based at the Chemeketa Community College near Salem.

The Eola Hills wine region has been more successful than any other in forging and maintaining a close relationship with the top Yamhill County producers. As many Yamhill County wineries purchase grapes or have vineyards established in the Eola Hills as the other way around, and the top Pinot Noir producers in the state seek out a diversity of plant material from both regions. The two areas share a strong Pinot Noir focus, and there are frequent discussions of merging the Yamhill County Wine Association with its Eola Hills equivalent, to create one broad promotional effort. Even without a joint marketing relationship, the two regions function virtually as one, both politically and socially.

Harry Peterson-Nedry of Chelahem; Lynn Penner-Ash of Rex Hill Vineyards; Ted Casteel of Bethel Heights Vineyard.

Notable producers

Bethel Heights Vineyard

☎ 503-581-2262 📠 503-581-0943
📧 info@bethelheights.com
🌐 www.bethelheights.com
6060 Bethel Heights Road NW, Salem, Oregon 97304
Acreage in production 12.4ha (30.5 acres) Pinot Noir, 4.8ha (11.8 acres) Chardonnay, 1.2ha (3 acres) Pinot Gris, 1.6ha (4 acres) Pinot Blanc
Production capacity 10,000 cases
2000 production 8,000 cases
Vineyard established 1977
Winery established 1984
First wines released 1985 vintage
Brothers Ted and Terry Casteel and their wives Pat Dudley and Marilyn Webb operate this well-regarded winery. Ted handles the vineyards, Terry makes the wine, Pat oversees marketing, and Marilyn serves as business manager. Estate wines include the elegant, well-structured Flat Block and Southeast Block *cuvées*. In 1996 Bethel Heights began purchasing Pinot Noir grapes from other vineyards including Freedom Hill Vineyard and Nysa Vineyard. The result in 1999 was two of the best wines Bethel Heights has ever produced.

Steve Doerner of Cristom Vineyards

Cristom Vineyards

☎ 503 375-3068 📠 503 391-7057
📧 Winery@cristomvineyards.com
6905 Spring Valley Road NW, Salem, Oregon 97304
Acreage in production 13.8ha (34 acres) Pinot Noir, 2.6ha (6.5 acres) Chardonnay, 2ha (5 acres) Pinot Gris, 0.5ha (1.3 acres) Viognier
New plantings 9.09 acres Pinot Noir; Production capacity 10,000 cases
2000 production 7,000 cases
Winery **established** 1992.
First wines released 1992 vintage
Crackerjack winemaker Steve Doerner, makes some of Oregon's best wines, very complex, well-structured Pinot Noirs. The original vineyards were planted in 1983 by the former owners, the Mirassous of the eponymous California winery. Thanks to Cristom owner Paul Gerrie's fondness for Viognier, Cristom grows and produces one of the richest, wood-aged versions in the Northwest.

Evesham Wood Vineyard & Winery

☎ 503-371-8478 📠 503-763-6015
📧 evewood@open.org
3795 Wallace Road NW, Salem, Oregon 97304

Acreage in production 2.4ha (6 acres) Pinot Noir, 0.4ha (1 acre) Chardonnay, 1.2ha (3 acres) Pinot Gris, 0.3ha (0.8 acres) Gewürztraminer
New plantings 0.4ha (1 acre) Pinot Noir, 0.2ha (0.4 acres) Chardonnay
Production capacity 4,000 cases
2000 production 3,000 cases
Established 1986
First wines released 1986 vintage
Russ Raney makes concentrated wines including seductive Pinot Noir (and the highly-sought-after Cuvée J), Chardonnay, and Pinot Gris, and a terrific Gewürztraminer, no doubt a homage to Raney's winemaking training in Germany.

Stangeland Vineyards & Winery

☎ 503-581-0355 📠 503-540-3412
📧 Stanglnd@open.org
🌐 www.open.org/stanglnd
8500 Hopewell Road NW, Salem, Oregon 97304
Acreage in production 0.6ha (1.5 acres) Pinot Noir, 0.4ha (1 acre) Chardonnay, 0.4ha (1 acre) Pinot Gris
Production capacity 3,000 cases
2000 production 1,000 cases

Established 1978
First wines released 1991 vintage
A small facility whose production has been increasing as owners Larry and Kinsey Miller find acceptable fruit to purchase. Besides Pinot Noir, Chardonnay, and Pinot Gris, they make a blend of Chenin Blanc and Pinot Noir and Gewürztraminer.

Witness Tree Vineyard

☎ 503-585-7874, 888-478-8766
📠 503-362-9765
📧 info@witnesstreevineyard.com
🌐 www.witnesstreevineyard.com
7111 Spring Valley Road NW, Salem, Oregon 97304
Acreage in production 17.5ha (43.3 acres) Pinot Noir, 0.8ha (2 acres) Chardonnay, 0.4ha (1 acre) Viognier, 0.4ha (1 acre) Pinot Blanc, 0.1ha (0.3 acres) Lagrein, 0.1ha (0.3 acres) Dolcetto
Production capacity 7,000 cases
2000 production 5,500 cases
Established 1982
First wines released 1988 vintage
Pinot Noir is the focus here, although winemaker Bryce Bagnal operates an experimental vineyard planted with a wide range of varieties. Quality has been uneven, but when it's good, it's very good.

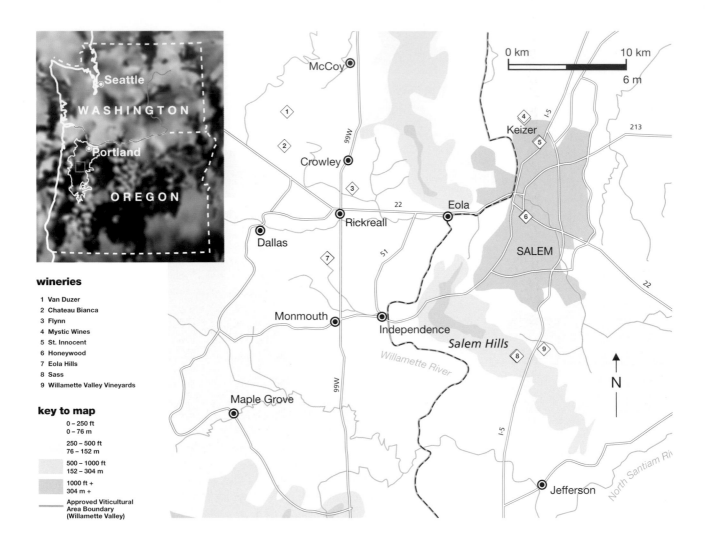

key to map

0 – 250 ft
0 – 76 m

250 – 500 ft
76 – 152 m

500 – 1000 ft
152 – 304 m

1000 ft +
304 m +

Approved Viticultural
Area Boundary
(Willamette Valley)

South Salem Hills

The black dashed lines represent the county borders.

Fanning out south of the Eola Hills, this **geographically diverse area** stretches down the Willamette Valley from the Eola Hills, over the Salem Hills to Benton County, crossing the Willamette River from Marion County into Polk County. Scattered vineyards and wineries ring the city of Salem, Oregon's state capital. This chapter also collects a number of properties that lie in the Willamette Valley, but not within Yamhill County, the Eola Hills, or Benton County, and the southern Willamette Valley that reaches down to the Eugene area.

While not boasting a central core of wine activity, a number of significant wineries – important for different reasons – make their

home in the greater Salem area. Within the city of Salem itself, historic Honeywood Winery has been in continuous operation since 1933, just after the repeal of Prohibition (however, it moved to its current location from the original building in 1990). When the winery first opened, production focused on fruit brandies and liquors; fruit wines followed. Today, fruit wines are still made (such as raspberry, loganberry, and rhubarb), as well as a number of vinifera wines blended with fruit juice; varietally labelled table wines have been produced since 1982.

St Innocent Winery is also based in the capital, producing well-made, *méthode* *traditionelle* sparkling wine as well as a number of well-respected, vineyard-designated Pinot Noir, Chardonnay, Pinot Gris, and Pinot Blanc wines sourced from some of the top vineyards in the Willamette Valley.

These are the Seven Springs Vineyard, O'Connor Vineyard, and Temperance Hill in the Eola Hills; Shea and Brick House Vineyards on Chehalem Mountains; and Freedom Hill. Owner/winemaker Mark Vlossak owns no vineyards, instead he chooses to work closely with established vineyard owners. Vlossak served as winemaker at Panther Creek Cellars in McMinnville from 1994-8, and still consults there.

Willamette Valley Vineyards – located just south of Salem and dramatically visible on an eastern rise up from the Interstate 5 freeway, sitting on top a vine-covered slope – is significant as the major player in this geographic area, as well as holding an important, if unique, commercial role in the state. Willamette Valley Vineyards was established in 1983 by Jim Bernau, the current President of the winery. He was attracted to the old plum orchard on the site – by then dead and overgrown – in part because of the soil and elevations: a gradually climbing slope of Jory soil at the lower elevation of 168 metres (550ft) and Nekia soil at 198–229 metres (650–750ft): very similar to the composition of the Eola Hills. (The fact that Jory soil – most prominent in the Red Hills of Dundee – is found in the Salem Hills is not very surprising: the soil was named after the Jory family, who homesteaded in the south Salem area in 1848.) The Nekia soil here offers similar characteristics, as well: lower yields, smaller clusters, smaller berries, and earlier ripening.

Willamette Valley's first estate vineyards (planted in 1983–5) contain the Wadensville clone of Pinot Noir (with some grafting over in the 1990s with Dijon clones), planted widely at 1.2 x 3.6 metres (4 x 12ft) at about 2,470 plants per hectare (1,000 plants per acre). All vines are trained in Geneva Double Curtain (GDC), a split canopy system that proved to be good for colour and flavour in trials run by the Oregon State University Research Station

Sustainable agriculture

Only five vineyards in the state have qualified for the Oregon Tilth certification (the local authority that certifies to US standards). These are two vineyards in the Yamhill County area of the Eola Hills owned by the Cattral brothers, whose grapes are sold to Amity Vineyards (the first producer of organically grown wine, in 1990); Brick House Vineyards on Chehalem Mountains, Cooper Mountain Vineyards in Washington County, and most recently, Evesham Wood in the Eola Hills. Cooper Mountain is working towards full biodynamic certification.

But a concept of sustainable agriculture has captured a broader viticultural audience: The Low Input Viticulture and Enology (LIVE) was founded in 1999 by Ted Casteel of Bethel Heights Vineyard, based on the Swiss Vinatura-integrated production programme – a system with which Oregon-State-University-Viticulture Professor Carmo Candolfi-Vasconcelos had prior experience.

LIVE is a voluntary programme. Its objectives are holistic in approach. Treating the farm as the basic unit, its aims include creating and maintaining a viticulture that is economically viable over time, maintaining the highest level of quality in fruit production, minimizing the use of agricultural chemicals and fertilizers, promoting and maintaining high-biological diversity, and encouraging responsible soil stewardship.

The grape grower must have professional, trained vineyard management, continuing education and LIVE training, as well as keeping complete records on fertilization, pesticide application, pruning, and soil management. LIVE also prescribes how to establish a vineyard. Site inspections and score cards assess the level of compliance with LIVE objectives. LIVE now boasts sixty participating vineyards in Oregon, encompassing 1,012 hectares (2,500 acres).

at the time of Bernau's original planting. Ripening with the GDC brings a different rate of maturity on each side of the curtain: the eastern face of the canopy matures the fruit faster, seeing more summer morning sun; the earlier maturing grapes are tagged at *veraison*, and harvested before the other grapes. On the south and southeast slopes, where the Pinot Noir vines are planted, they are thinned to one cluster per shoot and yields are kept under 28 hectolitres per hectare (2 tons per acre); estate Pinot Gris is cropped higher, to 49 hectolitres per hectare (3.5 tons per acre).

Willamette Valley Vineyards is large by Oregon standards, producing more than 80,000 cases of wine each year. That production number, though, includes all the three brands that it owns: Willamette Valley Vineyards, Tualatin Estate (purchased from Bill Fuller in 1997), and Griffin Creek – a joint venture begun between Rogue Valley grape growers

Don and Traute Moore and the winery, which makes wines that were first released in 1998.

Willamette Valley also follows the classic model of a large winery, but does it more successfully than most. A winery of this size makes a significant volume of wine destined for the supermarket shelves; selling that quantity of basic wines pays for the more labour-intensive, upper-end wines produced. Willamette Valley's talented winemaker Joe Dobbes crafts solid wines at all levels. His single-vineyard Pinot Noirs can compete with the best of those in Oregon – made from fruit purchased from some of the top vineyards in the state, including Freedom Hill and Hoodview, a vineyard Willamette Valley controls, located on the Yamhill County side of the eastern slope of the Eola Hills. Dobbes additionally now serves as winemaker for Torii Mor Winery (in Yamhill County) as well. He is one of the few Oregon winemakers who manages to juggle the production of wine at disparate locations. The commuting is made easier by Willamette Valley's deeply supportive staff: the winery has a full-time enologist and a production manager to help ease Dobbes' load.

Winemaker Joe Dobbes crafts solid wines at all levels ... He is one of the few Oregon winemakers who juggles the production of wine at disparate locations.

What separates Willamette Valley Vineyards from other Oregon wineries is its structure; it is a publicly traded company, listed on the Nasdaq stock exchange (and currently not performing terrifically well). In 1989, Jim Bernau and Willamette Valley Vineyards created the first Regulation A: a public stock offering that was self-underwritten, a novelty not only in Oregon but also in the United States. All first 871 shareholders were wine *afficianados*; that number is now higher than 4,500 due to subsequent offerings.

Across the freeway from Willamette Valley Vineyards, the **St Jory Vineyard** is also visible from the highway. This is Duck Pond's (the giant operation based in Yamhill County) newest venture, and it is a 40.5 hectare (100 acre) parcel with 3 hectares (7 acres) of Pinot Noir and 36 hectares (90 acres) of Pinot Gris,

planted in 1998 and 1999. The entire property produces its first light crop in 2001. These vines are spaced 1.5 x 2.4 metres (5 x 8ft), with approximately 2,500 plants per hectare (1,010 plants per acre).

Duck Pond also owns two other south Salem area vineyards, each planted in 1990–2 with Pinot Noir and Pinot Gris. These sites – 26 hectare (65 acre) and 37 hectare (90 acre) parcels – are even less densely planted than the St Jory Vineyard, with wide spacing of 1.5 x 3 metres (5 x 10ft), with 2,152 plants per hectare (871 plants per acre). Duck Pond plans to build another production facility – in

addition to their winery in Dundee – at The St Jory Vineyard site.

Other **nearby wineries** include Flynn Vineyards and Eola Hills Wine Cellars – both near Rickreall, west of Salem and southwest of the Eola Hills. Each of these wineries produces about 30,000 cases of wine themselves from estate vineyards (and parcels in the Eola Hills), but are also known for doing custom crushes for wineries lacking production facilities.

Within this broadly defined wine-producing region, there are a number of vineyards without associated wineries such as the neighbouring Croft Vineyard and Freedom Hill Vineyard, one of the most respected sites in the state. The fact that Freedom Hill Vineyard lies outside of the more well-known soils and concentration of wineries should raise questions about whether the best vineyard sites in the state still remain to be discovered.

Located 8km (5 miles) south of Rickreall, .Freedom Hill sits on 57 sloped hectares (140 acres), 26 hectares (65 acres) are currently planted, mostly with Pinot Noir (19.4 hectares/48 acres), but also Pinot Gris (4

While usually recognized as a cool and damp region, Oregon really does see many glorious, cloudless days! Shown here is Willamette Valley Vineyards.

hectares/10 acres), Pinot Blanc (1.2 hectares/3 acres), and Chardonnay (1.6 hectares/4 acres). Elevations range from 107–183 metres (350–600ft), and all elevations possess a southeast exposure.

The soil here...is called Bellpine, a sedimentary, silty clay loam that may be the oldest in the Willamette Valley.

The soil here – and travelling further down the valley, as well – is called Bellpine, a sedimentary, silty clay loam that may be the oldest in the Willamette Valley. Bellpine has a very high mineral content, a depth of 1–1.2 metres (3–4ft) or less, and is moderately well drained. The weather here is similar to that of the Eola Hills, with a bit less wind and very little marine cooling influence from the Van Duzer Corridor.

Freedom Hill's Vineyards have a greater rangerange of trellising systems than most: the oldest block is supported on single wires and cane-pruned, which creates "hanging" trellises; one block (3.2 hectares/8 acres) sports Lyre trellising, and the new Pinot Noir plantings use the more classic Vertical Shoot Positioned (VSP) trellises, with double Guyot canes. The Pinot Gris and Pinot Blanc use the Geneva Double Curtain (GDC) system. Freedom Hill's owner Dan Dusschee has a commitment to dry farming by managing water needs by reducing competition among the plants.

Producers who buy in the rich, well-structured Freedom Hill grapes include such respected names as Ken Wright Cellars, Panther Creek Cellars, Bethel Heights Vineyard, Willamette Valley Vineyards, St Innocent Winery, Cristom Vineyards, Lange Winery, and the King Estate.

Freedom Hill Vineyard, Seven Springs Vineyard (in the Eola Hills), and Shea Vineyard (in Yamhill County) command justified top billings as named vineyards on many of the most highly rated bottles of wine in the state.

Notable producers

Chateau Bianca Winery
☎ 503-623-6181 ☏ 503-623-6230
✉ chateaubianca@qwest.net
🌐 www.chateaubianca.com
17485 Highway 22, Dallas, Oregon 97338
Acreage in production 0.8ha (2 acres) Gewürztraminer, 0.8ha (2 acres) Riesling,2.4ha (6 acres) Pinot Noir, 2ha (5 acres) Chardonnay, 1.2ha (3 acres) Pinot Blanc, 0.4ha (1 acre) Cascade, 0.4ha (1 acre) Pinot Gris
New plantings 1.6ha (4 acres) Marechal Foch
Production capacity 13,000 cases
2000 production 10,000 cases
Established 1989
First wines released 1990 vintage
Family operation producing thirteen different varietals and blends, including a sparkling wine.

Eola Hills Wine Cellars
☎ 503-623-2405 ☏ 503-623-0350
✉ eolahills@eolahillswinery.com
🌐 www.eolahillswinery.com
501 S Pacific Highway 99W, Rickreall,
Oregon 97371
Acreage in production 21ha (52 acres) Pinot Noir, 10ha (25 acres) Chardonnay, 3.6ha (9 acres) Sauvignon Blanc, 6ha (15 acres) Pinot Gris, 0.6ha (1.5 acres) Viognier, 0.8ha (2 acres) Marechal Foch
Production capacity 80,000 cases
2000 production 32,000 cases
Established 1986
First wines released 1989 vintage
This winery is not technically located in the Eola Hills, but named instead for its vineyards, which are. A wide range of wines is produced. Known for very popular Sunday brunches, themed parties, and events at the winery, made possible by a full-time culinary director. A number of wineries without their own facilities have used the Eola Hills production space.

Flynn Vineyards
☎ 503-623-8683 ☏ 503-623-0908
✉ flynnwine@aol.com
🌐 flynnvineyards.com
2200 W. Pacific Highway, Rickreall,
Oregon 97371
Acreage in production 20.3ha (50 acres) Pinot Noir, 4.1ha (10 acres) Pinot Gris, 1.6ha (4 acres) Chardonnay
New plantings 19ha (47 acres) Pinot Noir
Production capacity 90,000 cases
2000 production 30,000 cases
Established 1982
First wines released 1984 vintage
A solid operation, making good quality wines, including a sparkling wine *méthode traditionelle*. Flynn does a large amount of custom crushing for others.

Honeywood Winery
☎ 503-362-4111 ☏ 503-362-4112
✉ info@honeywoodwinery.com
🌐 www.honeywoodwinery.com
1350 Hines Street SE, Salem,
Oregon 97302
Production capacity 70,000 cases
2000 production 16,000 cases
Established 1934

Joe Dobbes of Willamette Valley Vineyards

First wines released 1934 vintage
Oregon's oldest, continuously running winery,
historically and currently focusing on fruit wines.
The current facility has been in operation since
1990. All fruit is purchased, and increasingly,
varietal wines have been produced as well as
fruit and fruit-varietal combinations.

Mystic Wines

☎ 503-581-2769 ℻ 503-581-2894
✉ rmafit@viser.net
3995 Deepwood Lane NW, Salem,
Oregon 97304
Production capacity 1,000 cases
2000 production 650 cases
Established 1992
First wines released 1992 vintage
All fruit is sourced from the Columbia Valley,
near The Dalles. Merlot, Cabernet Sauvignon,
and Syrah varietal wines are produced in
small quantities.

Sass Winery

☎ 503-391-9991
✉ Wildwindswinery@email.msn.com
PO Box 13662, Salem, Oregon 97309;
9092 Jackson Hill Road SE, Salem,
Oregon 97306

Acreage in production 2ha (5 acres)
Pinot Noir, 1.2ha (3 acres) Pinot Gris
New plantings 0.2ha (0.5 acres) Pinot Noir
Production capacity 5,000 cases
2000 production 1,000 cases
First wines released 1994 vintage
Formerly known as Wild Winds Winery, Jerry
Sass's small winery lies across the highway from
Willamette Valley Vineyards, producing solid Pinot
Noir, Pinot Gris, and Chardonnay from both estate
grapes (planted in 1989) and purchased fruit.

St Innocent Ltd

☎ 503-378-1526 ℻ 503-378-1041
✉ Markv@stinnocentwine.com
🌐 www.stinnocentwine.com
1360 Tandem Avenue NE, Salem,
Oregon 97303
Production capacity 7,000 cases
2000 production 6,600 cases
Established 1988
First wines released 1988 vintage
Mark Vlossak produces Pinot Noir from some
of the top vineyards around including Shea,
Freedom Hill, and Seven Springs; his wines tend
to be big and tannic in youth. His white wines can
carry a slightly bitter edge from extended skin
contact. He also produces a pleasant sparkling

wine, *méthode traditionelle*. Vlossak also served
as winemaker at Panther Creek Cellars from 1994
to 1998, and still consults there.

Van Duzer Vineyards

☎ 503-623-6420 or 800-884-1927
℻ 503-623-4310
✉ Kathy@vanduzer.com
🌐 www.vanduzer.com
11975 Smithfield Road, Dallas, Oregon
97338
Acreage in production 26.3ha (65 acres)
total of Pinot Noir, Pinot Gris, and Chardonnay
New plantings 6ha (15 acres) Pinot Noir
Production capacity 15,000 cases
2000 production 15,000 cases
First wines released 1989 vintage
The current property was purchased in 1998, by
new owners venture capitalist Carl Thoma and his
wife Marilynn, who are also managing principals
of Parducci Wine Estates of California. The
property is located south of Amity and west of
Salem, due east of the Van Duzer Corridor. Field
grafting has brought in Dijon clones for Pinot Noir,
turning 15-year-old vines into modern clonal
selections. The changes should bring up the
quality and name of Van Duzer wines.

Willamette Valley Vineyards

☎ 503-588-9463, 800-344-9463
℻ 503-588-8894, 503-362-0062
✉ info@wvv.com
🌐 www.wvv.com
8800 Enchanted Way SE, Turner, Oregon
97392
Acreage in production Estate Vineyard:
8.7ha (21.5 acres) Pinot Noir, 3.4ha (8.5 acres)
Pinot Gris, 4.3ha (10.5 acres) Chardonnay;
O'Connor Vineyard: 8.9ha (22 acres) Pinot Noir,
6ha (15 acres) Pinot Gris, 5.7ha (14 acres)
Chardonnay, 1.4ha (3.5 acres) Gamay noir, 0.6ha
(1.5 acres) Auxerrois
New plantings Estate Vineyard: 1.6ha
(4 acres) Pinot Noir
Production capacity 100,000 cases
2000 production 70,000 cases
Established 1983
First wines released 1989 vintage
One of Oregon's largest producers, especially
when you factor in the other brands they own:
Tualatin and Griffin Creek. In spite of the volume,
the reserve and vineyard-designated Pinot Noirs
crafted by winemaker Joe Dobbes are among
the best Oregon has to offer. The single vineyard
wines come from some of the top vineyards in
the state, including Hoodview and Freedom Hill.

Southern Willamette Valley

The **southern Willamette Valley** (entirely within the Willamette Valley formal appellation) begins for this chapter's purposes near Monmouth – just south of the Salem Hills – where the Willamette Valley starts to narrow, as it makes its way towards the city of Eugene, just north of the point at which the Coast and Cascade Mountain Ranges converge. The southern Willamette Valley follows the (north-flowing) Willamette River and its fertile valley south to where the river's

The black dashed lines represent the county borders.

originating forks meet – one winds its way up from a point a bit further south, and the other comes from the east, right up into the Cascade Range.

The southern Willamette Valley is mostly a flat, agricultural corridor – its produce is diverse and includes grass seed, mint, poultry, livestock, and dairy goods. Beyond the river valley, the farmland disappears into densely wooded land. Away from the valley floor, sloped vineyard land lies to the west of

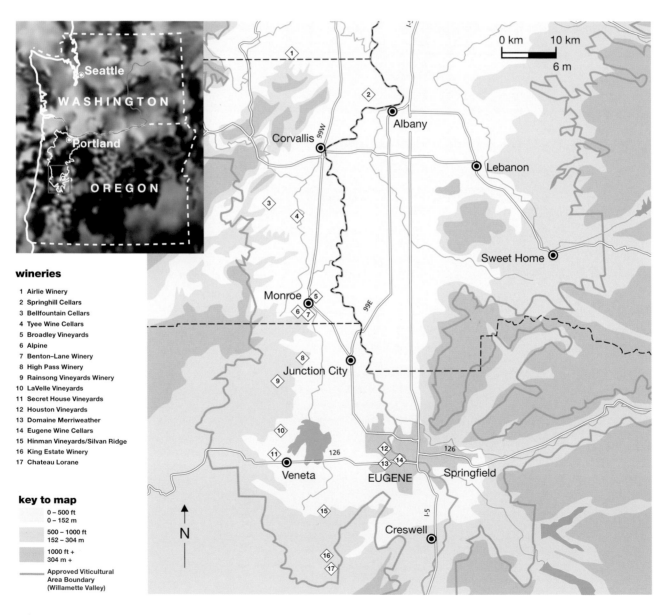

wineries

1 Airlie Winery
2 Springhill Cellars
3 Bellfountain Cellars
4 Tyee Wine Cellars
5 Broadley Vineyards
6 Alpine
7 Benton–Lane Winery
8 High Pass Winery
9 Rainsong Vineyards Winery
10 LaVelle Vineyards
11 Secret House Vineyards
12 Houston Vineyards
13 Domaine Merriweather
14 Eugene Wine Cellars
15 Hinman Vineyards/Silvan Ridge
16 King Estate Winery
17 Chateau Lorane

key to map

0 – 500 ft
0 – 152 m

500 – 1000 ft
152 – 304 m

1000 ft +
304 m +

Approved Viticultural
Area Boundary
(Willamette Valley)

the river, snuggling up against the leeward foothills of the Coastal Range.

The southern valley is warmer than the more northern reaches; while the south is slower to heat up in spring than the northern region, the northern region cools off more quickly and is susceptible to autumn rain. The south retains heat longer into the autumn, but as the Willamette Valley narrows and the mountain ranges converge, the resulting winds are a cooling, tempering influence on the grapes, helping the retention of acidity during the maturation period. Rainfall averages about 89cm (35in) during the mild winter months.

This region offers a variety of different soil types almost pocketed throughout the valley. The silty Bellpine clay loam, familiar in the south Salem Hills area, can be found as far south as the King Estate and Hinman/Silvan Ridge, both southeast of the city of Eugene in Lane County, as well as in various patches in other spots, including parts of the Woodhall Vineyard and Benton Lane Vineyards near Monroe. But elsewhere in this region, many other soils dominate: Tyee, near Corvallis, sits on Willamette soil, a deep, rich, and well-drained soil type. Vines at Broadley and some at Benton Lane near Monroe, on the Benton County-Lane County border, are planted on Hazelair, a well-drained, rockier soil of varying depths, from 0.3 metres (1ft) to more than 3 metres (10ft) deep. Benton Lane even has a bit of iron-rich Jory soil, as well.

The **first vineyards** in the southern Willamette Valley were planted in the early 1970s, near Corvallis, the home of Oregon State University. Tyee Wine Cellars was planted in 1974 by owner David Buchanan, on the century-old farm that had been his grandfather's base for sheep ranching, dairy farming, and horse racing. A self-taught interest in home winemaking led Buchanan in 1984 back to his alma mater OSU and to

Barney Watson, a University-of-California-at-Davis enology graduate who then, as now, was in the process of conducting research on winemaking and the Oregon wine industry. Watson teamed up as winemaker with the Buchanans, and began to focus on estate-grown Pinot Noir, Pinot Gris, Chardonnay, and – in particular – good Gewürztraminer.

Tyee's property – like nearby Bellfountain Winery – sits in the rain shadow of Mary's Peak, which is the highest elevation of the Coastal Range, at 1,149 metres (4,097ft). Afternoon drying sea breezes provide a positive effect on the grapes, cooling them, and preserving acidity. Only 17km (10 miles) further south, the area around the town of Monroe is often described as the Banana

The Oregon wine country sports a homey and humble demeanour, with many small towns still boasting a country charm.

Belt, as it is the warmest, driest autumn mesoclimate in the Willamette Valley.

Neighbouring Alpine and Woodhall Vineyards were each planted in this area around 1976, by neighbours and medical doctor colleagues Dan Jepson (and his wife, Christine) at Alpine and Frank Baynes at Woodhall. They each planted a wide variety of grapes – Riesling, Chardonnay, Pinot Noir, and Cabernet Sauvignon – which they crop to about 42 hectolitres per hectare (3 tons per acre), not perhaps the most focused concentration, especially for Pinot Noir.

Woodhall Vineyard has significant importance to education in Oregon; it was donated to the state in 1988...for use as a research vineyard

Today, Alpine itself produces very little commercial wine – about 20 cases of Chardonnay and 50 cases of Cabernet Sauvignon – instead preferring to sell the majority of its grapes to Willamette Valley Vineyards, Edgefield Winery, Chateau Lorane, and (Pinot Noir only) to Broadley.

Woodhall Vineyard has significant importance to education in Oregon; it was donated to the state in 1988 by Dr Frank Baynes for use as a research vineyard. While

Oregon's two largest state universities make their home in the southern Willamette Valley – Oregon State University (OSU) in Corvallis and the University of Oregon in Eugene. Of these two, it is OSU that serves the role of an agricultural college, with a famously strong viticulture and enology department that works very closely with the Oregon wine industry.

At any one time, OSU conducts six to eight wine industry-related research trials. The Department of Horticulture oversees the viticultural studies at Woodhall (and cooperative studies conducted at commercial vineyards around the state), while the Department of Food Science and Technology – where Barney Watson is based – covers enology research.

Woodhall is a 5.6 hectare (14 acre) property, planted on Bellpine soil with elevations ranging from 152–198 metres (500–650ft); the vineyards all face south. Like the other Monroe area vineyards, Woodhall is a warm site, where fruit ripens two to three days earlier than in the northern Willamette Valley. Until the 2001 vintage, by the terms of Dr Baynes' donation, the public could pay to pick grapes. Beginning with the 2001 vintage, grapes at Woodhall will be sold to wineries.

The early plantings – the commercial grapes – are spaced 1.8 x 2.7 metres (6 x 9ft). Newer grapevines have been planted at 1.2 x 2.1 metres (4 x 7ft) and include the OSU rootstock trials, with four varieties planted on twenty different rootstocks, plus trials of eleven Chardonnay clones (planted in 1989), and twenty Pinot Noir clones.

Current **viticulture research** projects use Woodhall for about half of the research load. At Woodhall, the rootstock trials are ongoing, with growth and ripening data recorded annually. Nitrogen studies are underway as joint-ventures at Benton Lane Winery in nearby Monroe and Argyle's Knudsen Vineyard in Dundee. Experiments on crop load are conducted at Woodhall, as well as at WillaKenzie Estate in Yamhill and Hyland Vineyard near McMinnville. Barney

Vine pruning and training systems

Grape clusters only develop on shoots that grow out of buds retained on canes that grew in the prior year. There are two basic types of pruning to retain the bearing buds: spur pruning and cane pruning. In spur pruning, the buds grow on spurs of a cordon or trunk of the vine. Spur pruning is best suited to a warm climate. For cane pruning, the whole cane is retained. Cane pruning can be a safer bet in cool climates.

Training systems define how the vine is arrayed on a trellis.

Cordon training is the simplest form of spur pruning: the trunk of the vine terminates in a permanent branch (cordon) with upward spurs. The Guyot system is a training system for cane pruning, leaving a cane (from the prior years' growth) with six to ten buds and a spur near the trunk. (Shoots from the spurs form the cane the following year.).The Smart-Dyson training system (for spur pruning) is also a vertically-divided canopy similar to the Scott Henry system (see page 83), but the vine is cordon-trained and there are upward-and downwards-pointing spurs. The Geneva Double Curtain training system (spur pruned) divides the canopy into two hanging curtains trained downwards from high canes. A Lyre training system can use either cane or spur pruning; it also has a divided canopy, divided horizontally into two parallel canopies with upward-pointing shoots. VSP, or vertical shoot positioning, (cane or spur pruning) describes the support of annual vertical shoot growth by moveable horizontal foliage wires.

Watson leads the winemaking end of similar research projects, focusing on the analysis of the wines produced from the experimental grapes. These experiments receive their funds in large part from the Oregon Wine Advisory Board.

One of the more important recent conclusions of this research involves nitrogen levels; the studies showed that must samples at harvest are often deficient in fermentable nitrogen content, and that there are differences within vineyard blocks as well as vintage and variety variations. Results showed a relationship between grapevine-nitrogen content found in the petiole (the branch of a grapevine's leaf) and must-nitrogen content, suggesting that petioles collected at *veraison* may be able to predict low nitrogen levels in the must. The *veraison* levels, of course, are affected by the typical drought conditions Oregon sees each August, as well.

More research will be conducted, but these preliminary results have helped winemakers to make more knowledgeable nutrient supplement decisions prior to fermentation to avoid potential problems.

In addition to having a research vineyard, the Monroe area is significant for being home to two wineries that produce the greatest quality of estate Pinot Noir – and only Pinot Noir – in the southern Willamette Valley: Broadley Vineyards and Benton Lane Winery.

Broadley was planted in 1982 by Craig and Claudia Broadley, who first made wine in 1986. They planted Pinot Noir on a northeast slope; they chose the coolest site on their property in order to maintain acidity. Early plantings were spaced at 1.2 x 3.4 metres (4 x 11ft), with 2,718 plants per hectare (1,100 plants per acre), to accommodate a tractor and their Lyre trellising system. The yield is kept to 28–30.8 hectolitres per hectare (2–2.2 tons per acre). Harvest can be as early as 1 September, but averages 25 September (in contrast to 1 October in Yamhill County). The block for its reserve wine always ripens first; Broadley's top *cuvée*, Claudia's Choice, always comes from a discrete block of fruit, which is harvested one week later.

Broadley ferments **whole clusters** in open-top fermenters, for up to a month, at times intentionally creating a slightly tannic wine intended for ageing. And in order to compete with the better known Yamhill County wines, Broadly crafts its wine to be big, backed by the tannin and a firm natural acidity.

Nearby Benton Lane crafts three different *cuvées*, including their workhorse bottling, an oppositely styled wine from Broadley's, made to be soft and ready to drink on release; reserve wines are more structured. Pinot Noir and Nebbiolo were planted on the former Sunny Mountain Ranch in 1989 by California winemakers Steve Girard of Girard Wines (which has now been sold) and Carl Doumani of Stags Leap Winery, both in Napa. The Nebbiolo has since been grafted over with Pinot Noir since it never came close to ripening before frost set in. (A very small amount of Viognier has been planted and early trials show great promise.) Yields vary according to vineyard block and ultimate destiny: the grapes for the basic cuvée are harvested at 42 hectolitres per hectare (3 tons per acre); the goal for the reserve wines is 28 hectolitres (2 tons). The vines on Hazleair soil struggle to produce one cluster per shoot, and typically yield less than 28 tons per hectare (2 tons per acre).

Benton Lane (the name of the two counties the property straddles) sits on a sloped rise, ranging in elevation from 106–220 metres (350–725ft), with a southeast orientation. The property is shielded from the west by a mountain that divides the cloud cover; Benton Lane stays sunny when other area properties can be overcast. This exposure allows grapes to ripen easily and develop into very full-flavoured wines.

Moving further south in the Willamette Valley, a number of wineries dot the landscape due west of the university-dominated city of Eugene, and a few facilities have sprung up within the city of Eugene itself. Many of these properties choose to purchase grapes rather than grow them. A comparison can be made to the wineries in or near Portland; winemakers

Harvest can be as early as 1 September, but averages 25 September (in contrast to 1 October in Yamhill County).

in these cities choose to live and work in an urban setting, without a commitment to farming grapes.

West of Eugene, Hinman Vineyards/ Silvan Ridge began early, first planting grapes in 1979. The property sits on Bellpine soil, at relatively low elevations that find themselves are susceptible to spring and autumn frosts. This area – as well as at the King Estate and Chateau Lorane – sits in a cool zone. Only 2 hectares (5 acres) of grapes (Pinot Gris) are still under cultivation, Hinman now purchases most of its fruit for its basic wines (labelled Hinman), and reserve level wines (labelled Silvan Ridge). South of Hinman by only a few miles, King Estate is one of Oregon's largest wineries, perched on over 220 hectares (550 acres) of pastoral landscape. Approaching it is like coming upon Xanadu, the grandeur totally unexpected – its appearance is more like Napa than Oregon. Even the philosophy is more California-like in demeanour. King Estate is not just a winery making 75,000 cases per year, it also boasts a culinary programme that has so far produced two cookbooks with nationally-recognized chefs and a television programme about food and wine based on the books. Additionally, the kitchen staff use estate fruits and vegetables to create lovely jams, relishes, and vinegars.

Unlike most Oregon wineries, King Estate had set its sights on a **national wine profile**. The winery purchases most of its grapes, from over forty growers throughout the state. Blending has been at the core of its identity since the winery was established in 1992; the goal has been a widely distributed, consistent product, not *terroir*-driven wines. The King Estate is one of Oregon's largest wineries, with Pinot Gris its largest production, but also with a focus on Pinot Noir. The Pinot Gris has a good varietal character and price value.

That original blended approach began to undergo a shift with the 1997 vintage, when the grapes from King Estate's own vineyards began producing enough fruit to bottle. The blended wines are still a focus, but the

Domaine wines – as King Estate calls its estate-grown wine – have been a new development at the winery.

The Estate boasts 92 hectares (230 acres) of vines – Pinot Gris, Pinot Noir, and Chardonnay – planted on Bellpine soil at elevations of 260–305 metres (850–1000ft). The higher elevations affect ripening; typically, the fruit is picked five days after most other grapes comes in. Weather is moderated by cooling coastal breezes. While nearby Hinman doesn't boast the higher elevations necessary for quality-fruit production, the King Estate would appear to be better sited for that purpose.

The King Estate owns and operates the on-site Lorane Grapevines, which is Oregon's largest grapevine nursery and propagation facility. The nursery ships about 250,000 grafted grapevines each year, primarily to Oregon vineyards. Of the plant material, 81 per cent is Pinot Noir, seven per cent Pinot Gris, four per cent Chardonnay, and one per cent Merlot, with the remaining seven per cent devoted to assorted varieties. The broad portfolio of plants is made up of more than twenty available rootstocks.

The King Estate has seen a high turnover of personnel over its life. The early days were free spending, with a large staff in every department and ambitious in-house culinary programmes. In recent years, the team has slimmed down considerably, with the players changing a bit more frequently than at other large operations in the state. Turnover or not, the King Estate looms overall as an extremely large player in the Oregon wine market; it distributes internationally and has one of the strongest Oregon wine presences in Great Britain.

This chapter's winery listings also include the few wineries located on the Oregon Coast. These facilities do not boast vineyard land (the seaside location would not be a compatible site for vinifera), but they represent a lifestyle choice for their owners, who purchase fruit from vineyards around the state.

The King Estate is one of Oregon's largest wineries, with Pinot Gris its largest production, but also with a good focus on Pinot Noir.

Not all vineyards in Oregon – including this one near the university town of Corvallis – are sited on sloped hillsides.

Notable producers

Airlie Winery

☎ 503-838-6013 ℹ 503-838-6279
✉ airlie@airliewinery.com
🌐 www.airliewinery.com
15305 Dunn Forest Road, Monmouth, Oregon 97361
Acreage in production 2.8ha (7 acres) Pinot Noir, 2.4ha (6 acres) Pinot Gris, 2.4ha (6 acres) Chardonnay, 1.6 ha (4 acres) Marechal Foch, 0.8 ha (2 acres) Gewürztraminer, 1.2ha (3 acres) Riesling, 1.6ha (4 acres) Müller-Thurgau
Production capacity 8,000 cases
2000 production 6,000 cases
Established 1986
Solid, commercial quality wines, with clear varietal character. Good value wines.

Alpine Vineyards

☎ 541-424-5851 ℹ 541-424-5891
✉ alpinewine@aol.com
25904 Green Peak Road, Monroe, Oregon 97456
Acreage in production 1.2ha (3 acres) Chardonnay, 3.2ha (8 acres) Pinot Noir, 2.8ha (7 acres) Riesling, 1.6ha (4 acres) Cabernet Sauvignon, 0.8ha (2 acres) Pinot Gris, 0.2ha (0.5 acres) Gewürztraminer, 0.2ha (0.5 acres) Merlot
Production capacity 5,000 cases
2000 production 70 cases
Established 1976
First wines released 1980 vintage
Tiny producer, selling a majority of the grapes each year to other wineries including Willamette Valley Vineyards, Edgefield Winery, and nearby Broadley Vineyard. Alpine wines are sold only at the winery and sell out quickly.

Bellefountain Cellars

☎ 541-929-3162
✉ winemaker@proaxis.com
🌐 www.bellefountaincellars.com
25041 Llewellyn Road, Corvallis, Oregon 97333
Acreage in production 1.4ha (3.5 acres) Pinot Noir, 1.4ha (3.5 acres) Chardonnay, 0.6ha (1.5 acres) Pinot Gris, 0.6ha (1.5 acres) Cabernet Sauvignon
Production capacity 7,000 cases
2000 production 2,500 cases
Established 1989

Morgan, Claudia, and Craig Broadley of Broadley Vineyards

First wines released 1990 vintage
Well-focused, pleasant wines, although the Cabernet Sauvignon can show a slightly green edge due to lack of optimal ripeness.

Benton-Lane Winery

☎ 541-847-5792 ℹ 541-847-5791
✉ Sharon@Benton-lane.com
🌐 www.benton-lane.com
PO Box 99, 23924 Territorial, Monroe, Oregon 97456
Acreage in production 43.7ha (108 acres) Pinot Noir
New plantings 2.4ha (6 acres) Pinot Noir
Production capacity 25,000 cases
2000 production 22,000 cases
Established 1988
First wines released 1992 vintage
Carl Duomani (from Stags' Leap Winery in Napa) and Steve Girard (whose eponymous Napa winery was sold to the Rudd Estate) produce very ripe, focused Pinot Noir. Until the 1998 vintage (the same year winemaker Gary Horner joined the team) Benton-Lane made its wine at Flynn Vineyards. The name Benton-Lane reflects the two Oregon counties their property straddles.

Broadley Vineyards

☎ 541-847-5934 ℹ 541-847-6018
✉ claudiab@peak.org
Box 160, 265 South 5th Street, Monroe, Oregon 97456
Acreage in production 7.7ha (19 acres) Pinot Noir
New plantings 3.6ha (9 acres) Pinot Noir
Production capacity 3,000 cases
2000 production 2,300 cases
Established 1986
First wines released 1988 vintage
A family-owned property focusing on Pinot Noir. Claudia's Choice their top cuvée.

Brad Biehl of King Estate Winery

Eugene Wine Cellars

☎ 541-342-2600 ⓕ 541-342-1132
ⓔ ewcmon@aol.com
ⓦ www.areawine.com
255 Madison Street, Eugene,
Oregon 97402
Production capacity 10,000 cases
2000 production 7,100 cases
Established 1999
First wines released 1999 vintage
These long-time (1983) vineyard managers and consultants under the name AREA Inc now make wine themselves in a production facility in downtown Eugene. Grapes are purchased from sites around the state, including properties they farm: Pinot Noir, Syrah, Viognier, Melon, Pinot Blanc, Pinot Gris, and Chardonnay. Owner Bruce Biehl is the brother of King Estate viticulturist Brad Biehl.

Flying Dutchman Winery

☎ 541-765-2553 ⓕ 541-765-2554
ⓔ CMI@Actionnet.net
915 1st Street, Otter Rock, Oregon 97369
Acreage in production None
Production capacity 800 cases
2000 production 800 cases
Established 1997
First wines released 1997 vintage
One of the three Oregon-coast based wineries, this one located near Lincoln City at the popular Inn at Otter Crest resort, at its Flying Dutchman restaurant. Pinot Noir, Chardonnay, Pinot Gris grapes are purchased from Salem-area vineyards.

Hinman Vineyards – Silvan Ridge

☎ 541-345-1945 ⓕ 541-345-6174
ⓔ staff@silvanridge.com
ⓦ www.silvanridge.com
27012 Briggs Hill Road, Eugene, Oregon 97405
Acreage in production 2.8ha (7 acres) Pinot Gris
Production capacity 35,000 cases
2000 production 25,000 cases
Established 1979
Credible winery near Eugene, producing two labels: Hinman Vineyards and the higher-end Silvan Ridge reserve line, begun in 1993. For Hinman Vineyards, wines produced (mostly from purchased grapes) include Pinot Gris, Pinot Noir, Chardonnay, Cabernet Sauvignon, and Riesling.

Chateau Lorane Winery

☎ 541-942-8028 ⓕ 541-942-5830
ⓔ linde@chateaulorane.com
ⓦ chateaulorane.com
27415 Siuslaw River Road, Lorane, Oregon 97451
Acreage in production 2.4ha (6 acres) Pinot Noir, 1.2ha (3 acres) Marechal Foch, 0.4ha (1 acre) Leon Millott, 0.4ha (1 acre) Pinot Meunier, 0.8ha (2 acres) Riesling, 0.4ha (1 acre) Sauvignon Blanc
New plantings 1.6ha (4 acres) Dijon closes of Pinot Noir, 1.2ha (3 acres) various German hybrids
Production capacity 6,000 cases
2000 production 4,000 cases
Established 1992
First wines released 1992 vintage
Located in the pretty foothills of the Coastal Range, Linde and Sharon Kester first planted their vineyards in 1984.

Domaine Meriwether

☎ 541-345-5224 ⓕ 541-431-0476
ⓔ meriwetherwines@earthlink.net
ⓦ www.meriwetherwines.com
255 Madison Street, Eugene, Oregon 97402
Acreage in production None
New plantings 4.1ha (10 acres) Pinot Meunier, 6.1 ha (15 acres) Pinot Noir
Production capacity 8,000 cases
2000 production 6,200 cases Meriwether, 1,800 cases Discovery (second label)
Established 1998
First wines released 1998 vintage
New sparkling wine producer, using *méthode traditionelle*.

For Silvan Ridge, the lineup is similar: Pinot Gris, Pinot Noir, Chardonnay, Gewürztraminer, Merlot, Syrah, early Muscat, and dessert wines (ice Gewürztraminer and a Port-style Syrah). In the early 1990s, Joe Dobbes (now winemaker at Willamette Valley Vineyards and Torii Mor) served as winemaker here, raising the quality; winemaker Bryan Wilson continues the drive.

Houston Vineyards

☎ 541.747.4681 ⓕ 541.342.5121
ⓔ mailbox@HoustonVineyards.com
ⓦ www.HoustonVineyards.com
86187 Hoya Lane, Eugene, Oregon
97405-8633
Acreage in production 2.1ha (5.2 acres)
Chardonnay, 0.4ha (1 acre) Muscat Blanc
Production capacity 2000 cases
2000 production 1600 cases
Established 1980
First wines released 1983 vintage
Chardonnay producer which has its own grapes custom-crushed at other wineries. Distribution is limited (and somewhat erratic); the wines tend to be sweet and fruity.

King Estate Winery

☎ 541-942-9874 ⓕ 541-942-9867
ⓔ info@kingestate.com
ⓦ www.kingestate.com
80854 Territorial Road, Eugene,
Oregon 97405
Acreage in production 31.2ha (77 acres)
Pinot Noir, 1.2ha (30 acres) Chardonnay, 43.3ha (107 acres) Pinot Gris
Production capacity 75,000 cases
2000 production 75,000 cases
Established 1992
First wines released 1992 vintage
A very visible brand, especially strong for Pinot Gris. The King Estate's early Pinot Noir style (still made) produced a consistent, blended wine that did not represent the taste of any one vineyard or even one growing region. With the increasing maturity of its own estate vineyards, that blended commitment is changing for the better, with good, firmly structured wines labeled as Domaine.

Mountain View Winery

☎ 541-388-8339 ⓕ 541-388-4175
ⓔ debons@attglobal.net
61905 Gosney Road, Bend, Oregon 97702
Acreage in production None
Production capacity 700 cases

2000 production 600 cases
Established 1991
First wines released 1991 vintage
Oregon's only winery in the central Oregon high desert area. Owner/winemaker Al Debons brings grapes in from the Willamette, Rogue, and Columbia Valleys to produce varietal wines: Cabernet Sauvignon, Pinot Noir, Merlot, Chardonnay, Riesling, Müller-Thurgau, and Gewürztraminer.

Nehalem Bay Winery

☎ 503-368-9463 ⓕ 503-368-5300
ⓔ NBWines@hotmail.com
ⓦ nehalembaywinery.com
34965 Highway 53, Nehalem, Oregon
97131
Production capacity 5,000
Established 1977
First wines released 1977 vintage
A tasting room is maintained at this coastal facility, but the wines are now made at Honeywood (in Salem). Production is divided among fruit wines, vinifera-fruit blends and vinifera varietals, the fruit of which is sourced from vineyards on the Chehalem Mountains.

Secret House Winery

☎ 541-935-3774 ⓕ 541-935-3774
ⓔ secrethouse@worldnet.att.net
ⓦ www.secrethousewinery.com
88324 Vineyard Lane, Veneta,
Oregon 97487
Acreage in production 3.2ha (8 acres) Pinot Noir, 1.6ha (4 acres) Riesling, 1.2ha (3 acres) Chardonnay
New plantings 3.6ha (9 acres) Pinot Noir, 0.4ha (1 acre) Pinot Gris, 0.4ha (1 acre) Pinot Meunier
Production capacity 14,000 cases
2000 production 10,000 cases
Established 1989
First wines released in 1991 from 1989 vintage
First established by the Benoit family in 1972 (who later relocated to Dundee and Chateau Benoit), the winery and vineyards were purchased by the Chappel family in 1989 and now produces Pinot Noir, Chardonnay, Riesling and sparkling wines (*Méthode Traditionelle*) from its estate grapes. They also craft blends, as well as a white Pinot Noir.

Springhill Cellars

☎ 541-928-1009 ⓕ 541-928-1009
ⓔ springhill@proaxis.com
ⓦ www.springhillcellars.com
2920 NW Scenic Drive, Albany,
Oregon 97321
Acreage in production 2.7ha (6.7 acres)
Pinot Noir, 1.3ha (3.3 acres) Pinot Gris
Production capacity 2,000 cases
2000 production 1,000 cases
Established 1988
First wines released 1988 vintage
A small family-owned winery producing Pinot Noir, Pinot Gris, and small lots of Chardonnay, all with a combination of French and American barrel ageing, plus some Riesling. Most, though not all, of the fruit comes from the estate vineyards, planted in 1978.

Tyee Wine Cellars

☎ 503-753-8754 ⓕ 503-753-8754
ⓦ www.tyeewine.com
26335 Greenberry Road, Corvallis,
Oregon 97333
Acreage in production 1ha (2.5 acres) Pinot Noir, 0.6ha (1.5 acres) Pinot Gris, 0.6ha (1.5 acres) Chardonnay, 0.2ha (0.5 acres) Gewürztraminer
New plantings 1ha (2.5 acres) Pinot Noir, 0.4ha (1 acre) Pinot Gris, 0.2ha (0.5 acre) Gewürztraminer
Production capacity 3,000 cases
2000 production 2,500 cases
Established 1985
First wines released 1987 vintage
Known for consistently good, varietally strong Gewürztraminer, as well as good-value Pinot Noir, Pinot Gris, and Chardonnay.

Shallon Winery

☎ 503-325-5978
ⓔ shallon@pacifier.com
ⓦ www.shallon.com
1598 Duane Street, Astoria,
Oregon 97103
Production capacity 835 cases
2000 production 200 cases
Established 1978
First wines released 1980 vintage
This north-coast winery produces berry wines, fruit, and other flavoured wines (including flavoured whey-based wines), and "foot stomped" Zinfandel, all from purchased fruit.

Umpqua Valley

Moving southwest from Eugene, the **Umpqua Valley** appellation follows the Umpqua River, zigzagging up and down a series of low-lying hills. Wineries are located here in a broad west-facing crescent, northwest to southwest of the city of Roseburg, as far north as Elkton. Here the low hills flatten to a valley out towards the Pacific Ocean, where maritime breezes help keep Elkton the coolest growing area of the appellation. But west of the central core of this region, the tall mountains of the southern end of the Coastal Range rise, offering other valleys that bring cool marine air to the vineyards. This reduces evening temperatures in relief to the hot summer days. Further south still, the region is much warmer.

The higher daytime heat and length of the growing season means that a range of varieties that cannot grow and ripen in the Willamette Valley can reach maturity here.

The varied climates of the Umpqua region, resulting from the maritime breezes and differing elevations, mean that the range of planted varieties is broad: Cabernet Sauvignon, Pinot Noir, Chardonnay, Sémillon, Sauvignon Blanc, Riesling, Gewürztraminer, and a few French hybrids are grown. Recent plantings of Syrah, Grenache, Dolcetto, and Malbec are starting to bear fruit and offer good varietal character. But it is Tempranillo, amazingly, that shows the most promise.

Writers Ernest Hemingway and Zane Grey came to fish in the Umpqua region, where nature-based recreations still predominate, and where wineries now bring many visitors to the area too. Pioneer Richard Sommer came to this area in 1961 from California, bringing with him the first modern-era commitment to grape growing in Oregon; Sommer still produces the famous HillCrest wine today, including Riesling from his original plantings, produced in an off-dry style.

Other **local wineries** planted grapes early in Oregon's modern viticultural history; in 1972, Scott Henry of the Henry Estate planted a vineyard (Chardonnay and Pommard-clone Pinot Noir) on his family's 75-year-old prune orchard. The vineyard at Giradet Wine Cellars also dates to 1972, when Swiss-born Philippe Giradet settled in the Umpqua, a region which strongly reminded him of his native Switzerland.

Each of these pioneers brought a different contribution to Oregon's identity. The Henry Estate sits on the Coles Valley bench, at about a 122 metre (400ft) elevation, making the site more of a plateau than a sloped location. The soils on the property are a rich, but not heavy, clay-loam type that vary in depth from 0.6–4.6 metres (2ft–15ft), a volcanic soil on a bedrock base. The many varieties under cultivation include the original Chardonnay and Pinot Noir plants, plus Pinot Gris, Riesling, Gewürztraminer, Müller-

The Steamboat Pinot Noir Conference

As the International Pinot Noir Conference was established to share the glory of Pinot Noir – and help market Oregon's most important varietal wine – an adjunct conference for winemakers-only was created to attempt a better understanding of how to get the best expression out of that notoriously temperamental grape.

In 1979, a serious wine workshop was convened at one of the gem getaway locations in Oregon: The Steamboat Inn, a simple but charming fishing lodge on the banks of the North Umpqua River, due east from Roseburg. For the four days prior to IPNC, winemakers make a pilgrimage to Steamboat, a three-hour drive from McMinnville. First attended by the California and Oregon Pinot producers who planned to go to the IPNC conference in McMinnville later in the week, there is now such demand to attend (from the international winemakers at IPNC as well) that the conference now uses a lottery system for admission. Not only are all rooms, cabins, and houses filled with winemakers, a number camp out as well in order to be included. For many of the visiting winemakers, Steamboat is the highlight of their Oregon IPNC experience.

Steamboat really is all about learning, all about the quest for quality in Pinot Noir. In the spirit of collegiality – Oregon's mantra – each attendee brings a "problem" wine to discuss. Scary stuff, since each winemaker shows off his or her mistakes, seeking help to understand what not to do in the future. The winemakers then break up into smaller groups to taste and deconstruct the wines.

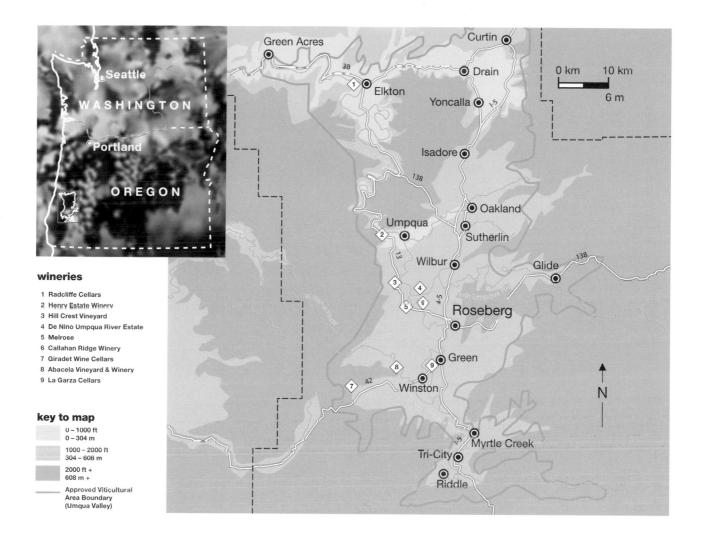

The black dashed lines represent the county borders.

wineries

1 Radcliffe Cellars
2 Henry Estate Winery
3 Hill Crest Vineyard
4 De Nino Umpqua River Estate
5 Melrose
6 Callahan Ridge Winery
7 Giradet Wine Cellars
8 Abacela Vineyard & Winery
9 La Garza Cellars

key to map

0 – 1000 ft
0 – 304 m

1000 – 2000 ft
304 – 608 m

2000 ft +
608 m +

Approved Viticultural
Area Boundary
(Umqua Valley)

Thurgau, Cabernet Sauvignon, Cabernet Franc, Merlot, Petit Verdot, Syrah, and additional plantings of Chardonnay and Pinot Noir. Henry plants the Bordeaux varieties, Syrah, and a little Pinot Noir in the shallow soils, and the earlier ripening grapes – some Pinot Noir, Chardonnay, Riesling, Gewürztraminer, Müller-Thurgau, and Pinot Gris in the deeper soils. The Pinot Noir is planted in both soil types to add a range of complexity to the finished wines.

All yields average 56 hectolitres per hectare (4 tons per acre) – high by Oregon standards in comparison to the cooler north – although there is variation by variety: the Estate crops to even higher tonnage for Müller-Thurgau, Riesling, Gewürztraminer, Chardonnay, and some of the deep-soil Pinot Noir. Lower yields can be found with the shallow-soil Pinot Noir, and with the

Bordeaux varieties (to encourage ripening that can be a challenge); with Petit Verdot, getting as high as 14 hectolitres per hectare (1 ton per acre) is unusual. Henry says that all cropping levels are geared to creating a balanced vine. Not surprisingly, all vines at the Henry Estate, including table grapes, are trained on the Scott Henry trellising system (see page 83).

Philippe and Bonnie Giradet first discovered the Umpqua when they came up from California on vacation in the 1960s and stopped by at Richard Sommer's HillCrest Vineyard. Inspired by his wines and the landscape of the region, they returned in 1971 to plant their own vineyard at a site at the confluence of two weather patterns, a sunny slope between cooler coastal

Not surprisingly, all vines at the Henry Estate, including table grapes, are trained on the Scott Henry trellising system

81

UMPQUA VALLEY

influences and the warmer southern, interior Umpqua Valley.

While the Giradets produce Chardonnay, Pinot Noir, Cabernet Sauvignon, Riesling, and White Zinfandel, they are best known for the French hybrids they champion. Of the more than thirty hybrids they grow, many are used to blend into Giradet's Grand Rouge and Grand Blanc wines, as well as blended into their varietal wines. Additionally, Baco Noir, Marechal Foch, Seyval Blanc, and De Chaunac wines – all hybrid varietals – are produced.

A few **new arrivals** in the Umpqua area, though, are helping to give the Umpqua a wide reputation for high quality. Thomas Stutz, winemaker at Mirassou Vineyards in San Jose, California, happened upon the Umpqua Valley on his way to a family event; as he drove through the region near Elkton, the landscape struck Stutz, a winemaker by occupation, as a possible vineyard site. He also remembered reading about the area in the mid-1970s, when he saw early local climate data in a wine journal. He later returned to buy grapes and plan a winery.

Stutz was attracted to the northernmost part of the appellation, where the climate becomes increasingly continental in character with greater temperature swings summer to winter and with generally warm growing seasons. He purchases fruit from Elkton area vineyards and makes his Radcliffe Cellars wine – Pinot Noir only – at the Henry Estate. Stutz purchased 15.2 hectares (38 acres) of land in 2001 – the land boasting a red clay loam soil very similar to Jory – near Elkton and intends to plant it with Pinot Noir in 2003.

While Stutz makes Pinot Noir at Mirassou in California, the wines he produces in Oregon under his own Radcliffe Cellars label are made for ageing and are intentionally less friendly when young. The Radcliffe Pinot Noir, like other Umpqua Pinots, tends to be less fruity, with more body and a slightly higher alcohol due to higher sugar levels at harvest. There is no rush to market with the Radcliffe (or Henry Estate wines); the current Radcliffe release vintage in 2001 was the 1996 vintage.

The most **interesting property** in Oregon, however, may be Earl and Hilda Jones' Abacela Vineyards and Winery. The success they have seen with Tempranillo – a wonderful wine, full of varietal flavour with good concentration and structure – keeps the discussion going as to whether Oregon has yet found all the appropriate varieties and all the best locations to plant them.

The Joneses were interested in Tempranillo, and only Tempranillo. While they had spent time in the Rioja and Ribera del Duero regions of Spain to learn more about growing the grape, they did not want to live in Spain. Their research showed them that they needed a shorter and cooler growing season than in Napa, but with the necessary blistering heat during July and August. The Joneses looked for vineyard land in New Mexico, Arizona, California, and Washington and were about to give up when they hit upon southern Oregon in 1992.

These old Umpqua-area ungrafted vines in Scott Henry training seems to be invading the parking area.

The Scott Henry trellising system

Early in his viticulture career, Scott Henry understood that too much vigour in a vineyard could be a problem, creating over-shading, reduced colour, bunch rot, fungus susceptibility, and less varietal character in the wine.

As a result of extensive research in the late 1970s, Henry discovered two basic principles: irrespective of soil depth, the best wines carry a balanced (and moderate) crop load and growth of vegetation; and that increased fruit exposure on the vine improves the colour, ripeness, and general quality of the finished wines. To get the crop level in balance, he unintentionally caused over crowding in the fruit zone, resulting in bunch rot. He then thought to grow two levels of fruit without a split canopy, but the lower canopy shaded out the upper. He next tried changing the direction of the fruit, and turning the lower canopy down and the upper canopy up, creating a window between the supporting vines. The results allowed all fruit to be in the sun with good air movement between the canopies, and with drying action after morning fog or rain (creating a decrease in fungus).

Henry attended the 1984 Cool Climate Symposium, and introduced himself to noted New Zealand viticulturist Dr Richard Smart. Smart was intrigued enough by Henry's trellis description to come down to the Henry Estate to see the system for himself. At the 1988 Cool Climate Symposium in Auckland, New Zealand, Henry went to visit wineries, and found his system in wide use. When he inquired about it, vineyard workers kept referring to it as the "Scott Henry System" (as named by Smart), and then responded with disbelief that their visitor really was *the* Scott Henry. Smart spread the use of Henry's trellising in New Zealand and Australia, where it is applied more frequently than in Oregon.

At first, the Joneses were concerned about the risk of frost near Medford, due south of the Umpqua area in the Rogue Valley. They travelled a little north and west to higher elevations in the southern end of the Umpqua Valley and were attracted to the landscape that they ultimately purchased: sloped land 153–229 metres (500–750ft) of elevation. While they bought the land for its topography, the soil was the surprise bonus: the lower vineyard offered shallow, rocky soil on a base of bedrock; Earl Jones had to clear boulders to plant vines. The upper vineyard lies across a fault line, with a deep soil studded with angular pieces of stone, very cobblestoned in appearance.

The average growing season is 220 days, with no risk of frost... the grapes hang until ripe with no pressure to bring them in early.

The weather made the Joneses very nervous; the Tempranillo was ripening late September–early October, later than other varieties in the region. To hedge their bets, they planted other varieties, hoping for the best: Syrah, Grenache, Merlot, Dolcetto, Malbec, Cabernet Franc, and Cabernet Sauvignon. The average growing season is 220 days, with no risk of frost; as a result, the Joneses let their grapes – including the Tempranillo – hang until ripe with no pressure to bring them in earlier. All their vines are drip irrigated.

The Joneses experimented with grapevine spacing, planting rows at 15cm, 30cm, 60cm, 90cm and up to 305cm (6in, 1ft, 2ft, 3ft and up to 10ft) apart. The 305 cm (10 ft) spacing won out since it was the most convenient for tractor use. The vigour of the different varieties varied, with Tempranillo, Syrah, and Malbec as the most vigorous growers; Earl Jones trained these early plantings on a Scott Henry system although nowadays he believes that the trellising is too costly to maintain for all three varieties, and is changing the Tempranillo and Syrah to a Sylvos system: a Geneva Single Curtain system with a fruiting wire at 152cm (5ft), allowing the vines to hang down and flop over it. The Joneses aim for 42 hectolitres per hectare (3 tons per acre) for everything.

The winery was designed to be a gravity-fed facility, with the Joneses believing that gentle handling and limiting oxidation best preserves the natural fruit flavours. Unusual perhaps for the varieties they have chosen, but the wine they produce indicates that it works extremely well for Abacela.

Scott Henry himself, next to his namesake split-canopy training system.

Notable producers

Abacela Winery

☎ 541-679-6642 ℻ 541-679-4455

✉ wine@Abacela.com

Ⓦ www.Abacela.com

12500 Lookingglass Road, Roseburg, Oregon 97470

Acreage in production 4 acres Tempranillo, 1.5 acres Syrah, 3 acres Merlot, 0.5 acres Dolcetto, 1.5 acres Malbec, 1.5 acres Cabernet Sauvignon, 1 acre Cabernet Franc, 0.2 acres Grenache, 0.3 acres Petit Verdot, 0.3 acre Graciano, 0.2 acres Bastardo, 0.2 acres Sangiovese, 0.2 acres Refosco, 0.2 acres Fresia, 0.2 acres Viognier

New plantings 8 acres Tempranillo, 7 acres Syrah, 2 acres Dolcetto, 0.8 acres Grenache, 0.5 acres Petit Verdot, 0.5 acres Viognier

Production capacity 5,000 cases

2000 production 4,000 cases

Established 1994

First wines released 1997 vintage

The quality leader is Southern Oregon, not just within the Umpqua Valley, producing big, deeply colored wines and a particularly impressive Tempranillo. New winery employs gravity-flow principles. Owners Earl and Hilda Jones have sparked new life and respect into the Umpqua region.

Callahan Ridge Winery

☎ 541-673-7901 ℻ 541-673-5580

✉ winenet@rosenet.net

Ⓦ www.callahanridge.com

340 Busenbark Lane, Roseburg, Oregon 97470

Acreage in production 4.5 acres total, including Chardonnay, Pinot Noir, Cabernet Sauvignon

2000 production 6,000 cases, growing to 8,000 in 2001

Established 1987

First wines released 1987 vintage

Grapes are sourced from a variety of sites in addition to the estate vineyard, planted in 1982. The winery and tasting room are located in a restored 1878 hay barn.

DeNino Estate Umpqua River Vineyards and Winery

☎ 541-673-1975 ℻ 541-673-1975

✉ vivovino@internetcds.com

451 Hess Lane, Roseburg, Oregon 97470

Acreage in production 10 acres Cabernet Sauvignon, 8 acres Merlot, 4 acres Sauvignon

Blanc, 2 acres Chenin Blanc, 4 acres Semillon, 2 acres Cabernet Franc, 2 acres Marechal Foch

Production capacity 1,500 cases **2000 production** 1,200 cases

Established 1982

First wines released 1988 vintage

Small family-run operation crafting big, hearty wines.

Giradet Wine Cellars

☎ 541-679-7252 ℻ 541-679-9502

✉ genuine@girardetwine.com

Ⓦ www.girardetwine.com

895 Reston Road, Roseburg, Oregon 97470

Acreage in production 3 acres Pinot Noir, 4 acres Riesling, 2 acres Chardonnay, 3 acres Cabernet Sauvignon, 1 acre Syrah, 1 acre Tempranillo, 1 acre Zinfandel, 3 acres Baco Noir, 3 acres Marechal Foch, 8 acres French hybrids

Production capacity 12,000 cases **2000 production** 10,000 cases

Established 1983

First wines released 1983 vintage

The vineyards were first planted in 1971 by Philippe Giradet in a valley reminiscent of his native Switzerland. A particular focus on French hybrids and blended wines.

Henry Estate Winery

☎ 541-459-5120, 800-782-2686

℻ 541-459-5146 ✉ henryest@wizards.net

Ⓦ www.henryestate.com

687 Hubbard Creek Road, Umpqua, Oregon 97486

Acreage in production 15 acres Pinot Noir, 15 acres Chardonnay, 5 acres Gewürztraminer, 3 acres Pinot Gris, 3 acres White Riesling, 1 acre Müller-Thurgau

Production capacity 16,000 cases **2000 production** 16,000 cases

Established 1978

First wines released 1978 vintage

Revered name not only in Oregon, but world-wide for the eponymous trellising system pioneered by owner Scott Henry. The vineyards were first planted in 1972 on Henry's family's farm

HillCrest Vineyard

☎ 541-673-3709 ✉ finewine@sorcom.com

Ⓦ www.HillCrestwine.com

240 Vineyard Lane, Roseburg, Oregon 97470

Acreage in production 20 acres Riesling, 5

acres Pinot Noir, 3 acres Sauvignon Blanc, 2 acres Semillon, 3 acres Cabernet Sauvignon, 2 acres total Chardonnay, Zinfandel, and Gewürztraminer

Production capacity 10,000 cases **2000 production** 3,000 cases

Established 1961

First wines released 1968 vintage

HillCrest is still producing the Riesling and Gewürztraminer wines that original Oregon pioneer Richard Sommer was convinced could shine when he arrived in Oregon in 1960. Quality has been uneven over HillCrest's long history, but Sommer has now returned to a prominent role at the winery and there is hope that quality can rise once again. The winery still offers for sale such older vintages of its wines as 1984 and 1988.

La Garza Cellars

☎ 541-679-9654 ℻ 541-679-3888

✉ lagarza@rosenet.net

Ⓦ www.winesnw.com/LaGarzaCellars.htm

491 Winery lane, Roseburg, Oregon 97470 **Acreage in production** 3.5 acres Cabernet Sauvignon

New plantings 3 acres Syrah, 3 acres Cabernet Sauvignon

Production capacity 5,000 cases **2000 production** 5,000 cases

Established 1992, **First wines** released 1992 vintage

These vineyards were planted in 1968 and used for Jonicole Winery in 1975; the winery was abandoned by the early 1980s. Donna Souza-Postles revived the vineyards as La Garza in 1992, and also opened a restaurant on the property. The Cabernet Sauvignon wins many state fair gold medals.

Radcliffe Cellars

☎ 408-238-0836 ℻ 408-238-0836

✉ Tom@Radcliffe-Cellars.com

3255 Heritage Estates Drive, San Jose, California 95148

Production capacity 3,000 cases **2000 production** 1,000 cases

Established 1996

First wines released 1996 vintage

Thomas Stutz, winemaker at Mirassou Vineyards in San Jose, California currently owns no vineyards, but has purchased land in Elkton for a future vineyard site. He produces ripe, slightly tannic Pinot Noir from grapes purchased from other Elkton-area vineyards.

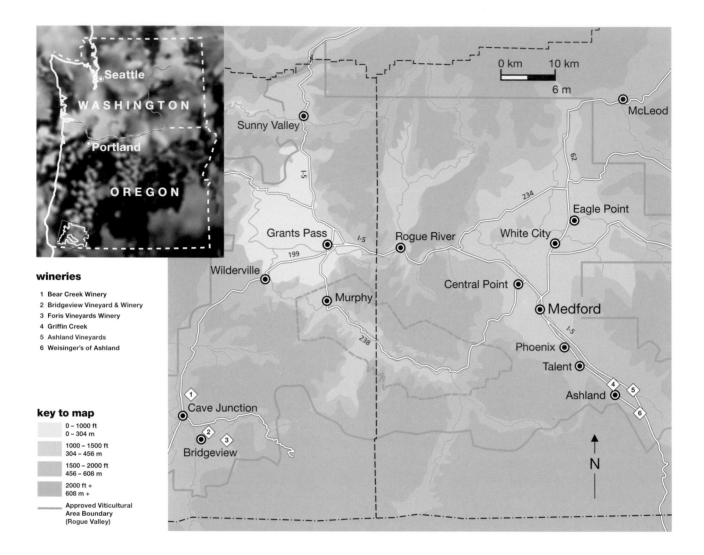

Rogue Valley

*The black dashed
lines represent the
county borders.*

The **Rogue Valley** forms almost a square at the southwest corner of Oregon – just north of California – about 112km (70 miles) wide by 97km (60 miles) long. Three mountain ranges and the river valleys between them geographically define the AVA: the Klamath Mountains to the west (with the Pacific Ocean just beyond), the Cascades to the east, with the Siskiyou Mountains in between.

For generations, the Rogue Valley's signature crop was pears, but in the last decade, new vineyards have sprung up, potentially challenging the dominance of other crops due to the affordability of suitable land for grapes.

Wineries and vineyards dot the river valleys: the Illinois River creeps up from California, travelling north to the east–west flowing Rogue River, around the Klamath peaks; the Applegate River also flows north through the centre of the appellation to the Rogue River, defining the new Applegate AVA granted in 2001 (see page 92). Bear Creek establishes the eastern edge of the Rogue Valley, flowing between the two major cities in the area, Medford and Ashland.

The Rogue Valley boasts a recreational wonderland, a beautiful wilderness area known for winter skiing, white-water rafting, hiking, fishing, and visiting the Oregon Caves

National Monument. Cultural attractions include the nationally recognized Oregon Shakespeare Festival in Ashland, offering an almost-year-round, high-quality programme of Shakespearean and modern theatre. The Shakespeare Festival makes Ashland a well-known holiday destination, with access from the Interstate 5 highway that passes through it on its route between Canada and Mexico. Ashland is also home to Southern Oregon University, many restaurants, bookstores, and a professional community. Two wineries are located in the Ashland area to take advantage of its more urban location: Weisinger's and Ashland Vineyards.

Given the outstanding **natural beauty** of the area and the range of activities throughout the Rogue Valley, it is unfortunate the region isn't more visited year round. Access is one problem: the airport at Medford is small, public transport is limited, and the drive between activities and sites is long, meaning a car is absolutely necessary to enjoy the valley, and an overnight stay required for nearly all. For those who live outside the area, the Rogue Valley is a destination, not a casual visit – a disappointing reality for the wineries who struggle to be better known and recognized for wines they consider are among the best in Oregon.

The remoteness of the Rogue is also what attracted some people to the region in the first place; the Rogue is filled with a varied cast of characters, many of whom have chosen to live there specifically because of its wild and isolated geography.

The geography hinders the marketing of the Rogue wines as well. In areas such as the Eola Hills and Yamhill County, the sheer number of wineries there helps to promote the wines. There is a collegiality of winemakers in the north, people who get together regularly to discuss wines, and how best to present them to the public. The Rogue doesn't boast a dense community of producers; there aren't a great number of wineries in operation and they don't have the closeness of geography or cooperation. The producers here tend to rely on the

promotional efforts of the state and the winery-supported Oregon Wine Advisory Board (OWAB) alone.

And Rogue Valley producers haven't chosen a **varietal flag** to wave as the north has done: Pinot Noir has become the well-known theme of the Willamette Valley – accomplished through the International Pinot Celebration, Oregon Pinot Camp (an annual, producer-supported long weekend of workshops aimed at the wine-trade market only), media invitations, and a general energetic group effort to promote Pinot Noir in Oregon, independent of the OWAB. Sub-marketing groups have developed in the north as well to focus on Pinot Blanc, and there is even one that is trying to revive an interest in Müller-Thurgau.

In contrast, the Rogue region produces a wide range of wines based on the varied mesoclimates that exist. In the cooler Illinois Valley, Pinot Noir, Pinot Gris, Gamay Noir, Chardonnay, Riesling, and Gewürztraminer predominate, which is similar to the Willamette Valley. In the warmer Bear Creek Valley, Merlot, Cabernet Sauvignon, Syrah,

Mountains rise as a backdrop to the almost flat vineyards of South Oregon's Rogue Valley. Height is deceptive, as most vineyards here are at elevations between 1200 and 1800 feet.

Cabernet Franc, Sauvignon Blanc, Tempranillo, Dolcetto, Sangiovese, Viognier, Malbec, and Chardonnay are grown.

Syrah makes sense in the Applegate and Bear Creek Valles, but **stunning Syrah** – the likes of which is now emerging from a similar climate in Washington – hasn't yet made its mark in southern Oregon. New plantings are just coming on, and overall quality is still an issue. Sarah Powell, the winemaker at Foris Vineyards Winery, produced a very fine 1999 Syrah, a one-time-only release that was bottled under her own label.

Weather in the Rogue Valley, as the choice of grapes illustrates, is quite varied and defined by geography; annual rainfall can be as low as 38cm (15in) in the Bear Creek Valley to an remarkable 127–153cm (50–60 in) in the Illinois Valley, where the cooling mountain and oceanic influences are the most profound. Warmth (and degree days) increase the further east and south towards Ashland you travel.

> **Greg Jones' research on all of the existing vineyards – eighty-two in total – uses a satellite-based global-positioning system.**

Vineyards in the Rogue Valley can claim the highest elevations in Oregon: the lowest vineyard sits at 22.6 metres (890ft) west of Grants Pass; the highest at Yank Gulch Vineyard at 63 metres (2,490ft) in the Bear Creek Valley. The mean elevation for vineyards is 40.6 metres (1,600ft).

This data on **elevations** has been collected by Greg Jones PhD, assistant Professor of Geography at Southern Oregon University in Ashland. Jones is a climatologist who studies the effect of weather on grapevines and other agricultural farming. He has collected data for a vineyard-mapping project, evaluating all the potential vineyard sites in the Rogue and Umpqua Valleys for elevation, aspect, slope, soil, and zoning.

His research on all of the existing vineyards – eighty-two in total – uses a satellite-based global positioning system, and Jones adds information on the varieties grown, clones and rootstocks planted, trellis systems and pruning decisions, and the cycle of bud break, flowering, and *veraison*. By combining all the data (of existing and potential sites), he hopes to help the region's viticulturists become better growers, as well as provide vineyard-siting tools for potential growers. He believes that if the Rogue Valley is to succeed as a grape-growing region, there needs to be a greater mass of vineyards and wineries to make it happen.

Jones is also the son of Earl and Hilda Jones of Abacela Vineyards and Winery, and he worked with his parents to find their land in the Umpqua region. At that time, Jones was finishing the dissertation for his PhD at the University of Virginia (he had previously studied viticulture and climate in Bordeaux); it was serendipitous that he was offered his university position in the Rogue Valley soon after completing his PhD.

Vineyards in the Rogue Valley face a few problems that are not found elsewhere in Oregon. Frost is a major, especially near Medford, both at bud break in spring, and in the autumn near harvest. Underground water is also a problem. The Rogue Valley Basin has a complex underground water reserve, and the mix of soil types means that vineyards – or even small areas lying within vineyards – have different ranges of water-holding capability depending on the amount of clay in the soil.

Frost is an issue for the estate vineyard at **Bridgeview Vineyards**, Oregon's largest winery. Located in Cave Junction, in the Illinois Valley, the winery is very close to the entrance of the Oregon Caves tourist attraction, bringing a large number of visitors to the area. Bridgeview was first planted in 1980; the winery was completed in 1986. Bridgeview owns its estate vineyard as well as another vineyard in the warmer Applegate Valley, and works closely with a number of Rogue Valley growers. The estate vineyards near the winery are mostly flat, sitting on mineral-rich and rocky river-bottom soil in a sunny inland valley dotted with old gold mines, but a frost problem – not mitigated by sloped vineyards – occasionally means ripening can be difficult. Bridgeview also buys

Vineyards outnumber the wineries in the rugged Rogue Valley.

a large number of grapes from growers around the state, as well as on the bulk market each year.

The range of varieties on the 70 hectares (175 acres) that Bridgeview controls is very broad, covering Müller-Thurgau to Merlot and virtually everything else in between. More than 80,000 cases of wine are produced annually (with the capacity to increase production to over 100,000 cases) making Bridgeview Oregon's largest producer.

The winery has positioned itself as a major supermarket-shelf brand, producing an affordable, commercial product. Bridgeview enters many state fairs and local wine competitions, coming away with an array of ribbons. Its packaging is eye-catching: Bridgeview's Blue Moon series of wines come in distinctive blue glass bottles; a series bottled in blue crescent moon-shaped bottles is of almost novelty – but popular – status.

Forest Vineyards Winery owner Ted Gerber realized early that Pinot Noir and Oregon were often uttered in the same breath...

Nearby, some of the highest quality in the Rogue Valley comes from **Foris Vineyards Winery**, first planted in 1975. Of all the Rogue Valley wineries, Foris is the most Willamette Valley-like in terms of varieties grown with its commitment to Pinot Noir, yields, quality-focus, and marketing savvy. Owner Ted Gerber realized early that Pinot Noir and Oregon were often uttered in the same breath, and recognized the advantage of being associated with that identity. Foris also produces uniquely Rogue-style wines, including Merlot, Syrah, and a Bordeaux-style blend called "Fly-Over Red" in reference to the Rogue Valley's less visited, more "flown-over" status.

The estate vineyards at Foris are planted on soils very different from one another; they all can be described as having a clay-loam profile, with the top soil on the best sites only 0.6–1.2 metres (2–4ft) deep. Some areas boast more small rocks than others; other sites consist of a denser clay with resulting high-water retention. The sticky clay soil areas need drip irrigation, especially if they are sitting on serpentine subsoil, which can be very problematic because of its soil chemistry. Serpentine soils are high in nickel, chromium, and magnesium, and have difficulty taking up necessary potassium, making frequent potassium adjustments necessary. The best soils at Foris are at its Maple Ranch vineyard, with its rockier-soil and low-frost potential, producing Foris' highest quality Pinot Noir.

Owner Ted Gerber planted his initial vineyards in 1.8 x 3.6 metres (6 x 12ft) rows, with a unique trellising system: he wanted movable vines and kept two canes: on one side in Vertical Shoot Positioning (VSP), the other side loose with floppy foliage. New plantings are at 1.8 x 2.4–2.7 metres (6 x 8–9ft) rows, with both canes of the vine on a VSP system. Yields are kept at around 42 hectolitres per hectare (3 tons per acre).

The Rogue Valley's other quality leader is the jointly owned **Griffin Creek Vineyards**: vineyards are owned and operated by the Moore family and Willamette Valley Vineyards (WVV) with WVV producing the wine.

While working as winemaker at Silvan Ridge, current WVV winemaker Joe Dobbes purchased Merlot from Don and Trauge Moore, owners of the Quail Run Vineyard in the Rogue appellation. The Griffin Creek brand grew out of that relationship, which followed Dobbes to Willamette Valley Vineyards where the brand was created. Merlot – an early focus of the Moores – was planted in 1989. Viognier, Syrah, Cabernet Sauvignon, Cabernet Franc, Tempranillo, Pinot Noir, Pinot Blanc, Pinot Gris, and Chardonnay are also being cultivated. The Viognier in particular shows great promise, with true aromatic varietal character.

Del Rio Vineyards is another newer Rogue vineyard with good potential, located along the Rogue River near Gold Hill between Grants Pass and Medford, and owned by viticulturists Clay Shannon and Lee Traynham of Arbuckle, California. This is the largest vineyard in the Rogue Valley, growing a wide range of grapes. The first few harvests have shown well-structured, balanced fruit.

Notable producers

Ashland Vineyards

☎ 541-488-0088 ⑤ 541-488-5857
ⓔ wines@compuserve.com
Ⓦ winenet.com
2775 East Main Street, Ashland, Oregon 97520
Acreage in production 10.1ha (25 acres) producing acres, including Merlot, Cabernet Sauvignon, Cabernet Franc, Pinot Gris, and Müller-Thurgau
New plantings 20.2ha (50 acres), including Merlot, Cabernet Sauvignon, Syrah, Viognier, Sangiovese, Dolcetto, and Tempranillo
Production capacity 10,000 cases
2000 production 6,000 cases
Established 1987
First wines released 1989 vintage
One of the few wineries in the warm Bear Creek Valley. New plantings in a range of varieties might help discover the most appropriate variety for the area, with good possibilities for Syrah, Sangiovese, and Tempranillo.

Bear Creek Winery of Oregon

☎ 541-592-3977 ⑤ 541-592-2127
ⓔ Rene@bridgeviewwine.com
6220 Caves Highway, Cave Junction, Oregon 97523
Acreage in production 2.4ha (6 acres) Pinot Noir, 0.4ha (1 acre) Cabernet Sauvignon, 0.4ha (1 acre) Chardonnay, 0.4ha (1 acre) Gewürztraminer
New plantings 3.7ha (1.5 acres) Pinot Noir, 0.4ha (1 acre) Pinot Blanc
Production capacity 5,000 cases
2000 production 2,800 cases, of which 1,800 cases are under the Bear Creek label, 1,000 cases under the Siskiyou Vineyards label
Established 1997
First wines released 1997 and 1998 vintages
Bridgeview winemaker Rene Eichmann purchased the former Siskiyou Vineyard property in the Illinois Valley (originally planted in 1978), not far from his family's Bridgeview Vineyards and Winery. The Bear Creek name is misleading, given that the winery is not located there.

Bridgeview Vineyards & Winery

☎ 541-592-4688 ⑤ 541-592-2127
ⓔ bvw@bridgeviewwine.com
Ⓦ www.bridgeviewwine.com
4210 Holland Loop Road, Cave Junction, Oregon 97523
Acreage in production 2.4ha (6 acres) Chardonnay, 10.1ha (5 acres) Gewürztraminer, 14.1ha (35 acres) Merlot, 1.2ha (3 acres) Müller-Thurgau, 6ha (15 acres) Pinot Noir, 6ha (15 acres) Pinot Gris, 8ha (20 acres) Riesling, 0.2ha (0.5 acre) Muscat
Production capacity 100,000 cases
2000 production 80,000 cases
Established 1986
First wines released 1986 vintage
Oregon's largest producer, with a strong supermarket shelf presence and name familiarity.

Foris Vineyards Winery

☎ 541-592-3752 ⑤ 541-592-4424
ⓔ foris@foriswine.com Ⓦ foriswine.com
654 Kendall Road, Cave Junction, Oregon 97523
Acreage in production 14.5ha (36 acres) Pinot Noir, 2.8ha (7 acres) Chardonnay, 2.4ha (6 acres) Gewürztraminer, 1.6ha (4 acres) Pinot Gris, 0.4ha (1 acre) Gamay Noir, 0.8ha (2 acres) early Muscat
New plantings 2ha (5 acres) Gewürztraminer, 1.2ha (3 acres) Pinot Blanc
Production capacity 30,000 cases
2000 production 25,000 cases
Established 1986
First wines released 1986 vintage
Ted Gerber first planted his vineyards in 1975. Talented winemaker Sarah Powell crafts the Rogue Valley's best and most-consistent wines.

Griffin Creek Vineyards

☎ 800-883-6063 ⑤ 503-588-8894
ⓔ gphillip@jeffnet.org Ⓦ www.wvv.com
1257 Siskiyou Boulevard, Suite 162, Ashland, Oregon 97520
Acreage in production 20.6ha (51 acres) Merlot, 3.6ha (9 acres) Cabernet Sauvignon, 10 acres Cabernet Franc, 4ha (7 acres) Syrah, 1ha (2.5 acres) Tempranillo, 3.6ha (9 acres) Pinot Noir, 5ha (12.5 acres) Viognier, 2.4ha (6 acres) Pinot Blanc, 8.9ha (22 acres) Pinot Gris, 2.8ha (7 acres) Chardonnay
Production capacity 15,000 cases
2000 production 10,000 cases
Established 1989
First wines released 1996 vintage
While the vineyards for this label are located in the Rogue Valley, the brand is a joint venture with Willamette Valley Vineyards, which produces the wines. The Viognier in particular shows clean varietal character without the presence of oak.

Weisinger's of Ashland Vineyard & Winery

☎ 541-488-5989 ⑤ 541-488-5989
Toll free: 800-551-9463
ⓔ wine@weisingers.com Ⓦ www.weisingers.com
3150 Siskiyou Boulevard, Ashland, Oregon 97520
Acreage in production 1.6ha (4 acres) Gewürztraminer
Production capacity 5,000 cases
2000 production 3,000 cases
Established 1988
First wines released 1989 vintage
A family operation using both estate fruit and red grapes from the Pompadour Vineyard nearby. Wines produced include Gewürztraminer, Chardonnay, Sémillon, Merlot, Cabernet Franc, Cabernet Sauvignon, and two red blends, Mescolare, and Petite Pompadour. Fewer than 100 cases each are produced of the reserve wines, and about 400 cases of the signature Petite Pompadour, a Bordeaux-style blend.

Sarah Powell of Foris Vineyards Winery

Applegate Valley

Until January 2001, the area now designated as the **Applegate Valley** was included in the Rogue Valley appellation, the middle valley between the Illinois Valley and Bear Creek Valley. The Applegate Valley and appellation is located entirely within the boundaries of the larger Rogue Valley appellation.

The Applegate Valley is approximately 80km (50 miles) long, running alongside the Applegate River from its origins south near the California border generally northwest to where the river joins the Rogue River, just west of Grants Pass. The surrounding Siskiyou Mountains are believed to have been created during the Jurassic period by volcanic eruptions caused by the sliding of the heavier ocean floor under the ligher continental crust.

Soils in the Applegate Valley are of two basic and similar types, both well-drained and deep, generally granitic in origin: Ruch, found in the more sloped vineyards, and Kerby, found on the flatter terrace areas of the appellation (both soil types are named after area towns). Compared with the soil types found in other parts of the Rogue Valley, soils in the Applegate Valley tend to be less acidic than Illinois Valley soils and slightly more acidic that Bear Creek Valley soils.

Weather is also a defining factor in the Applegate Valley appellation. The Illinois Valley's closer proximity to the ocean ensures that the area remains cooler; the Siskiyou Mountains that envelop the Applegate Valley keep the Valley's weather patterns more

The black dashed lines represent the county borders.

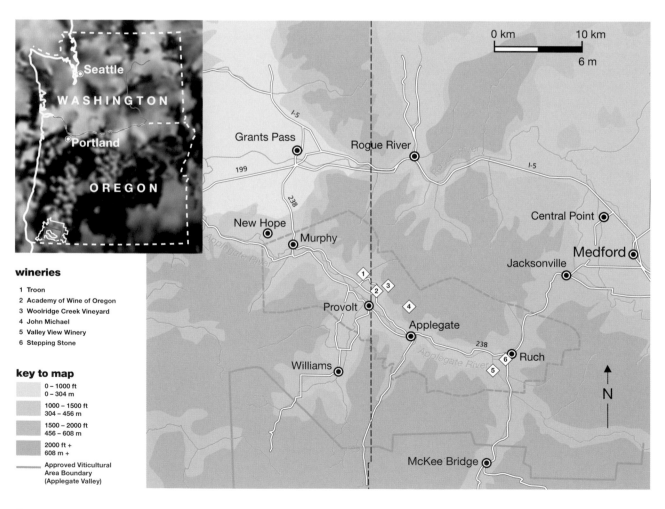

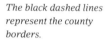

wineries

1 Troon
2 Academy of Wine of Oregon
3 Woolridge Creek Vineyard
4 John Michael
5 Valley View Winery
6 Stepping Stone

key to map

0 – 1000 ft
0 – 304 m

1000 – 1500 ft
304 – 456 m

1500 – 2000 ft
456 – 608 m

2000 ft +
608 m +

Approved Viticultural Area Boundary (Applegate Valley)

moderate in rainfall and temperatures – warmer and drier than the Illinois Valley due to less of a marine influence, and a little moister and cooler than the Bear Creek Valley. Rain averages about 64cm (25in) per year and temperatures are typically two to three degrees cooler than in the eastern areas of the Rogue (including Bear Creek Valley) that lack any marine cooling.

The Applegate Valley can be **classified as Region II**, out of the five categories of the Amerine and Winkler-defined degree day system for the growing season, with an average of 1,371 degree days Centigrade (2,500 Fahrenheit), with two to three weeks earlier ripening than in the Illinois Valley. Vineyards may be at high elevations, but nevertheless many aren't planted on slopes. Smith's Academy sits on flat land at 396 metres (1,300ft) but frost is a risk in spring and autumn. Owner Barney Smith planted all his vines at 2 x 3 metres (7 x 10ft) spacing, all trained on Geneva Double Curtain to mitigate vigour. The warm weather with cool nights translates to a long ripening period, giving growers the ability to allow grapes to hang on the vine into November, if necessary, to reach optimal sugars and acids.

The region is planted with Chardonnay, Cabernet Sauvignon, Merlot, and Zinfandel. A small amount of Syrah and Cabernet Franc are planted, and a tiny bit of Pinot Noir can also be found at Smith's Academy.

Given that the greater Rogue Valley contains such diverse growing regions as exist in the Illinois, Applegate, and Bear Creek Valleys, it follows that it shouldn't be unusual for the Applegate Valley to have a distinct AVA. But with only a handful of wineries – and all but one of them tiny, with very limited distribution – and a total of just 94 hectares (235 acres) within the appellation (almost half of them planted and owned by Bridgeview of the Illinois Valley), you wonder why it was only the Applegate that bothered to make the break from the overall Rogue appellation.

The Rogue Valley – until the January 2001 approval of the Applegate Valley – was the last

Not all wine matures in oak...

appellation granted in Oregon, in 1991. One of the reasons it took so long to claim the Rogue AVA, in spite of its long history of wine-grape growing, was the controversy within the Rogue Valley wine community. The committee proposing the Rogue appellation was initially deadlocked over the creation of the appellation, and there wasn't broad support for the appellation. Some people found the name "Rogue" too negative an identity (but in reality, perhaps, an appropriate link given the isolated aspects of the region); others were concerned about the very divergent growing conditions within the large region. Despite these concerns, the Rogue AVA was finally granted in 1991.

Barney Smith of Smith's Academy winery (in the heart of the Applegate appellation) began to work on the Applegate AVA request in 1998, feeling that the Applegate Valley should claim its own identity distinctly separate from the rest of the Rogue Valley. Smith made the appellation his personal crusade and the Bureau of Alcohol,

The warm weather with cool nights translates to a long ripening period, giving growers the ability to allow grapes to hang on the vine into November.

As in the surrounding Rogue Valley, Applegate Valley vineyards tend to be at higher elevations, and they also lack significant slope.

Tobacco and Firearms (BATF) granted AVA status to the Applegate Valley in January 2001. Ideally, the three growing regions within the Rogue should each claim an independent AVA; just having the Applegate region singled out is odd, as it's the growing region that is the least likely to use a separate appellation status to its best possible advantage.

While some of the producers in the Applegate Valley will use the new appellation name on labels, there is no organized effort to band together and market the wine as an appellation. The region needs to have a greater number of growers and producers and to improve quality in order to gain the kind of attention some of the area producers think is due them.

The Applegate's **early history** is synonymous with Oregon's early history. Winemaking dates back to the 1850s and pioneer Peter Britt, whose name is associated with an annual music festival held on the property of his former home in historic Jacksonville. Additionally, anecdotal story claims that A II Carson planted 12 hectares (30 acres) of Tokay grapes in 1870; he shipped as far as New York, but whether he shipped grapes or wine is questionable. Britt's original winery was named Valley View Vineyard. In 1972, the Wisnovsky family purchased the winery (near the town of Ruch) and replanted it with grapes. The winery was established in 1976. Today, Valley View can claim to be the Applegate Valley's largest and loudest-promoting producer, turning out 14,000 cases each year.

Other than the small number of producers, another reason the appellation hasn't yet banded together to market its wines is Valley View's counter efforts. Valley View does not intend to use the Applegate appellation on its labels; instead it is the driving force behind another proposed AVA application, developed by Earl Jones of Abacela Winery. Jones has submitted an application to the BATF for the creation of a gigantic "Southern Oregon" appellation, encompassing the existing Applegate, Rogue, and Umpqua appellations. The goal of this new Southern Oregon appellation would be to eliminate the names Umpqua and Rogue, which proponents of the new appellation find distasteful. They would like to contrast the entire southern region of the state – including the Willamette-like Illinois Valley – against the Willamette Valley (the target of Valley View's frequent complaints of being unjustly ignored).

Valley View is not alone. Other producers in the Rogue and Umpqua Valleys correctly see their region as distinctly different from the larger, better known Willamette Valley, and want the broader appellation to justify that distinction. But to create such a large Southern Oregon appellation would obliterate the dramatic climate and soil differences that exist throughout the southern part of the state – significant though (as it is argued) that the region generally shares a uniform warmth in contrast to the cool Willamette Valley. That the Applegate Valley convinced the BATF to

create a distinct appellation argues instead for the codification of the other discrete growing areas within the Rogue (at least the Illinois and Bear Creek Valleys), not necessarily the creation of one huge super-region.

Vineyards have always greatly outnumbered wineries in the Applegate Valley; by the early 1980s, such vineyards existed as Layne Vineyard, Valley View Vineyard, Farrell Vineyard, Troon Vineyards, and Whittaker Vineyard (sold initially to Drobney Vineyards and Winery which has since closed; nowadays it is called Rosella's Vineyard). But the number of producers has always been slim.

Bridgeview Winery – which is based in the cooler Illinois Valley to the east – has purchased grapes for years from Woolridge Creek and Layne Vineyards, as well as from a number of smaller growers. The winery purchased 40 hectares (100 acres) of its own in 1997 and planted 35.6 hectares (88 acres), across the Applegate River from the Academy of Wine. Most of the vineyard is planted with Merlot: 16.1 hectares (40 acres) containing 2,718 per hectare (1,100 plants per acre). Bridgeview's 4 hectares (10 acres) of Riesling boast 4,942 vines per hectare (2,000 vines per acre). Other varieties planted include Cabernet Sauvignon and Syrah and small lots of Viognier, Cabernet Franc, Sangiovese, and the Dijon clones of Chardonnay.

The vines are still very young; there have only been two harvests of the fruit so far, and yields have been tiny as a result of the immaturity of the plants. Bridgeview's ideal yield will be in the order of 56–70 hectolitres per hectare (4–5 tons per acre) for everything, but there is still a lot of experimenting to be done.

The irrigated vineyard sits at about 366 metres (1,200ft) of elevation, but on relatively flat land. The soil there is a silty loam, which is lacking in decent water-retention capacity. Bridgeview intends for this vineyard to bear fruit destined for its premium wines, using the Applegate AVA on the labels. While the acreage of grapes in the area is increasing

Valley View can claim to be the Applegate Valley's largest and loudest-promoting producer, turning out 14,000 cases each year.

slowly, the number of producers continues to be slim.

Valley View was certainly a pioneer. Troon Vineyards began producing its own wine in 1993; Barney Smith planted Smith's Academy Vineyards in 1989, although he didn't actually make any commercial wine until the 1995 vintage and current production stands at 300 cases per annum.

Until the region is more planted with grapes and ... populated with wineries, it will be hard for producers to form a critical mass for marketing their wines.

Until the region is **more densely planted** with grapes and more populated with wineries, it will be extremely hard for producers to form a critical mass for marketing their wines. The Applegate Valley has not been a region identified either with quality or large production. Having a formal AVA doesn't change that reality. And a Southern Oregon AVA wouldn't solve the problem either.

As to Valley View and others' complaints of being ignored, attention is bound to reach quality. In the slightly less remote Umpqua Valley, Abacela's efforts have brought that winery more-than-regional praise. There is reason to believe that if the Applegate Valley wines improved in quality, more attention would naturally follow.

If the southern producers are able to understand the benefit of banding together in order to sell their warm-weather varietals, why do they need a broad appellation to back that up? Their joint-marketing efforts can be accomplished with coordination and cooperation.

Notable producers

The Academy of Wine of Oregon, Inc

☎ 541-846-6817 ⓕ 541-846-6817
ⓔ academy@internetcds.com
ⓦ www.home.internetcds.com/~academy
18200 Highway 238, Grants Pass, Oregon 97527

Acreage in production 0.6ha (1.5 acres) Merlot, 0.6ha (1.5 acres) Cabernet Sauvignon, 0.6ha (1.5 acres)) Chardonnay, 0.2ha (0.5 acre) Pinot Noir
Production capacity 600 cases
2000 production 300 cases
Established 1993
First wines released 1995 vintage
Retired engineer Barney Smith has been the strongest advocate of the new Applegate AVA, proudly crafting small quantities of its wine.

Troon Vineyards

☎ 541-846-6562 ⓕ 541-846-6562
1475 Kubli Road, Grants Pass, Oregon 97526

Acreage in production 2.8ha (7 acres), Cabernet Sauvignon, 0.8ha (2 acres) Chardonnay, 0.4ha (1 acre) Zinfandel
Production capacity 1,800 cases
2000 production 1,500 cases
Established 1972
First wines released 1993 vintage
With vineyards that were planted in 1972, Dick Troon sold his fruit to area wineries and only started making his own wine in 1993. He also produces an unusual sparkling Cabernet Sauvignon.

Valley View Winery

☎ 541-899-8468, 800-781-9463
ⓕ 541-899-8468
ⓔ info@valleyviewwinery.com
ⓦ www.valleyviewwinery.com
1000 Upper Applegate Road, Jacksonville, Oregon 97530

Acreage in production 4ha (10 acres) Merlot, 4ha (10 acre) Cabernet Sauvignon, 1.2ha (3 acres) Syrah
New plantings 1.4ha (4 acres) Syrah
Production capacity 14,000 cases
2000 production 14,000 cases
Established 1976
First wines released 1976 vintage
The largest producer in the new Applegate Valley appellation, a long-time champion of southern Oregon in frequent opposition to the Willamette Valley. Located at the site of southern Oregon wine pioneer Peter Britt's Valley View Winery.

Woolridge Creek Vineyard

☎ 541-846-6310
ⓔ wooldridgecreek@aol.com
818 Slagle Creek Road, Grants Pass, Oregon 97527

Acreage in production 1.2ha (3 acres) Pinot Noir, 6ha (15 acres) Chardonnay, 4ha (10 acres) Cabernet Sauvignon, 0.4 (1 acre) Cabernet Franc, 4.9ha (12 acres) Merlot, 2ha (5 acres) Zinfandel, 0.8ha (2 acre Viognier
Production capacity 1,000 cases
2000 production 1,000 cases
Established 1978
First wines released 1994 vintage
Small-production winery, but a long-time vineyard owner who continues to sell fruit to other area wineries.

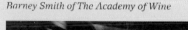

Barney Smith of The Academy of Wine

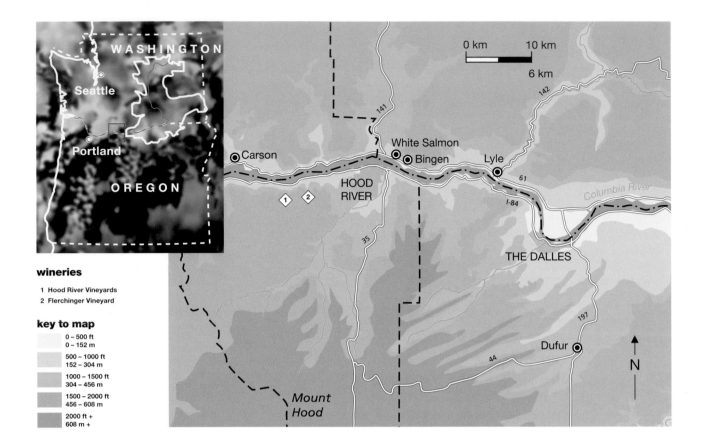

wineries

1 Hood River Vineyards
2 Flerchinger Vineyard

key to map

	0 – 500 ft 0 – 152 m
	500 – 1000 ft 152 – 304 m
	1000 – 1500 ft 304 – 456 m
	1500 – 2000 ft 456 – 608 m
	2000 ft + 608 m +

Columbia & Walla Walla Valleys

The black dashed lines represent the county borders.

The **Columbia Valley** and **Walla Walla Valley** are geographically located in Oregon, but as formal appellations they are shared with Washington. These wine-producing regions span the length of the Columbia River that divides the two states, and continue to the east where the river curls up into Washington and the two states border one another. The bulk of the two appellations lies in Washington. Although there are several important vineyards on the Oregon side, not one winery is located in the Oregon portion of these formal appellations.

There have been vineyards in this region since at least the turn of the century. Prior to the 1920s, over 1,600 hectares (4,000 acres) of vinifera were planted in Wasco County in Oregon alone (lying now in the Columbia Valley appellation), which at that time also included the town and area around Hood River. Today, this area is not within any formal appellation, but serves as home to Oregon's only two wineries in this broad region.

Despite a rather promising beginning, Prohibition curtailed most of the grape-growing activity in the region. Grape farming was revived in the 1940s and 1950s, when both Rhône and Bordeaux grapes (at least Syrah, Grenache, Cabernet Sauvignon, and Merlot) were planted in Oregon. Some Zinfandel was planted even earlier and is still farmed today.

The Columbia Valley was made an **appellation** in 1984, dipping down into Oregon as far south as Pendleton and to the Dalles to the west. A number of Willamette Valley growers at the time of the initial appellation discussions argued to include the vineyards along the Oregon side of the Columbia – in order to give appellation status to the warm-climate fruit that some of them purchased from the Columbia Valley in the early days of winemaking in Oregon .

The initial intention upon the creation of the AVA was to include all old-growth vines (especially Zinfandel, Cabernet Sauvignon, and Merlot) near the Dalles, but strangely, when the appellation lines were drawn, the boundaries bypassed existing vineyards near there and Hood River.

The mighty Columbia River forms the northern border of Oregon for most of its length, cutting a deep gorge through the towering Cascade Ranges. Across the appellation – and stretching west into Hood River and the Dalles grape-growing areas as well – elevations vary. Some vineyards planted along the river are almost flat, while on the gentle slopes leading away from the river, there are some vineyards – these slopes historically have been covered with apple, pear, and cherry trees.

Wind is an issue in the **vineyard-dense Hood River area**, known better as the Columbia River Gorge, a location well respected for the world-class wind-surfing activity that dominates the area each summer. Here the arid climate of eastern Oregon to the east of the Cascades virtually collides with the damper and more moderate maritime patterns of the western part of the state. This causes a vortex of wind action that creates very changeable weather in the region – and makes grape growing a challenge. Wind is a bigger problem in the Dalles; closer to Hood River, trees break the force of the gusts.

Rainfall increases from east to west along the river; in the Walla Walla area, the rain can be less than 64cm (25in) per annum. The closer towards Portland you travel, the rainier it becomes, up to 114–127cm (45–50in) each year in the west of the Columbia Gorge.

Degree days and warmth follow the same east–west variation. In the drier eastern Walla Walla Valley, warm, even hot, summer weather can compute to 1,648 degree days Centigrade (3,000 Fahrenheit); the Boardman and the Dalles areas see more moderate weather and about 1,538–1,593 degree days Centigrade (2,800–2,900 Fahrenheit). The bulk of the Hood River area has about 1,260–1,316 degree days Centigrade (2,300–2,400 Fahrenheit).

Clay loam is the basis of most of the soils – presenting a high-water retention ability, but with good drainage, especially on the gentle

This is young Syrah near Hood River along the Oregon side of the Columbia Gorge.

slopes that dominate the area. Most vineyards are dry-farmed. Vineyards in the Walla Walla Basin have a sandier soil base.

Within the **Columbia** and **Walla Walla Valley appellations**, there are approximately 560 hectares (1,400 acres) of vineyards; vineyards outside the appellations total about 200 hectares (500 acres). In 1989, this large region along the Columbia produced an amazing 22 per cent of all grapes grown in Oregon.

The largest vineyard in the Columbia Valley appellation is Boardman Farms, a 280-hectare (700-acre) parcel that suffered a severe freeze in 1990 and is just now beginning to produce fruit again. Most of the grapes (Merlot and Cabernet Sauvignon) since the freeze have been sold to the bulk market in Washington; Bridgeview in the Rogue Valley buys Riesling and Chardonnay from here as well. Other varieties grown in the smaller, 4–10-hectare (10–25-acre) vineyards that dot the region include Cabernet Sauvignon and Merlot, and are sold to Washington wineries.

Hood River Vineyards' Bernie Lerch has planted 47 varieties in nine different sites in the Hood River area.

Old-vine Zinfandel, Cabernet Sauvignon, and Merlot can be found in the area that stretches west of the appellation, from Hood River east to the Dalles. This is also where the two wineries south of the river along the north border of Oregon can be found: Hood River Vineyards and Flerchinger Vineyard. The combined Hood River and the Dalles area is now being considered for a new Columbia Gorge appellation, filed for approval with the Bureau of Alcohol, Tobacco, and Firearms in early 2001. It has been proposed that the appellation should span the river to include the vineyards and wineries left out of the Columbia Valley designation in both states. In addition to Hood River Vineyards and Flerchinger Vineyard in Oregon, it proposes to include the three wineries in Washington that are also located within the Columbia Gorge: Wind River Cellars, Klickitat Canyon Winery, and Cascade Cliffs Winery.

Hood River Vineyards grows the widest range of **grape varieties** of almost any vineyard in Oregon; owner Bernie Lerch – a former research chemist from California – purchased the winery in 1993. The original vineyard block of Pinot Noir and Chardonnay was first planted in 1975, but now Lerch has become interested in discovering what other varieties thrive in his location. He has planted forty-seven varieties including Syrah, Cinsault, Malbec, Grenache, Petite Syrah, Viognier, Nebbiolo, Barbera, Dolcetto, Arneis, Sangiovese, Tempranillo, and Graciano in nine different sites in the Hood River area; elevations vary from nearly flat near the river to 122 metres (400ft).

Yields vary as well. The old block Pinot Noir and Chardonnay are kept at 42 hectolitres per hectare (3 tons to the acre). Some varieties such as Tempranillo in one site are cropped at 77–84 hectolitres per hectare (5.5–6 tons an acre); Lerch claims that his Bordeaux varieties can produce 56–63 hectolitres per hectare (4–4.5 tons per acre) without no discernible quality' loss, but the resulting quality is perhaps not the highest achievable.

Dolcetto, Barbera, Sangiovese, Malbec, and Petite Syrah are grown on head-pruned vines, and carry low crop loads of 21 hectolitres per hectare (1.5 tons per acre). Lerch is still in an experimental phase, figuring out what grows well where. Quality is good at present; with greater understanding of his vineyards and varieties, quality will probably improve. The vines of his newer "experimental" plantings are still very young; as the plants reach greater maturity and root depth, it will be interesting to see what kind of fruit develops.

The quality of grapes grown in the Walla Walla appellation of Oregon is high. No winery is located there anymore, since Seven Hills Vineyard relocated in 2000 to the town of Walla Walla, Washington. This high-desert plateau supports a number of top-quality vineyards for such well-regarded Washington producers as Cayuse, Seven Hills, Leonetti, and Pepper Bridge (see pages 181–185).

Notable producers

Flerchinger Vineyards and Winery

☎ 1-800-516-8710 ☏ 541-386-2882
✉ winery@flerchinger.com
🌐 www.flerchinger.com
4200 Post Canyon Drive, Hood River, Oregon 97031
Acreage in production 2.4ha (6 acres) in Riesling and Chardonnay
Production capacity 4000 cases
2000 production 3500 cases
Established in 1994,
First wines released 1994 vintage.
Family operated winery, producing a commercial range of fruity, simple wines: White Riesling, Merlot, Syrah, Pinot Gris, Cabernet Sauvignon, Cab-Merlot, Riesling, Blush Riesling (blended with Merlot), and Chardonnay, from both vineyard fruit (planted in 1983) and purchased fruit. Little or no French oak is used.

Hood River Vineyards

☎ (541)386-3772 ☏ (541)386-5880
✉ hoodriverwines@gorge.net
🌐 www.hoodriverwines.com
4693 Westwood Drive, Hood River, Oregon 97031
Acreage in production 2ha (5 acres) Pinot Noir, 2ha (5 acres) Chardonnay, 1.2ha (3 acres) Riesling, 1.6ha (4 acres) Pinot Gris, 1.6ha (4 acres) Syrah, 2ha (5 acres) Petit Syrah, 0.8ha (2 acres) Viognier, 1.6ha (4 acres) of Sangiovese, 1.6ha (4 acres) Tempranillo, 1.2ha (3 acres) Barbara, 0.8ha (2 acres) Dolcetto, 0.8ha (2 acres) Grenache, 0.8ha (2 acres) Sémillon, 1.6ha (4 acres) Zinfandel, 0.8ha (2 acres) Cabernet Franc, 0.8ha (2 acres) Malbec, 0.4ha (1 acre) Petit Verdot, 1.2ha (3 acres) Cinsault, 0.8ha (2 acres) Mourvèdre.
Production capacity 10,000 cases
2000 production 5,500 cases
Established 1978
First wines released 1981 vintage
Originally planted with Pinot Noir and Chardonnay in 1975, owned and operated by Hood River orchardist Cliff Blanchette. Bernie and Annie Lerch purchased the winery in 1993 and have been planting a wide range of Italian and Spanish grapes – forty-seven varieties in all – as experiments to see what works best in this region. Quality is good, but should improve as Bernie and Annie Lerch discover which varieties work best in which locations, and how best to farm them.

Bernie Lerch of Hood River Vineyards

Vintages

Why Oregon red wines are consumed young has always been a curiosity; like their Burgundian counterparts, Oregon red wines typically take on more complexity and nuance with age. White wines, though, generally should be drunk early, due in part to Oregon's drought-at-*veraison* problem that can make white wines short lived.

With the individual growing regions within the state experiencing slightly different vintage variations (and the southern areas seeing very different climate conditions), it can be difficult to generalize about all varietals and all regions. And even in the difficult vintages, some fine wines certainly did emerge.

2000 This is a very promising vintage, with wines of good concentration and structure. The conditions were very similar to both 1998 (ripe fruit with moderate to high pHs) and 1999 (higher yields), with a dry harvest period. Thankfully, this is the third year of great quality wines in the Willamette Valley. Further south, the Umpqua, Rogue and Applegate Valleys saw an equally fine growing season and harvest.

1999 A superb vintage, perhaps the top vintage Oregon has ever seen. The early growing season was actually cool, following a very late bloom period, making it unlikely that grapes would ripen before the arrival of the wet, cold winter. Most people severely crop-thinned as a hedge against the threat of a cool autumn and the likelihood of unripe clusters, Remarkably, all fruit ripened beautifully (for those who were patient enough to wait it out). While there is some variation in quality – largely dependant on when the grapes were picked – the later-harvested grapes were rewarded with ripeness and a good long hang time, which translates to higher acidity and beautifully balanced wines; most wines of this vintage are perfect candidates for ageing.

1998 Following the large 1997 crop, this vintage was subjected to damp, cool weather just after an early flowering (with shot berries in most places), adding up to dramatically reduced yields around the state – on average, 40 per cent of the normal volume. Crop loads were very short, under 14 hectolitres per hectare (1 ton per acre) at many properties. A dry, otherwise normal ripening season created some deeply extracted wines from the smaller berries and low surface-to-volume ratio of skins to juice. Some of the wines are certainly well-structured; most will be enjoyed for their lush texture and ripeness, but their higher pHs call for more immediate drinking.

1997 Crop loads were so high most producers green harvested at least one-third of their fruit and still brought in a large volume of grapes. Relentless rain at harvest created hard, lean, slow-to-evolve wines, with too-firm a tannic structure. Botrytis pressure was high, and those who crop-thinned earlier and hand-sorted at harvest fared better.

1996 This was a variable vintage in Oregon, with top wines developing well. A cool May delayed the bloom, but the summer was warm and dry. September cooled nicely, which was good for developing flavour. Serious rain arrived when most grapes were already close to fully ripe. This is the best of the "rain years" of 1995–1997.

1995 These wines are lean due to rain – and lots of it. The rain hit after a good growing season, with moderate to good yields. Many Pinot Noirs lack colour and depth of fruit due to dilution. That said, there are a number of well-structured, more concentrated single-vineyard and reserve-level wines.

1994 The hot, short season in Oregon made lush, less-structured but flashy wines, well-loved by the public and press who are used to

California-style, jammy big wines. Most vineyards saw yields well below 28 hectolitres per hectare (2 tons per acre), accomplished without crop thinning, due to poor fruit set. Many wines have an over-ripe character. The lack of acid and firmness has meant many 1994 wines have started to fade.

1993 This was a somewhat varied vintage, but with top Oregon wines showing particularly well. Before the 1999 vintage, this year can be considered to be Oregon's best, with elegant, nicely structured wines. Bloom was late, as was harvest, but the autumn was warm and relatively dry, allowing for the long hang time most associated with fine wines. Those who crop thinned saw more concentration. Wines from this vintage are still showing well, with many more years of ageing possible.

1992 This was a good vintage, with strong balanced wines. It was a hot year, with an early harvest taking place in September. The heat relented somewhat towards the end of the harvest season, resulting in quality wines, often boasting high alcohol. Those growers who had crop thinned were more successful than others.

1991 A cool, long spring delayed the bloom until July, but the remaining growing season was almost too dry, with a long still-dry autumn. Oregon saw a good ripe harvest. Because the harvest was late, quality was better for those who had severely crop thinned earlier to get more concentrated, ripe grapes. In youth, the wines were hard and tannic, but these are now softening.

1990 Very cold conditions in December 1989 caused some bud damage, leading to a reduced crop (for the third year in a row). In addition, a cool spring caused poor set; autumn and harvest were dry. The small berries and low yields, though, produced some wines of great intensity and depth.

Other notable vintages:

1989 A warm late spring resulted in an early flowering. By mid-June, rain descended and caused low yields at the higher elevations; at the lower elevations, yields were low to normal. Harvest was early and the fruit quality was high. Those who picked late lost delicacy. Otherwise, the vintage was like a more elegant version of the fine 1985 and 1988 vintages.

1988 A wet cool spring for this year, but warmth arrived in time for some flowering late in May. Rain and cool returned in June and it didn't warm up until mid-July, lasting through mid-September. The harvest was dry. Yield was down by almost fifty per cent; quality good to very good. The wines still show well, but are reaching a plateau of maturity.

1985 Warmth arrived by late May after a cool spring. There was rain in early June, but the weather was warm and dry for flowering, the growing season and harvest. Most grapes were picked at perfect maturity. The wines still show class. A number of 1985 Oregon Pinot Noirs scored well at Competitions.

1983 A cool spring, but by June, there was perfect weather and bloom. A warm dry growing season followed, including a little rain in late August. Harvest commenced in early October, right on schedule. The crop was large but on the whole these wines have aged well.

1980 A wonderful vintage for Oregon wines. June was wet and cool and bloom was delayed until July. The growing season was warm and dry and harvest was complete by mid-October. Yields were reduced and the wines are well-structured, and still very good.

Don't overlook the still-wonderful wines from the fine 1975 and 1976 vintages – particularly from the Eyrie and Knudsen-Erath – in short supply but a joy to discover.

Washington

Seattle is Washington's major metropolis, complete with high-rise office towers and an electric bus system.

As early as 1825, there were grapes growing in Washington, at Fort Vancouver, across the Columbia River from what would later become Portland, Oregon. Many settlers along the Columbia river were either English-born or French fur trappers and traders, and it is likely they brought with them the seeds of grape varieties they would have known best: *Vitis vinifera*. There is no record of wine production at Fort Vancouver. Table grapes, though, have a long history in many regions of Washington; Concord grapes were planted in the Yakima Valley as early as 1904 and continue to be a solid agricultural product today.

Historically, the early settlers of the state initiated the grape industry. By 1859, there was an influx of settlers to a large number of areas across Washington. In the Walla Walla Valley (in the far southeastern corner of the state), A B Roberts planted grapes that he purchased from the Willamette Valley and also imported eighty different varieties from France.

The *Walla Walla Statesman* in 1876 reported ... that there were a total of about 12 hectares (30 acres) of vines under cultivation in the Walla Walla Valley

Italian-immigrant Frank Orselli became a home winemaker and sold the wine at his California Bakery in Walla Walla. The *Walla Walla Statesman* in 1876 reported that Jean Marie Abadie produced both red and white wines, and that there were a total of about 12 hectares (30 acres) of vines under cultivation in the Walla Walla Valley, although the percentage of table grapes versus wine grapes was not reported. A severe winter freeze in 1883, however, devastated the nascent industry that would not rise again as a major winemaking region until almost a century later.

Meanwhile, in the **Yakima Valley** of central Washington – east of the Cascade Mountains, German-immigrant Anthony Herke homesteaded at Tampico in 1871 and planted a vineyard, which probably included Lemberger and Riesling. Nearby, in Union Gap, the Schanno family planted grapes and irrigated them, using water from the Yakima River and Ahtanum Creek. Philip Miller, a German immigrant, settled in the Wenatchee area in 1872, and developed 3.2 hectares (8 acres) of grapes. By 1900, he was making 5,678 litres (1,500 gallons) of wine each year; the vines are said to have come from the Schanno vineyard. Another German, John Galler, planted vines in the area in 1873, and was said to have made "sour German wine."

Across the state, over the Cascade Mountains and in the Puget Sound islands and the peninsula west of Seattle, grape growing was also developing. In 1872, Florida native Lambert Evans planted American grapes on what is now known as Stretch Island, but was then called Evans Island.

In 1889, the state of **Washington** was admitted to the union. That year, upstate New Yorker Adam Eckert established a grape nursery on Stretch Island, and planted Island Belle, a variety now determined to be Campbell Early, a cross between *Vitis labrusca* and *Vitis vinifera*. It was well suited to the wet – and cool – growing conditions of the Puget Sound it is a variety that ripens early and is mildew-resistant. Until Prohibition, Island Belle was grown as a productive table and juice grape; with Washington's ratification of Prohibition Law in 1919 (effective in 1920), Island Belle gained popularity for home winemaking, which was permissible under the law for personal use.

By the early 1900s, irrigation transformed the mostly desert-like landscape east of the Cascade Mountains into profitable farmland. American table grapes flourished. Vinifera was planted as well: Riesling, Muscat, Carignane, Sauvignon Blanc, Sémillon, and Zinfandel have been documented. Growers found, though, that the American labrusca fared better in the long hot summers and potentially devastating winter freezes.

William B Bridgman, a young attorney from Canada, arrived in Sunnyside (in the

Yakima Valley) in 1902; he was to draft Washington's first irrigation laws. Bridgman managed a small irrigation company supplying local farmers.

By 1914, Bridgeman had also planted Black Prince, Flame Tokay, and Ribier grapes on Harrison Hill in Sunnyside, a modern-day top vineyard site. A few years later, he brought grape cuttings from Europe and California and established a vineyard on nearby Snipes Mountain, this time including vinifera: Sauvignon Blanc, Sémillon, and Zinfandel. Snipes Mountain continues to play an important role in growing high-quality wine grapes to this day.

As early as 1905, Seattle attorney E F Blaine grew grapes and operated Stone House Winery near Grandview in the Yakima Valley. He and winemaker Paul Charvet made wine from Concord, White Diamond, Black Prince, and Zinfandel grapes, shipping wines to customers around the state. Charvet also made wine at his own winery. When Prohibition took effect, table grapes such as Bridgman's and Blaine's became in demand for home winemaking purposes.

Washington wines at the time were primarily low-quality fruit-based or labrusca wines, and winemakers had no incentive to improve quality.

After Prohibition was repealed in 1933, St Charles Winery on Stretch Island in Puget Sound became Washington's first bonded winery, known for wines using local grapes including Island Belle. The winemaker was Erich Steenborg, who had trained in Germany.

The year 1934 was a big one for Washington wine. In the Yakima Valley, W B Bridgman opened Upland Winery in 1934. By that time, Bridgman controlled 36 hectares (90 acres) of grapes, soon producing 26,495 litres (7,000 gallons) of wine. And he hired Erich Steenborg – Washington's only university-trained winemaker – to help him. That same year, the National Wine Company (Nawico) of Grandview and Pommerelle Winery of Seattle each obtained winery bonds. Nawico produced sweet, low-alcohol table wines; Pommerelle, fruit, and berry wines.

Also in 1934, the Washington State Liquor Board (WSLB) – the regulatory agency that exists today – was created by the Washington Legislature's Steele Act, which also permitted wines made from Washington grapes to be sold directly to wholesalers and taverns; out-of-state wines had to go through the newly created Liquor Board. This protectionism was designed to insulate and protect the wines of Washington against the "foreign" (that is California) competition.

As a result, very little outside wine came into the state thereafter; the little that did enter was heavily taxed and highly expensive. Washington wines at the time were primarily low-quality fruit-based or labrusca wines, and winemakers had no incentive to improve quality. In fact, it wasn't until 1940 that wines made from grapes outsold wines made from other fruits.

There were exceptions, of course. Upland Winery hired Julian Steenbergen as winemaker (to assist Erich Steenborg) in 1938, and Bridgman began to import vinifera to plant in his vineyards. Upland became known for such varietal wines as Zinfandel, Sémillon, Cabernet Sauvignon, and Washington's first dry Riesling, laying the foundations for Washington's modern wine industry.

Upland Winery's importance continued, with Bridgman's leadership in grape varieties and Steenborg's commitment to higher quality wines. However, freezing winters in 1949 and 1950 killed most vinifera at Upland (and elsewhere in the Yakima Valley). Upland struggled. In 1960, the winery was sold to the short-lived Santa Rosa Winery. Bridgman died in 1968, but his name lives on in Washington as the name of one of Washington Hills Cellars' three wine brands.

Following World War II, Washington's **fledgling wine industry** continued to develop. In 1945, twenty-one Washington wineries sold a total of 106 million litres (28 million gallons), a record that stood until 1987; much of what was produced at that time, though, was not high quality.

During the post-war years, the vibrant Concord grape industry created an interest outside Washington. In 1949, E & J Gallo Winery of Modesto, California bought 4,000 tons of Yakima Concord juice for the first time, destined for Gallo's Cold Duck sparkling wine. In the 1950s, Gallo bought much more. Although Concord production had been increasing even prior to World War II, there was an ever-growing interest in vinifera grapes in Washington. With Bridgman's encouragement (and in some cases, with his plant material), horticulturist Walter J Clore PhD began planting vinifera in 1937 for research studies at Washington State College's Irrigation Branch Research Station (today called the Irrigated Agriculture Research Extension Center or IAREC) at Prosser in the Yakima Valley. This effort would ultimately prove to the agricultural and wine industries that premium wine grapes could be grown successfully in eastern Washington. The IAREC still conducts wine-grape research today.

In the 1950s vineyards continued to thrive in eastern Washington; by 1955 (the year of another devastating autumn freeze which resulted in a production drop of 39 per cent the following year), Washington wineries sold 4,572,038 litres (1,207,936 gallons) of wine worth approximately $4 million dollars. There were 3,000 hectares (7,500 acres) of grapes planted in the state of Washington at this time, 97 per cent of which were planted east of the Cascades.

The seeds of **Washington's modern era** date from 1954, the year when Nawico of Grandview and Pommerelle Winery of Seattle merged to form American Wine Growers (AWG). They marketed Grenache rosé in cork-stopped bottles under the Granada brand name. Two years later, AWG purchased one of Bridgman's vineyards north of Grandview. Seattle, however, remained the administrative base for the company, even though the grapes were grown east of the mountains.

Wine writer Leon Adams visited Washington in 1966 and tasted a home-produced Grenache rosé made by Lloyd Woodburne, a psychology professor who enjoyed home winemaking and who, for one year, had studied wine in Germany. Adams suggested to Victor Allison, the manager of AWG, that a consultant like André Tchelistcheff, then-winemaker at Beaulieu Vineyard in Napa, California, could help better define Washington wines.

Tchelistcheff came to Seattle – where his nephew Alex Golitzen resided and who would later start the respected Quilceda Creek Vintners – but at first was not at all impressed. Again, it was an Associated Vintners' connection that sparked his interest: the three-year-old Gewürztraminer served to Tchelistcheff by Associated Vintner's Philip Church changed his tune. Tchelistcheff signed on to help AWG produce its first vinifera wine. In 1967, AWG released its first wines under the Chateau Ste Michelle label – a name that would become synonymous with high quality and later grow to become the largest winery in Washington.

Meanwhile, **Associated Vintners** had been developing. Associated Vintners was set up in the mid-1950s by some professors at the University of Washington, led by Lloyd Woodburne. In 1962, Woodburne formed the company with a group including Philip Church, a meteorologist who had studied Yakima weather records for thirty years and who determined that Sunnyside in the Yakima Valley got the same sun and heat as Beaune, France. They planted Chardonnay, Pinot Noir, Gewürztraminer, Riesling, and later, Sémillon, and Cabernet Sauvignon. The vineyard prospered. The group opened a production facility near Seattle and produced its first commercial wines in 1967 under the Associated Vintners' label. In 1983, Associated Vintners changed its brand name to Columbia Winery.

In 1969, Protectionist wine legislation was lifted in Washington, allowing **imported wines** to sell in grocery stores and forcing Washington winemakers to compete and focus on producing better wines. All but three Washington wineries closed within the next few years. But at the same time, more and more vineyard land was planted across the Yakima, Columbia, and Walla Walla Valleys. But like Oregon, the "mom-and-pop", family-owned wineries didn't become established until the mid-1970s. And quality didn't jump up until a number of years later.

In 1967, AWG released its first wines under the Chateau Ste Michelle label – a name that would become synonymous with high quality.

Washington identity

Washington's image is all about **Seattle**. The titans of Seattle offer a triumvirate of highly visible business enterprises: Boeing aircraft (which decided in 2001 to move its corporate headquarters from the state, leaving operations in place but surprising and angering many Seattle citizens), giant Microsoft – the computer gorilla, and ubiquitous Starbuck's Coffee, now a major world-wide caffeine phenomenon. You can't be in Seattle – the "sleepless", rainy city almost completely surrounded by water – and escape their presence.

Most visitors think they are seeing the Washington wine country when they visit the wineries clustered around Seattle. The many producers that are based near the city source their grapes elsewhere, however, from the warmer, drier regions of eastern Washington, on the other side of the Cascade Mountains. All but 28.5 hectares (70 acres) of the state's vines are grown in eastern Washington, following the pattern set by early wine pioneers, such as AWG and AV (now Chateau Ste Michelle and Columbia Winery, respectively). Those 28.5 hectares (70 acres) of vines, not far from Seattle, grow in the Puget Sound appellation – spread among the islands that lie west of the city, and are directly accessible only by ferry or boat – which boasts a cool, wet maritime climate best suited to early ripening grapes.

It's a long, scenic drive to reach the broad Columbia Valley, where the bulk of Washington's vineyards lie, and increasingly more wineries are located here.

It's a long but scenic three-hour drive to reach the broad **Columbia Valley**, where the bulk of Washington's vineyards lie, and increasingly more wineries are located here. A visitor must drive through cool pine forests over the mountains and down into a semi-desert landscape, where in summer months the sun shines for up to 17 hours each day while in the depth of winter an icy chill descends for weeks on end. Alternatively, access is by air to Richland or Walla Walla, from Seattle or Portland. For a visitor, Washington is not an easy wine country to access, which makes more sense of the decision made by many wineries to site their visitor centres and operational headquarters near Washington's major city, Seattle.

The landscape of eastern Washington looks more like Nebraska or Kansas, definitely conjuring middle American images, with its

arid wheat fields spreading across vast expanses of bare, rolling landscape. This is punctuated by an occasional stretch of green fertile land where apples, asparagus, stone fruits, corn, hops, and increasingly, more and more grape vines are grown. The vines are more likely to be Concord or other varieties for juice and jelly (14,580 hectares/36,000 acres) than wine grapes, but the total area of vinifera has been expanding fast, reaching a level of almost 13,500 hectares (30,000 acres) in 2001. These figures make Washington the United State's second biggest grape grower and producer of vinifera wine, albeit representing only a very small fraction of California's mammoth output.

The latitude of Washington's wine region is between Burgundy and Bordeaux, and the **continental climate** ensures that everything ripens well, from the thick-skinned Bordeaux and Rhône-style varieties to Alsatian and Burgundian grapes. The warm, dry growing season with its cool nights helps create good colour and brings out true varietal flavours. Washington lets Oregon focus on Pinot Noir,

No, this is not a medical procedure, but rather the racking of wine from one barrel to another. The worker is starting a syphon to empty a barrel of wine.

where the cooler weather creates better structured wines.

Grapes ripen successfully in arid eastern Washington thanks to irrigation, an absolute necessity for the now thriving agriculture industry there. Land prices are low – and whilst the number of vineyards is indeed expanding, the success of other crops in the area means that grapes are not the only choice for a farmer.

The biggest threat to grape farming in Washington is winter temperatures. Tender varieties such as Grenache just don't survive without dramatic protection, such as burying the canes. In 1996, when a winter freeze devastated many vineyards, Merlot in particular suffered and the crop was reduced by more than 60 per cent.

The icy winters, however, keep phylloxera at bay, as do the sandy, well-drained soils. As a result, Washington has had no incentive to take preventive action (by grafting vines on American rootstocks) and all vines in the state are self-rooted (see page 118).

Historically, the trend in Washington has been to **purchase grapes** in eastern Washington and truck then to a production facility nearer Seattle, or even to an additional facility within the Columbia or Walla Walla Valleys. With the exception of producers such as Chateau Ste Michelle, Columbia Crest, Hogue, Preston, and Canoe Ridge, most wineries have purchased grapes from many differing sources and blended them without vineyard distinction.

That may be a **changing trend**. Beginning in the 1990s, Washington wine producers have taken a stronger interest in the vineyard. Small, top-flight wineries such as Andrew Will, Quilceda Creek, L'Ecole No. 41, Leonetti, and DeLille have invested in vineyard land and are now growing a portion of their own grapes. The growth in the number of during the same period has been remarkable, with new wineries opening recently at a stunning rate of one every thirteen days (in the calendar year 2000). Many of these new wineries are located in the Walla Walla Valley, and a good proportion of them have planted their own vineyards, including Pepper Bridge Winery, Dunham Cellars, Glen Fiona Winery, Cayuse Vineyards, Colvin Cellars, Reininger, and Spring Valley Vineyard.

This rapid growth means that many of Washington's vines are young, planted on light soils, but reaching a concentration and focus very different from wines made from earlier plantings. The earlier plant material in Washington was often from single clones, and farmed by fruit farmers as opposed to winemakers. As a result, many Washington wines of the past have lacked a subtlety and core focus. However, that's changing. Washington fruit in general can be described as showing deep colour, crisp acidity, and soft varietal flavours. The newer vineyards typically have planted vines more densely, using an array of clonal material, and are farmed with more attention to crop load and ripening, thus creating wines with more depth and structure.

Washington's **wine style** development runs a course similar to national taste trends: as many US drinkers come to wine through slightly sweet wines, the Washington industry began its relationship with wine with sweet fruit wines; a drier style developed over time. Washington's historical success with Riesling – coming in a broad range of styles from crisp and dry to late-harvest dessert wines (but most often slightly sweet, lower-alcohol wines) – and its commitment to value pricing has kept Oregon's Riesling production low. Washington's Riesling image is more firmly established than Oregon's and Oregon certainly could not compete on price.

Value is, in fact, a Washington trademark, with a number of large producers consistently turning out high-quality wines at very competitive prices; examples of this include Columbia Crest, Hogue Cellars, Washington Hills, and Columbia Winery. But Washington wines in general are priced higher than those of California (an average of $10 for Washington compared to $6 or $7 in California). California's output stands at about 150 million cases of wine per year, but

Washington fruit in general can be described as showing deep colour, crisp acidity, and soft varietal flavours.

only a mere 35 million cases of that total are in the $8-per-bottle and above category. Washington produces nearly 5 million cases in total and its higher priced, high-quality wines are on a financial par with the quality wines of California or anywhere else.

As in California, the Bordeaux varieties (plus Chardonnay) have taken the most prominent role in production. Chardonnay, Merlot, and Cabernet Sauvignon are, in almost equal proportions, the three most planted grapes in the state. By the early 1990s, Washington had made Merlot its poster child, staking its claim and identity on a popular varietal that shows a much clearer identity in Washington than the more anonymous Merlots coming out of California. Unfortunately, Merlot as a vine is tender and inconveniently succumbs to eastern Washington's regular winter freezes.

Lemberger, long a Washington specialty, resembles California's Zinfandel, offering a similarly dense, purple, blackberry profile and a similarly "unique-in-the-US" status. Sémillon could be a winner in Washington, if given the chance; marketing the wine against Washington's other whites, though, has been tough going.

But it is now Syrah that is beginning to steal the show from Merlot. Syrah was first planted in the mid-1980s, but has been steadily gaining in popularity in the 1990s. Other Rhône varieties such as Viognier, Grenache, Cinsault, and Mourvèdre were also planted in the late 1990s. The amount of vineyard acreage of these varieties has increased dramatically each year, and several wineries now focus on Rhône-style wines, including McCrea, Glen Fiona, and Cayuse. Most of Washington's better wineries also nowadays make a Syrah or Viognier. Syrah, in fact, may well eclipse Merlot as Washington's signature wine in the coming years.

The **scale** of the Washington wine industry is impressive. It has become a major player in Washington's economy, with an estimated income of $2.4 billion and a workforce of more than 11,000 people throughout the state. In the year 2000, 162 wineries produced 4.9 million cases of premium wine at a retail value of $575.9 million. (The number of wineries keeps on increasing, and there are likely to be many more wineries by the time you read this book.)

Over 75 per cent of the wine produced in Washington is shipped out of state. During 1999, Washington exported 3.7 million cases, valued at $216 million, to other states, and between July 1999 and June 2000, Washington's international exports exceeded 200,000 cases valued at more than $8.8 million. Washington wines are now to be found all over the world. Top export markets were Canada ($2.2 million between July 1999 and June 2000), followed by Japan with $1.3 million, and the United Kingdom at $1.0 million. Most of the ultra-premium wines command very high prices and made in small quantities, and therefore are not often exported outside the United States.

Between 1990 and 1999, the annual wine grape crop increased by 64 per cent, at a value of $63.7 million and grower revenue increased from $654 per ton in 1995 to an average of $910 per ton in 1999. Increasingly Washington is becoming a major player in the wine world.

Most of the ultra-premium wines are priced high and made in small quantities, and therefore are not often exported outside the United States.

The Washington State Department of Tourism has realized that and joined with the very able Washington Wine Commission to market wine tourism (see page 157). The Washington Wine Commission biannually hosts one of the top wine conferences anywhere, the World Vinifera Conference in Seattle. It attracts an impressive collection of internationally known top wine producers from around the world for topical, sometimes controversial, panel discussions; the conference always brings in a remarkable showing of press and wine-trade professionals.

Stories and reviews about Washington wines in the **international press** have also been appearing with great frequency. No longer an ignored wine region, Washington wines are now being taken seriously.

Water defines the growing conditions in Washington. The Cascade Mountain Range divides Washington into two discrete climatic and growing regions. These mountains stop the west–east flow of cool, wet maritime conditions so prevalent near Seattle due to the influence of the nearby Pacific Ocean. This same mountain range that runs down the West Coast of North America from Canada to Mexico, here in Washington marks a definite viticultural dividing line, inducing precipitation on the western side and creating a dry, arid environment to the east. Water defines the growing conditions of eastern Washington

As in any large volume winery , barrels have to be stacked to fit.

region almost as much as it does to the west; its absence creates a desert that, without irrigation, could not be viable farmland.

Of the **five formal AVAs** that exist in the state – the Yakima Valley, Walla Walla Valley, Columbia Valley, Puget Sound, and Red Mountain – only the Puget Sound appellation lies west of the Cascades. In 1995, the Puget Sound appellation was awarded to the cluster of islands within the Puget Sound Basin, situated about one hour southwest of Seattle.

Stretch Island within this appellation was the site of an early commercial vineyard in 1872, which continued to thrive both during and after Prohibition. Weather in the appellation is cool and damp, with 76–152cm (30–60in) of rain per year; most of this rain falls between November and April. Frost is not a danger. However, temperatures during the growing season never rise to the warmth experienced by other growing regions of the Pacific Northwest.

Most of the vineyards are planted with dependably ripening hybrids and early ripening vinifera such as Campbell Early, Island Belle, Madeleine Angevine, Madeleine Sylvaner, Müller-Thurgau, Sieggerebe, Pinot Noir, Chardonnay, and Pinot Gris. Wines tend to be light and lean – frequently with lower alcohol; distinctly different from wines made from eastern Washington grapes. Fruit wines are also regularly produced in the Puget Sound appellation. Most of these wines are primarily made for a local market.

The **Columbia Valley** forms Washington's largest appellation, comprising 33 per cent of the land mass of the entire state, and producing 98 per cent of all wine grapes grown, with about 11,600 hectares (29,000 acres) of wine grapes under cultivation. All of the other eastern Washington formal appellations lie entirely within the Columbia Valley appellation, which was approved as an AVA in 1984.

The boundaries of the region extend from the hilly Okanogan Lobe and its forests in the north of the state, all the way south into Oregon. The Cascade Mountains mark a natural western boundary, with the Palouse formation – a large, fertile plateau to the northwest of Walla Walla running almost into Idaho – forming the eastern boundary. The Columbia Valley AVA stretches 177km (110 miles) east to west by roughly 121km (75 miles) north to south.

Besides the formal AVAs of Yakima Valley and Walla Walla, major grape-growing areas within the broad Columbia Valley AVA include the Pasco Basin around the cities of Pasco, Kennewick, and Richland (known as the Tri-

Cities, famous for its Cold War nuclear weapons research), and the Quincy Basin to the north, including the Saddle Mountains and the well-regarded vineyard areas of Mattawa and the Wahluke Slope.

The Columbia Valley sees only 51–23cm (6–9in) of rain per year; this dry environment is a challenge, requiring irrigation. Soils are primarily sandy, with low fertility and low water-holding capacity. Falling between Bordeaux and Burgundy in latitude, the region enjoys long daylight hours during the growing season, with up to two hours more light each day than some of California's more southerly growing regions. Summer daytime temperatures can rise above 37.8°C (100°F).

Within these AVAs lie the Tri-Cities area, Spokane Area and the Greater Seattle Area. The black dotted line shows Washington state border.

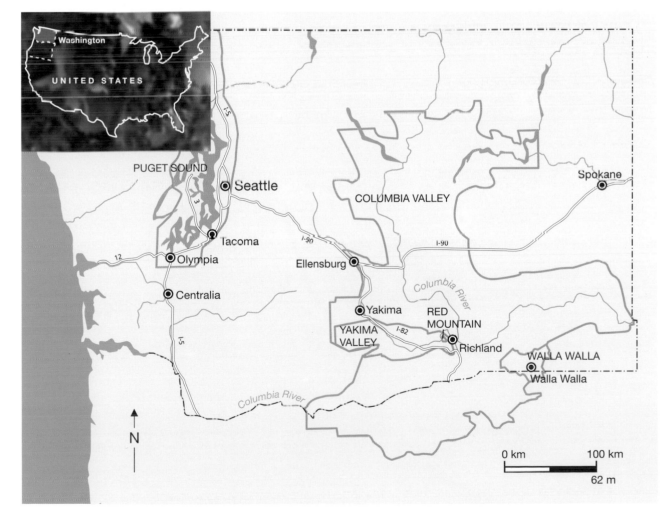

deposited basalt layers that cooled and subsided. Prehistoric floods caused many short-lived lakes and an ancient lake covered much of the area that is now the Yakima Valley, Walla Walla Valley, Pasco, and Quincy Basins. The lake repeatedly filled and emptied over time; with each flood came fine silt that filled the valley and basin floors and established the sandy soils of today that support grape and other fruit and vegetable farming. The Yakima Valley AVA boasts the greatest concentration of vineyards and wineries in the state. Once known for its white wines, red wines have now overtaken the whites in popularity.

The **Walla Walla Valley** stretches 48km (30 miles) east to west, roughly 32km (20 miles) north to south, forming a nearly self-contained basin. The hills that surround the Walla Walla Valley protect it from winter winds that can plague other parts of the Columbia Valley. Soils tend to be more gravel-laden and hold the heat better than in other areas. Syrah in particular shows great promise in this appellation.

Red Mountain, Washington's newest appellation, gained formal AVA status in April 2001. Encompassing approximately 1,360 hectares (3,400 acres), Red Mountain is part of the Yakima Valley. It is one of the smallest, most focused viticultural regions in the entire Pacific Northwest. Only 280 hectares (700 acres) of wine grapes are planted in this area, but there is the potential to expand to 680 hectares (1,700 acres). The wines from Red Mountain show unique properties: Merlot is generally full-bodied, with rough tannins that require bottle-ageing to soften. It displays a resemblance to Cabernet Sauvignon, which can also be a big, muscular wine when made from Red Mountain fruit. The individual vineyards of Red Mountain (including Klipsun, Taptiel, and Ciel de Cheval) are almost always designated on wine labels, which helps to make Red Mountain the most well-known, high-quality appellation in the state and ensures it is in demand by the state's top wineries, such as Andrew Will, Quilceda Creek, Woodward Canyon, L'Ecole No. 41, Hedges, and Wilridge.

The moderating influence of the Columbia River running to the east and the south of the appellation lowers the temperature by as much as 4.5°C (40°F) at night. This dramatic evening cooling is what gives Washington wines their crisp, acid structure, as the plant is able to respire at night, and build acidity in the fruit.

> **Red Mountain, Washington's newest appellation, ... is one of the smallest, most focused viticulture regions in the entire Pacific Northwest.**

The Columbia River also provides warmer temperatures in winter to nearby vineyards, as well as some protection from the freezes that so often hit the Valley. The **Yakima Valley** appellation was Washington's first formal AVA, created in 1983. The appellation stretches 129km (80 miles) long, and is bounded in the south by the Horse Heaven Hills, and to the north by the Ahtanum Ridge and Rattlesnake Hills, formed in ancient times when a volcano

Not all tanks are large, nor all barrels woods. And steel drums are not just for music.

Washington varieties

Chardonnay is Washington State's most widely planted grape, with results ranging from almost insipid, light, and crisp versions to oak-tinged, buttery wines. Growers tend to rely on a single clone, which can emphasize this variety's natural monotonous quality.
Statistics: 2,977 hectares (7,350 acres) planted; 2,037 hectares (5,030 acres) bearing.

Merlot has been Washington's flagship grape (with Syrah coming on strong). While frequently used in blends, Merlot gained popularity as a varietal wine in the 1970s. In Washington, Merlot wines tend to be more full-bodied, tannic, and alcoholic than Bordeaux versions, with higher acidity than California wines.
Statistics: 2,754 hectares (6,800 acres) planted; 1,636 hectares (4,040 acres) bearing.

Cabernet Sauvignon can be slightly grassy unless grown in an area warm enough to ripen it fully before temperatures start to fall. In youth, Cabernet Sauvignon seems subtler and more restrained than Washington Merlot, but with age emerges with typical black fruit, chocolate, and bell pepper characteristics. Several years of bottle ageing are usually necessary for the bigger-structured wines.
Statistics: 2,442 hectares (6,030 acres) planted; 1,090 hectares (2,690 acres) bearing.

Syrah may be the newcomer to Washington, but it keeps gaining popularity, and potentially poses a threat to Merlot as the state's most respected varietal wine. Increasingly planted on warmer sites across eastern Washington, Syrah has considerable promise as a savoury, complex addition to the state's roster of grapes.
Statistics: 1,215 hectares (3,000 acres) planted; 324 hectares (800 acres) bearing.

White Riesling was one of the original grape varieties in the state (as in Oregon), and also as in Oregon, the wines are usually produced with a bit of residual sugar. Occasionally, the appearance of *Botrytis cinerea* helps produce lovely late-harvest wines. Plantings in Riesling, in Washington and Oregon, have been decreasing since the early 1990s.
Statistics: 810 hectares (2,000 acres) planted; 721 hectares (1,780 acres) bearing.

Cabernet Franc has long been considered a blending grape, although good varietal wines have been appearing with greater regularity. Cabernet Franc is winter hardy and serves as a valuable sturdy core adding firm structure to softer wines. Vineyard average has tripled in the last five years.
Statistics: 340 hectares (840 acres) planted; 206.6 hectares (510 acres) bearing.

The Washington Wine Quality Alliance

The Washington Wine Quality Alliance (WWQA) exceeds the BATF standards, but it was intentionally created as a voluntary programme so as not to be a government-enforced law. WWQA members agree to follow these strictly defined production and labelling guidelines for their wines:

• The wines must contain 100 per cent Vitis vinifera grapes from Washington State or Washington State's American Viticultural Areas (AVAs), otherwise the label must identify the percentage of wine from each source.

• Wines must be produced without the addition of natural or artificial components not traditionally or historically added (to the extent that those additions would change the flavour, aroma, or colour of the wine).

• Most importantly, wines labelled as "Reserve" must be from grapes 100 per cent Washington State in origin, from any or all Washington AVAs and indicate the winemaker's designation of this wine as being of exceptional quality. The wine must also be among the higher priced wines produced by the winery in order to be identified as "Reserve". In addition, the "Reserve" label can apply to only the greater of 3,000 cases or 10 per cent of the member winery's production of the given varietal or blend.

• Varietal wines must contain at least 75 per cent or more of grape type indicated.

• The use of generic terms Burgundy, Bordeaux, Champagne, and Chablis is not permitted on labels.

• The term Johannisberg Riesling on labels was phased out in accordance with a 2000 BATF ruling.

These guidelines took effect for WWQA members beginning with the 2000 vintage. As of 2001, the programme has reached 60 per cent participation, with more than a hundred of Washington's 166 wineries committed to the programme.

Sauvignon Blanc, also known as Fumé Blanc, offers distinctive varietal character, with a fruit core, lively acid, and a touch of herbaceousness. As with Chardonnay, the styles vary from crisp grassy wines to ripe, tropical flavours overlaid with wood.
Statistics: 340 hectares (840 acres) planted; 243 hectares (600 acres) bearing.

Sémillon could be Washington's flagship white with a bit more marketing effort. In youth, the wines offer crisp citrus, melon, and fig flavours; with age, they can mellow into honeyed, nutty wines. Also susceptible to *Botrytis cinerea*, Sémillon is also made into lovely late-harvest wines by a few producers.
Statistics: 294 hectares (725 acres) planted; 239 hectares (590 acres) bearing.

Chenin Blanc wines in Washington are fruity and floral but lack complexity. They are produced in both dry and off-dry styles, and occasionally as a late-harvest dessert wine.
Statistics: 199 hectares (490 acres) planted; 162 hectares (400 acres) bearing.

Gewürztraminer was an early success because of its winter hardiness. This is the variety that enticed the legendary André Tchelistcheff (then at Beaulieu in Napa) to consult for Ste Michelle in 1967. Wines vary from the formerly more typical off-dry style to newer dry bottlings that capture the variety's aromas.
Statistics: 199 hectares (490 acres) planted; 26 hectares (310 acres) bearing.

Viognier, like its Rhône relative Syrah, has seen great growth in the state. Planted primarily along the Columbia Gorge, and the Mattawa and Yakima areas, the wines show an abundance of aromatic, floral fruit.
Statistics: 162 hectares (400 acres) planted; 41 hectares (100 acres) bearing.

Lemberger (Austria's Blaufränkisch) has long been a local specialty. These wines can be light, fresh, and fruity, almost like Beaujolais, or big purple wines, richly extracted, slightly dusty in character, and enrobed in oak. 71 hectares
Statistics: (175 acres) planted; 49 hectares (120 acres) bearing.

Pinot Gris and **Muscat Canelli** each claim about 41 hectares (100 acres). **Grenache** and **Mourvèdre** are also starting to catch on, as the Rhône fever continues. Grenache, however, is tender and susceptible to winter freezes. Growers want the fruity blending quality that the grape provides, so some are burying the canes in winter to protect them from frost.

Merlot has been Washington's identity grape, but Syrah is coming on strong (in quantity and quality) to challenge Merlot's dominance.

Sangiovese – made famous by Leonetti's Gary Figgins – rarely gets bottled as a varietal wine; Figgins in particular extols its benefit in blending. There are also about 81 hectares (200 acres) of **Pinot Noir**, almost all of it planted before 1985 in the Yakima Valley.

Notice the lack of a grafting union; all Washington vines are self-rooted. Who's afraid of phylloxera?

Grapes grown back west in the Puget Sound AVA in Western Washington are completely different – early ripeners such as Müller-Thurgau, Madeleine Angevine, and Siegerrebe – a group that would be more recognizable to those familiar with the cool, rainy climates of middle Europe.

Legal restrictions

All **Washington wine laws** follow the administrative rules and regulations for the production and sale of wines as required by the US Bureau of Alcohol, Tobacco, and Firearms (BATF). The Washington State Liquor Control Board (WSLCB) regulates and enforces BATF rules with its own administrative regulations covering label approval, monthly price posting, and a requirement similar to Oregon's that wine only be distributed through licensed wholesalers (although small wineries can claim exemption from that requirement). In an odd example of "competing in an area you regulate," the WSLCB also sells wine through its state-run liquor stores.

Washington State boasts one of the most successful and well-respected wine commission organizations of anywhere. The structure consists of three inter-related organizations: the Washington Wine Commission, the Washington Wine Institute, and the Washington Association of Wine Grape Growers.

The **Washington Wine Commission** (WWC) is a state mandated (since 1987), non-profit trade association dedicated to the marketing, promotion, and research of the wines and wine grapes of Washington State. All Washington vintners and wine-grape growers belong to the WWC. Of the ten commissioners serving for (rotating) three-year terms on the board, five are growers and five are vintners. Washington law specifies roles for each commission seat in terms of winery or vineyard size and location to ensure proper statewide and industry-wide representation on this board. Interestingly, although giant Stimson Lane could easily dominate this organization (as it is by far the largest producer in the state, owning more than one major brand), Stimson Lane has always taken the position that the promotion of any Washington wine benefits all producers. It has assumed a more back-seat role, and as a result the Commission allows other producers to demonstrate their leadership qualities as well.

90 per cent of the funding for the WWC (almost $1 million in 2000) is derived from an assessment of $6 per ton of grapes grown, $.04 per 3.8 litres (gallon) for wine produced, and $.025 per bottle on all wine sold in the state.

The Wine Advisory Board (WAB) is a subcommittee of the WWC that oversees and directs the viticultural and enological research activities of the Washington wine industry. The WAB is composed of vintners, growers, researchers, and nursery professionals; board members direct more than $500,000 to research every year through the Washington State University wine and wine-grape research system.

The **Washington Wine Institute** (WWI) was created in 1973 to represent the political voice for the Washington wine industry in Olympia (the state capital) and in Washington, DC. The WWI is a voluntary, vintner-only organization whose sole focus is to create a positive political and business climate for the Washington wine industry. Winery members support the budget in proportion to their production levels.

The **Washington Association of Wine Grape Growers** (WAWGG) is the grower counterpart to the WWI, a voluntary, grower-only organization dedicated to the education of the state's wine-grape growers, while at the same time being their voice in the state capital.

Established in 1989, the WAWGG hired its own executive director in 1999 and has become a marketing and promotional force in Washington agriculture as well as a driving force for quality in the state's vineyards. The budget is funded by fees assessed on wine-grape acreage.

Amazingly, you would be hard pressed to find a producer in Washington who doesn't think the WWC is doing a good job on his or her behalf. The attentive, focused staff manage to accomplish more than many larger staffed offices, and create goodwill.

The WWC has also developed an enology and viticulture academic programme in coordination with Washington State University (WSU), which already does most of the viticultural and enological research in the state. Together they will develop a coordinated teaching, research, and extension programme. Initial funding for the project has come from the WWC ($100,000).

The programme is being developed in three phases. The first phase began in 2000 with WSU working with Walla Walla Community College, Columbia Basin College, and Yakima Valley Community College to expand existing viticulture and enology programmes and training courses. Phase two began in 2001 with the appointment of two faculty members to build a detailed proposal for a permanent programme. The final phase will begin in 2003, with faculty additions and facility developments, with completion expected in 2005. The first Bachelor of Science degrees in viticulture and enology from Washington State University could be awarded as early as 2003.

Until now, Washington could not train and hire its own wine work force. As the second largest wine-producing state in the United States, Washington had to look outside the state to find university-trained winemakers and viticulturists. The new programme is a positive step in the Washington's maturity as a significant wine region.

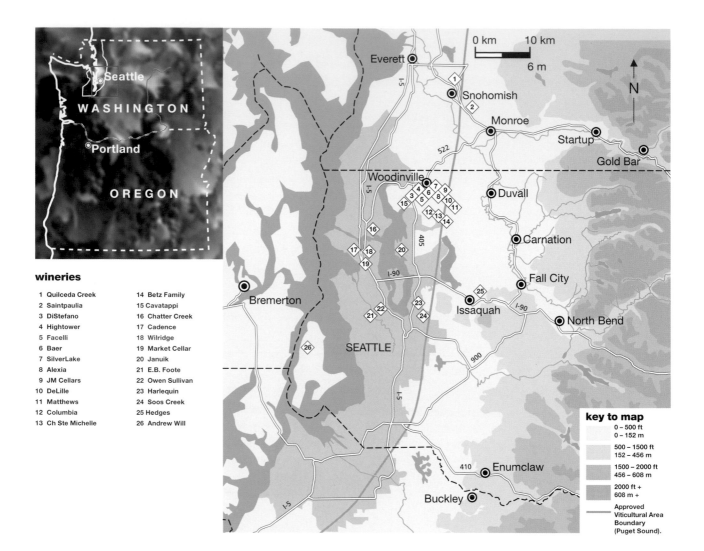

wineries

1	Quilceda Creek	14	Betz Family
2	Saintpaulia	15	Cavatappi
3	DiStefano	16	Chatter Creek
4	Hightower	17	Cadence
5	Facelli	18	Wilridge
6	Baer	19	Market Cellar
7	SilverLake	20	Januik
8	Alexia	21	E.B. Foote
9	JM Cellars	22	Owen Sullivan
10	DeLille	23	Harlequin
11	Matthews	24	Soos Creek
12	Columbia	25	Hedges
13	Ch Ste Michelle	26	Andrew Will

key to map

0 – 500 ft
0 – 152 m

500 – 1500 ft
152 – 456 m

1500 – 2000 ft
456 – 608 m

2000 ft +
608 m +

Approved
Viticultural Area
Boundary
(Puget Sound).

Greater Seattle area

The black dashed lines represent the county borders.

Seattle is Washington's largest, most important city. Although not its capital, Seattle has always been the jewel of Washington, but the city has suffered the same migration into the suburbs over the past decades that has plagued other US cities. In 2000, with its population of 563,374 people, Seattle finally surpassed its previous high of 557,087 residents in 1960.

The shift of population from the city of Seattle proper to the surrounding suburbs over that forty-year period was significant. The continued growth of the bordering counties of King, Snohomish, Pierce, and Kitsap had given the greater Seattle area a booming population of almost four million people by the recent turn of the century.

Key factors to Seattle's success as a community are its skilled workforce, manufacturing capability, education and research, quality transportation and infrastructure, and access to international and domestic markets. Other important factors include a broad cultural diversity, an international perspective, and a high quality of life. Arts and culture form an important thread that weaves through the fabric of Seattle, boasting many high-quality, well-funded museums, a vibrant arts community, and a strong commitment to music, from classical to grunge. The lure of Seattle is easy to understand; no other city in the state can offer the depth and breadth of business, cultural, and educational opportunities.

So it comes as no surprise that many wineries have chosen to anchor their operations near Seattle and its population base, not only to be near supplies and distribution, but also for a higher quality of life for the owners and employees and easy access for visitors. All grapes, of course, come from the vineyards east of the mountains. This trend towards Seattle-based wineries started early, and really defined the emerging wine industry in Washington. The wineries in the formal Puget Sound appellation – also close to Seattle – located among the islands south and west of the city, are discussed in the next chapter.

Both Associated Vintners (AV) and American Wine Growers (AWG), Washington's pioneer brands of the modern era, maintained Seattle-area operations: AV because the founders were based in Seattle and AWG because its precursor, the Pommerelle Winery, had been located there. Today, these two wineries are located directly across the road from each other in Woodinville, just northeast of the city, but still within the greater metropolitan area.

Under the tutelage of well-known winemaking "maestro" and consultant **André Tchelistcheff** (the then-recently retired winemaker of Beaulieu Vineyards in Napa, California), AWG launched Chateau Ste Michelle and before long the winery began to attract national attention. In 1968, a blind tasting was held by Darrell Corti of Corti Brothers in Sacramento, California. The Ste Michelle Sémillon beat all American competitors and was placed a fraction behind Y, the dry Sémillon of Château d'Yquem of Sauternes, Bordeaux. In a now-famous 1974 Los Angeles blind tasting, the Ste Michelle 1972 Johannisberg Riesling bettered all German, Australian, and other American Rieslings in the line up – all more expensive than the Ste Michelle entry – projecting the winery into a national spotlight.

Chateau Ste Michelle was sold to United States Tobacco in 1974, and had built new offices and a winemaking facility. Two years later, the winery moved from Seattle into the grand Chateau Ste Michelle in Woodinville, the company's current headquarters and white winemaking facility. The property sits on former lumber baron Frederick Stimson's wooded summer estate, Hollywood Farm, built in 1912. It is surrounded by 35 hectares (87 acres) of beautifully landscaped property, located 24 km (15 miles) northeast of Seattle.

Around 1980, a vital **new group of winemakers** came on the scene in the greater Seattle area to boost its image still further. André Tchelistcheff's nephew, Alex Golitzen,

This trend towards Seattle-based wineries started early, and really defined the emerging wine industry in Washington.

Chateau Ste Michelle joint ventures

Former Stimson Lane Chief Executive Officer Allen Shoup initiated a series of joint-venture wine projects at Chateau Ste Michelle (CSM) with some of the world's most respected names. The wines that have emerged now rank as the best wines in the CSM portfolio.

Piero Antinori and CSM jointly produce (in Washington) their Col Solare wine, first released as the 1995 vintage. The wines are superb: big, elegant Cabernet Sauvignon and Merlot blends, backed with a small amount of Syrah. Antinori helped CSM make changes in the vineyard to improve the ripeness of the fruit, and persuaded CSM to harvest later.

The second project focused on Riesling made with one of the Mosel's top producers, Dr Ernst Loosen of Weingut, who had approached CSM after tasting one of its dry Rieslings. Shoup's goal was to create a renaissance of Riesling to honour the roots of the Washington wine industry. Loosen worked with CSM white wine winemaker Eric Olsen to develop a minerally and well-balanced Riesling, named Eroica. The two also created a luscious TBA-style dessert wine, Single Berry Select.

Loosen encouraged Ste Michelle to shoot thin, increase canopy management, and lower the yields to 4 tons per 0.4 of a hectare (1 acre) at its Cold Creek Vineyard. In the cellar, Olsen says the changes he made with Loosen's advice – and has since applied to all Ste Michelle Rieslings – include pressing whole cluster and using a combination of yeasts for a long, slow fermentation.

Allen Shoup also teamed up with Brian Croser of Petaluma in Australia to make Petaluma's Bridgewater Mill wines. Stimson Lane has also become the exclusive agent for Petaluma wines in the United States. The current Chief Executive Officer Ted Baseler is eager to work with other European producers, perhaps with a Bordeaux property, or perhaps with Antinori as a partner as well. He is also conducting discussions with a Burgundian domaine for a joint-Chardonnay project.

The Seattle Public Market
serves as a tourist
attraction and a popular,
year-round greengrocer
and fresh-fish market.
Think salmon.

lived and worked as a chemical engineer just north of Seattle. Whenever Tchelistcheff came to Seattle to consult with Chateau Ste Michelle, the two got together to talk family and wine. Golitzen was intrigued by winemaking, and Tchelistcheff encouraged his nephew to make wine at home. Tchelistcheff would taste wines with Golitzen, advise him about how to proceed, and generally talk him through steps that at first Golitzen did not understand. By the mid-1970s, Golitzen was hooked. In 1978, his Quilceda Creek Vintners became Washington's twelfth bonded winery, based at Golitzen's Snohomish home, roughly forty-five minutes north of Seattle.

Quilceda Creek today produces one of Washington's most respected Cabernet Sauvignon wines, known for its sturdy, well-structured, and aromatic appeal, with an ability to age well and develop greater nuance. Cabernet is Quilceda's focus (a tiny amount of Cabernet Franc is also produced), and historically has been sourced from the state's best vineyards, including Taptiel, Ciel de Cheval, and Klipsun, all on Red Mountain. Golitzen now owns 20 per cent of the Champoux Vineyard (near Alderdale, west of Paterson and not far from the Columbia River) with its twenty-year-old vines; he has also purchased (and just begun to plant) 7 hectares (17 acres) on Red Mountain in a partnership with neighbouring Ciel de Cheval vineyard owner Jim Holmes.

Around the same time as Golitzen started Quilceda Creek, David Lake MW joined Associated Vintners (AV) as winemaker. Lake was, and still is, the only Master of Wine in the United States who works as a full-time winemaker. His interest, like Golitzen's, was to make high-quality red wines, something which had not yet become a Washington focus. He also hoped to restore Associated Vintners to its original glory; after all, it was an AV Gewürztraminer that first convinced Andre Tchelistcheff to become a consultant for American Wine Growers (AWG). For Lake, coming to AV/Columbia was a good

> **Stimson Lane owns more vineyard acreage than any other winery in the state (over 486 hectares/1,200 acres with Chateau Ste Michelle alone).**

opportunity to develop his winemaking career, but it was also a challenge, since the heady momentum of the early heady years of AV had been lost, and the quality had become somewhat uneven.

Lake concentrated on the vineyard, and developed relationships with several top-quality growers who continue to produce some of the best fruit for the Columbia label; most are destined for Columbia's vineyard-designated wines and the David Lake Signature Series. The sites on which Lake has built Columbia's reputation include the Red Willow, Otis, and Wyckoff Vineyards in the Yakima Valley and Alder Ridge, and Sagemoor in the Columbia Valley.

In 1980, **Allen Shoup** joined Chateau Ste Michelle as Vice President for marketing, and quickly established himself and Ste Michelle as leaders in the state. Shoup, like David Lake and Alex Golitzen, saw the need to develop quality in red wines as well as white wines, and developed Chateau Ste Michelle's production facility at Grandview in the Yakima Valley to handle Chateau Ste Michelle's red winemaking.

Shoup formed Stimson Lane Vineyards and Estates in 1986 as the marketing and administrative company to oversee Chateau Ste Michelle's growing portfolio of wineries, now including Columbia Crest, Snoqualmie, Domaine Ste Michelle, and Northstar, as well as Villa Mt Eden in Napa, California. Stimson Lane owns more vineyard acreage than any other winery in the state (over 486 hectares/1,200 acres with Chateau Ste Michelle alone). The size of the Stimson Lane operation is enormous: Chateau Ste Michelle produces more than 800,000 cases of wine per year; Domaine Ste Michelle produces 250,000 cases; Columbia Crest, 1.3 million; Snoqualmie, 53,000 cases; and Northstar produces 1,100 cases each year. This total is almost three times more than all Oregon wine production combined, and represents almost half of Washington's wine production. For all that size and scale, it is remarkable that the quality levels are so very high.

On Shoup's retirement in June 2000, Ted

Baseler became President and Chief Executive Officer, after overseeing all sales and marketing operations at Stimson Lane for more than a decade. Baseler shares Shoup's commitment to wine quality at Stimson Lane, and the desire to promote Washington wines in general. Soon after he took over from Shoup, Baseler announced that Stimson Lane would build a brand new winery in Walla Walla as a home for Northstar, the high-end Merlot that the company has been making since 1994.

Chateau Ste Michelle has served as a training ground for a number of the state's top winemakers, including Kay Simon (now of the Chinook Winery), Mike Januik (now of the Januik Winery), and Charlie Hoppes (now of the Three Rivers Winery).

Both Columbia Winery and Chateau Ste Michelle continue to loom large in the Washington wine world, but other **top-notch labels** are also based in the Seattle area, specifically in Woodinville, each a short distance from one another. DeLille Cellars was started by father and son Charles and Greg Lill. Greg Lill thought a winery would honour his ancestor Julius deLille's winemaking efforts in 16th-century Eastern Europe; deLille was a Huguenot who had fled the French city of Lille to escape religious persecution. The younger Lill thought a winery would be a great retirement project for his father, as well as a way to leave a legacy with the DeLille family name on it.

Founded in Woodinville in 1992 with the initial help of winemaker David Lake MW, the winery has always purchased grapes from top vineyards. Current winemaker Chris Upchurch focuses on lush, well structured Bordeaux-style blends of red and white wine, and on one of the top oak-enrobed Syrahs in the state.

Matthews Cellars in Woodinville produces some of the most impressive wines in Washington, most notably the Yakima Valley red wine, made from a blend of classic Bordeaux grapes (Cabernet Sauvignon, Merlot, and Cabernet Franc) from such vineyards as Elerding, Snipes Canyon, Portteus (all

Yakima Valley), and Hedges Red Mountain. The resulting wine expresses great depth and complexity, with good acid and tannin structure – the stuff for long ageing. Matt Loso is a young winemaker, having worked in a number of Seattle area restaurants and cellars before launching his own label in 1993. Loso's new winery was constructed in 1998 on a 3.2 hectare (8-acre) site just down the road from DeLille.

Not far away, Hedges Cellars was established in Issaquah in 1989, several years after Tom Hedges began blending Washington wines and selling them to buyers in Sweden. The winery maintains a tasting room in Issaquah, but a new production facility was built near its vineyards on Red Mountain in 1995.

Chris and Annie Camarda outgrew their original Seattle-based Andrew Will winery space and chose to relocate to the more rural environment on Vashon Island (half an hour by ferry, southwest of Seattle). Unlike most island-based wineries (who use locally grown grapes for their wines), the Andrew Will wines use fruit grown in many of the same top-rated vineyards in eastern Washington as Quilceda Creek. The Camardas produce extremely concentrated, stylish red single varietals and blend from such high-quality vineyards as Klipsun and Ciel de Cheval on Red Mountain as well as Champoux in the Columbia Valley near Alderdale); the Camardas own 10 per cent of these vineyards. In 2001, they purchased 14.4 hectares (36 acres) near Zillah in the Yakima Valley, and planted it with Cabernet Sauvignon and Cabernet Franc, along with a small amount of Merlot. Andrew Will also produces a rich Pinot Gris from the Celilo Vineyard near the Columbia River, and makes Pinot Noir from Chris Camarda's brother-in-law's vineyard in Clackamas County, Oregon.

Other wineries-without-vineyards of note in the area include Cavatappi and Betz Family near Woodinville, Januik Winery in Kirkland, and Wilridge Winery, located within the city of Seattle itself.

Chateau Ste Michelle has served as a training ground for a number of the state's top winemakers.

Notable producers

Andrew Will Cellars

☎ 206-463-9227 📠 206-463-3524
✉ awwines@msn.com
12526 SW Bank Road, Vashon,
Washington 98070
Acreage in production 1.8ha (4.5 acres)
Cabernet Sauvignon, 2.4ha (4.5 acres) Merlot,
2.4ha (6 acres) Cabernet Franc
New plantings 3.6ha (9 acres) Cabernet
Franc, 7.2ha (18 acres) Cabernet Sauvignon,
1.2ha (3 acres) Merlot
Production capacity 4,300 cases
2000 production 4,300 cases
Established 1989
First wines released 1989 vintage
A partner in Champoux Vineyards and another
vineyard in Walla Walla, Chris Camarda has
also planted grapes at an unnamed site near
Zillah, Yakima Valley. These wines are among
Washington's best, silky, elegant beauties.

Baer Winery

☎ 206-915-5086
✉ info@baerwinery.com
🌐 www.baerwinery.com
PO Box 1124, Woodinville, Washington
98072
Production capacity 3,500 cases
2000 production 200 cases
Established 2000
First wines released 2000 vintage
Very new producer, with a red blend (Cabernet
Sauvignon, Cabernet Franc, and Merlot) from
Alder Ridge that will not be released until 2003.

Betz Family Winery

☎ 425-415-1751 📠 425-415-1751
✉ betzwinery@aol.com
🌐 www.betzfamilywinery.com
Mailing address: 13506 NE 190th
Place, Woodinville, Washington, 98072
Winery address: 18512 142nd Avenue
NE, Woodinville, Washington 98072
Production capacity 1,000 cases
2000 production 800 cases
Established 1997
First wines released 1997 vintage
Bob Betz MW is Vice President of Enology
Research at Stimson Lane, where he has been
employed for twenty-five years. He and his wife
Cathy produce small lots of wines from the top
vineyards: focused Cabernet Sauvignon,
Syrah, and a terrific blend of Cabernet
Sauvignon, Merlot, and Syrah.

Cadence

☎ 206-381-9507 📠 206-860-6888
✉ info@cadencewinery.com
🌐 www.cadence winery.com
Mailing address: 1420 Lake
Washington Boulevard S, Seattle,
Washington 98144
Winery address: 432 Yale Avenue N,
Seattle, Washington 98109
New plantings 4.2ha (10.5 acres)
Cabernet Sauvignon, Merlot, Cabernet Franc,
Nebbiolo
Production capacity 1,500 cases
2000 production 1,000 cases
Established 1998
First wines released 1998 vintage
Quality producer of well-structured wines made
for ageing: a lovely, restrained Merlot blend as
well as a number of Cabernet Sauvignon
blends, with fruit sourced from Walla Walla
Valley and Red Mountain's top vineyards.

Cavatappi Winery

☎ 206-282-5226
✉ peter.dow@accessone.com

David Lake MW of Columbia Winery

835 8th Avenue N, Seattle, Washington
98109
Production capacity 1,000 cases
2000 production 800 cases
Established 1982
First wines released 1984 vintage
Peter Dow crafts one of the few Nebbiolo wines
in Washington, with grapes from the respected
Red Willow Vineyard. The winery was
previously located next to Dow's former
restaurant, Café Juanita in Kirkland, which he
sold in order to concentrate on wine.

Chateau Ste Michelle Vineyards & Estates

☎ 425-488-1133 📠 425-415-3657
✉ info@ste-michelle.com
🌐 www.ste-michelle.com
PO Box 1976, 14111 NE 145th Street,
Woodinville, Washington 98072
Acreage in production 103ha (256 acres)
Merlot, 98ha (242 acres) Chardonnay, 150ha
(371 acres) Cabernet Sauvignon, 28.4ha (70
acres) Sauvignon Blanc, 12ha (30 acres) Syrah,
65ha (159 acres) Riesling

Chris Upchurch of DeLille Cellars

New plantings (unspecified acreage)
Cabernet Sauvignon, Syrah, Sangiovese
2000 production 809,000 cases
Established 1934 (the year predecessors
Nawico and Pommerelle were bonded)
First European varietal wines released
1967 vintage
The flagship property and headquarters of
Stimson Lane, and Washington's leading
winery group in every way: volume, vineyard
ownership, funding, education, research,
community charity, and leadership. Size could
make Stimson Lane the 800-pound gorilla, but
the organization has used its position to
promote Washington wines specifically, and
wine in general, almost more than its own
brands. All CSM wines show a commitment to
quality, from the supermarket shelf bottlings all
the way up to the "Artist's Series" reserve wines
and the partnership wines produced with
international wineries (see Col Solare and
Eroica). Washington wine would not have
achieved the respect it now commands without
Stimson Lane's and Ste Michelle's leadership.

Chatter Creek Winery
☎ 206-985-2816
✆ gordyrawson@msn.com
W www.chattercreek.com
620 NE 55th Street, Seattle,
Washington 98105
Production capacity 1,400 cases
2000 production 1,000 cases
Established 1996
First wines released 1997 vintage
Originally established as Alexia Sparkling

Wines, the winery was renamed in 1999 to
Chatter Creek, to mark the inclusion of red wine
production and to resolve a trademark issue
with the name Alexia. Owner/winemaker Gordy
Rawson was cellarmaster at Columbia Winery
and later worked as winemaker at Cascade
Ridge before leaving to focus on Chatter Creek.

Col Solare
☎ 425-488-1133 ✆ 425-415-3657
✉ info@ste-michelle.com
Ⓦ www.ste-michelle.com
**One Stimson Lane, Woodinville,
Washington 98072**
New plantings Cabernet and Syrah at Horse
Heaven Vineyard
2000 production 4,600 cases
First wines released 1995 vintage
This Chateau Ste Michelle/Piero Antinori
partnership has a blend that changes each
vintage (usually a combination of Cabernet
Sauvignon, Merlot, and Syrah), but always
emerges as a magnificent, powerful wine
meant for ageing – one of the best wines in the
state. Fruit has always come from CSM's Horse
Heaven Vineyard, and a new Col Solare
vineyard has been planted.

Columbia Winery
☎ 425-488-8164 ✆ 425-488-3460
✉ contact@columbiawinery.com
Ⓦ www.columbiawinery.com
PO Box 1248, 14030 NE 145th Street,
Woodinville, Washington 98072
Acreage in production 12.2 (30 acres)
Chardonnay, 0.4ha (1 acre) Viognier, 58.7ha

(145 acres) Riesling, 9.3ha (23 acres)
Gewürztraminer, 4.9ha (12 acres Pinot Gris),
3.2ha (8 acres) Sémillon, 29.2ha (72 acres)
Merlot, 14ha (42 acres) Cabernet Sauvignon,
0.8ha (2 acres) Cabernet Franc, 14.6ha (36
acres) Syrah, 1.6ha (4 acres) Sangiovese
Production capacity 300,000 cases
2000 production 140,000 cases
Established 1962
First wines released 1962 vintage
The original Associated Vintners, now owned
by giant Canandaigua Wines, located in a
Victorian-styled building directly across the
street from Chateau Ste Michelle. David Lake
MW crafts gently understated, varietally true
wines, representing almost all of the varieties
grown in Washington State.

DeLille Cellars
☎ 425-489-0544 ✆ 425-402-9295
✉ info@delillecellars.com
Ⓦ www.delillecellars.com
14208 Woodinville-Redmond Road,
Woodinville, Washington 98052
Acreage in production 2ha (5 acres) Syrah,
6ha (15 acres) Cabernet Sauvignon
Production capacity 4,200 cases
2000 production 4, 200 cases
Established 1992
First wines released 1992 vintage
One of the best producers in the state, crafting
a big, muscular Chaleur Estate Bordeaux-blend
and a silkier, softer Harrison Hill Bordeaux-
blend, each good consumed young, but even
better with age. Its Doyenne Syrah is equally
fine, brawnier, rich fruit, blanketed in oak.

DiStefano Winery
☎ 425-487-1648 ✆ 425-452-1029
✉ mark@distefanowinery.com
PO Box 2048, 12280 Woodinville Drive
NE, Woodinville,
Washington 98072
Production capacity 5,000 cases
2000 production 4,600 cases
Established 1984
First wines released 1986 vintage
First established as a sparkling wine producer
under the name Newton & Newton (and the
Northwest's first producer of *méthode
traditionelle* wines), the name was changed
with the 1991 vintage, by which time only still
wines were being produced. Wines now
include varietally true Cabernet Sauvignon,

Merlot, Syrah, and Sauvignon Blanc, sourced from top vineyards in eastern Washington.

E B Foote Winery

☎ 206-242-3852 ☏ 206-433-0788
Mailing address: 221 SW 153rd Street, PMB 181, Burien, Washington 98166
Winery address: 127-B SW 153rd Street, Burien, Washington 98166
Production capacity 5,000 cases
2000 production 2,000 cases
Established 1978
First wines released 1978 vintage
Current owners Sherrill Miller and Rich Higginbotham purchased the winery – one of modern Washington's oldest – in 1991. They make good Chardonnay, Merlot, and Cabernet Sauvignon from grapes in the Yakima Valley.

Eroica

☎ 425-488-1133 ☏ 425-415-3657
✉ info@ste-michelle.com
🌐 www.ste-michelle.com
One Stimson Lane, Woodinville, Washington 98072
2000 production 4,722 cases
First wines released 1999 vintage
Another Chateau Ste Michelle joint venture with a top international producer. Ernie Loosen and CSM white winemaker Eric Olsen craft a good off-dry Riesling, floral and delicate, as well as a luscious dessert wine, Single Berry Select, made in tiny quantities. All the fruit comes from CSM's Cold Creek Vineyard, Columbia Valley.

Facelli Winery

☎ 425-488-1020 ☏ 425-488-6383
✉ facelliwinery@msn.com
🌐 www.facelliwinery.com
16120 Woodinville-Redmond Road NE #1, Woodinville, Washington 98072
Production capacity 5,000 cases
2000 production 4,000 cases
Established 1988
First wines released 1989 vintage
Red wines are the focus here, with quality that has been steadily improving.

Harlequin Wine Cellars

☎ 425-413-4633 ☏ 425-413-4644
✉ pinotboy1@home.com
🌐 www.harlequinwine.com
19264 208th Avenue SE, Renton, Washington 98058

Mike Januik of Januik Winery

Acreage in production Washington – 0.8ha (2 acres) Merlot, 1.2ha (3 acres) Cabernet Sauvignon, 1ha (2.5 acres) Syrah, 0.4ha (1 acre) Zinfandel; Oregon – 0.6ha (1.5 acres) Pinot Noir
Production capacity 2,000 cases
2000 production 1,100 cases
Established 1998
First wines released 1999 vintage
Robert Goodfriend was a cellar assistant at Silvan Ridge, Oregon before moving to the Seattle-area to start his own winery. The Pinot Noir grapes come from Oregon's terrific Hoodview Vineyard, Eola Hills (also a top vineyard site for Joe Dobbes at Willamette Valley Vineyards in Oregon). Harlequin makes very good Cabernet Sauvignon and Syrah too.

Hedges Cellars

Tasting Room/Offices –
☎ 425-391-6056 ☏ 425-391-3827
✉ rdmountn@nwlink.com
🌐 www.hedgescellars.com
195 NE Gilman Boulevard, Issaquah, Washington 98065
Acreage in production Hedges Estate Vineyard –7.3ha (18 acres) Merlot, 6.5ha (16 acres) Cabernet Sauvignon, 0.4ha (1 acre) Cabernet Franc, 0.3ha (0.7 acres) combined Tinta Cao/Touriga/Souzao
Bel' Villa Vineyard – 5.7ha (14 acres) Cabernet Sauvignon, 2ha (5 acres) Syrah, 3.2ha (8 acres) Merlot, 1.2ha (3 acres) Cabernet Franc
Production capacity 55,000 cases
2000 production 53,000 cases

Established 1986
First wines released 1987 vintage
See Red Mountain.

Hightower Cellars

☎ 425-788-2261 ☏ 425-788-2261
✉ handsorted@aol.com
🌐 www.hightowercellars.com
Mailing address: 18705 NE 165th Street, Woodinville, Washington 98072
Winery address: 18658 142nd Avenue NE, Woodinville, Washington 98072
Production capacity 1,300 cases
2000 production 950 cases
Established 1997
First wines released 1997 vintage
Tim and Kelly Hightower craft good, well-structured Cabernet Sauvignon and Merlot, sourced from Pepper Bridge Vineyards in Walla Walla, Alder Ridge Vineyard in the Columbia Valley, and Artz Vineyard on Red Mountain.

Januik Winery

☎ 425-825-5710 ☏ 425-825-9710
✉ contact@januikwinery.com
🌐 www.januikwinery.com
7401 NE 122nd Street, Kirkland, Washington 98034
Production capacity 3,000 cases
2000 production 3,000 cases
Established 1999
First wines released 1999 vintage
Talented former Chateau Ste Michelle head winemaker Mike Januik left Ste Michelle after

the 1999 harvest to focus on his own label. He has been buying fruit from many of the same vineyards as he did at CSM, as well as the Pepper Bridge Vineyard in Walla Walla, crafting small lots of elegant Chardonnay, Cabernet Sauvignon, and Merlot.

J M Cellars Company
☎ 206-321-0052 ℱ 206-522-4822
✉ jbig36@aol.com
🌐 www.jmcellars.com
14404 137th Place NE, Woodinville, Washington 98072
Production capacity 2,500 cases
2000 production 1,400 cases
Established 1998
First wines released 1999 vintage
John and Peggy Bigelow are producing premium wines with Cabernet Sauvignon, Cabernet Franc, Syrah, Merlot, and Sauvignon Blanc, sourced from prestigious vineyards in the Yakima Valley and Red Mountain AVAs. One label is designated "Tre Fancuilli" in homage to their "three treasured sons", a blend of Cabernet Sauvignon, Merlot, and Syrah.

Market Cellar Winery
☎ 206-622-1880 ℱ 206-264-7886
✉ marketcellar@uswest.com
🌐 www.marketcellarwinery.com
1432 Western Avenue, Seattle, Washington 98101
Production capacity 500 cases
2000 production 500 cases
First wines released 1996 vintage
A downtown Seattle wine and home brewers supply shop. A small amount of wine (Cabernet Sauvignon, Merlot, and a white blend called Pike Blanc) is made from grapes grown in the Yakima Valley.

Matthews Cellars
☎ 425-487-9810 ℱ 425-483-1652
✉ wine@matthewscellars.com
🌐 www.matthewscellars.com
16116 140th Place NE, Woodinville, Washington 98072
Production capacity 3,000 cases
2000 production 2,000 cases
First wines released 1993 vintage
One of Washington's star producers, Matt Loso crafts tightly structured, velvety Bordeaux-style wines from grapes he purchases from top vineyards in the Yakima Valley.

Owen Sullivan Winery
S 206-243-3427 F 206-243-3471
E osw@peoplepc.com
4497 S 134th Place, Tukwila, Washington 98168
Production capacity 4,000 cases
2000 production 2,400 cases
Established 1997
First wines released 1997 vintage
Excellent producer of big lush wines made from grapes from some of the state's finest vineyards.

Quilceda Creek Vintners
☎ 360-568-2389 ℱ 360-568-2389
✉ qcv@earthlink.net
🌐 www.QuilcedaCreek.com
11306 52nd Street SE, Snohomish, Washington 98290
Acreage in production 6.9ha (17 acres) Cabernet Sauvignon
New plantings 4ha (10 acres) Cabernet Sauvignon
Production capacity 5,000 cases
2000 production 4,700 cases
Established 1978
First wines released 1979 vintage
Alex Golitzin crafts elegant, powerful Cabernet Sauvignon made for long ageing. He sources his fruit from the state's top vineyards, including two in which he has partial ownership: Champoux, the former Mercer Ranch, and a new eponymous vineyard on Red Mountain in collaboration with Ciel de Cheval Vineyard.

Saintpaulia Vintners
☎ 360-668-8585 ℱ 360-668-9038
✉ paulshinoda@msn.com
18302 83rd Avenue SE, Snohomish, Washington 98296
2000 production 700 cases
Established 1994
First wines released 1994 vintage
Paul Shinoda named his small-production winery – crafting Cabernet Sauvignon only – after the African violets he has grown commercially for the past thirty years. The wines are available only through his mailing list.

SilverLake Winery
☎ 425-486-1900 ℱ 425-483-3523
✉ info@washingtonwine.com
🌐 washingtonwine.com
15029 Woodinville-Redmond Road, Suite A, Woodinville, Washington 98072
Acreage in production 22.7ha (56 acres) Riesling, 5.7ha (14 acres) Sauvignon Blanc, 1.6ha (4 acres) Chenin Blanc, 13ha (32 acres) Chardonnay, 14.6ha (36 acres) Merlot, 28.4ha (70 acres) Cabernet Sauvignon, 2ha (5 acres) Cabernet Franc, 0.8ha (2 acres) Zinfandel, 1.2ha (3 acres) Gewürztraminer
New plantings 3ha (7.5 acres) Syrah
Production capacity 60,000 cases
2000 production 22,000 cases
Established 1989
First wines released 1989 vintage
Formerly a producer of *méthode traditionelle* sparkling wines only, varietal wines are now being produced using fruit from the winery's own Yakima vineyard.

Soos Creek Wine Cellars
☎ 253-631-8775
✉ sooscreek@mindspring.com
20404 140th Avenue SE, Kent, Washington 98042
Production capacity 1,000 cases
2000 production 750 cases
Established 1989
First wines released 1989 vintage
David Larsen makes small quantities of concentrated, powerful Bordeaux-style wines, aged for three years in barrel. Larsen buys grapes from Ciel du Cheval, Champoux, Charbonneau, and Pepper Bridge Vineyards.

Wilridge Winery
☎ 206-325-3051 ℱ 206-447-0849
✉ wilridgewinery@earthlink.net
🌐 www.wilridgewinery.com
1416 34th Avenue, Seattle, Washington 98122
Production capacity 2,000 cases
2000 production 1,000 cases
Established 1988
First wines released 1990 vintage
Solid producer of very good Merlot, Cabernet Sauvignon, Cabernet Franc, and Syrah made from grapes from top eastern Washington vineyards. The Pinot Noir, from Oregon grapes, is pleasant. The Nebbiolo is less successful.

Puget Sound

The **Puget Sound** growing region was granted formal appellation status in 1995, largely through the efforts of Gerard and Jo Ann Bentryn (owners of Bainbridge Island Vineyards and Winery, and tireless promoters of the island community). The core of the region lies on the islands that occupy Puget Sound; appellation boundaries, however, extend across Puget Sound, west to Seattle and beyond to the Cascade Mountains. From the north, it begins at the Washington State border with British Columbia and runs south to Olympia (the state capital) and just beyond. Many of the wineries discussed in the previous Greater Seattle chapter are technically based in the Puget Sound appellation; but since those producers only use grapes grown in eastern Washington and don't consider themselves as part of the Puget Sound appellation, they were discussed separately. The islands themselves will be the focus of the wine region discussed here with two exceptions, the high-quality Andrake Cellars and McCrea Cellars, each located near Olympia.

Within the islands – the westerly portion of the appellation – the tall Olympic Mountains, which form the boundary of the region to the west, offer some protection from the wet influences of the Pacific Ocean. However, this region as a whole still sees up to 150cm (60in) of rain each year, about 38cm (15in) falls during the April to October growing season. The appellation was drawn to exclude areas over 183 metres (600ft) of elevation, where grape ripening would be further compromised by extremes of cold and wet.

Temperatures vary greatly throughout the region. Using the Amerine and Winkler's degree-day scale, degree days on the islands ranges from 704–943 degree days Centigrade (1,300–1,730 Fahrenheit), with greater warmth on the "mainland" around Seattle and south to the area surrounding Olympia.

The area was created geologically by the advance and withdrawal of the Vashon glaciation more than 10,000 years ago.

The area was created geologically by the advance and withdrawal of the Vashon glaciation more than 10,000 years ago. As a result, the soils are silty to sandy topsoils, with scattered small to moderate rounded stones. The subsoil is semi-permeable cemented, at depths of 0.3–3 metres (1–10ft) and it holds water well.

Most grapes are not well adapted to the generally **cool climate** of the Puget Sound region. The earliest grape growing in the region favoured table grapes and Island Belle (Campbell Early), which are well suited to the wet and cool growing conditions of the Puget Sound, as the variety ripens early and is mildew-resistant. During Prohibition, Island Belle gained popularity for home winemaking, permissible under the law for personal use; Hoodsport Winery near Hood Canal (south of the islands) still produces Island Belle from fruit grown on Stretch Island, where Island Belle was so popular a century ago. As a wine grape, Island Belle tends to produce thin, acidic wines.

By the 1950s, the planting of vinifera (and hybrid vines) began. Varieties now growing in the region include Madeleine Angevine, Madeleine Sylvaner, Müller-Thurgau, Sieggerebe, Pinot Noir, Chardonnay, Pinot Gris, and Chasselas. Wines tend to be lower in alcohol, reflecting the difficulty of producing truly ripe grapes in this cool climate. In order to promote ripeness, plants are generally spaced closely together, with low yields to further maximize the possibility of ripening. Vines are trained low to be able to absorb the heat radiating from the ground. Fruit wines are still popular in this region too.

Production tends to be small at most Puget Sound wineries; with only 24 hectares (60 acres) of grapes planted in total, most of the appellation's wine is sold at the wineries themselves, with only limited distribution to the Seattle area.

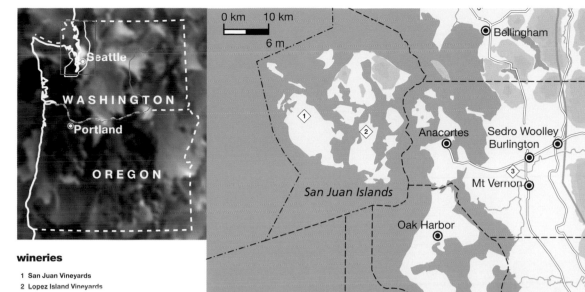

wineries

1 San Juan Vineyards
2 Lopez Island Vineyards
3 Pasek Cellars
4 Fairwinds
5 Sorensen
6 Camaraderie
7 Olympic
8 Lost Mountain
9 Greenbank
10 Whidbey Island Vineyards
11 Bainbridge Island
12 Rich Passage
13 Hoodsport
14 Andrew Will
15 Vashon Winery
16 Baron Manfred Vierthaler
18 McCrea Cellars
17 Andrake

key to map

	0 – 1000 ft 0 – 304 m
	1000 – 1500 ft 304 – 456 m
	1500 ft + 456 m +
	Approved Viticultural Area Boundary (Puget Sound).

*The black dashed
lines represent the
county borders.*

Bainbridge Island Vineyard and Winery owners Gerard and Jo Ann Bentryn proudly champion their appellation. They firmly believe in demonstrating responsible stewardship of the land. Their own 3.2 hectares (8 acres) of grapes are farmed sustainably, with the Bentryn family doing almost all of the work themselves. The family have also turned it into a very popular tourist destination.

A few of the island wineries follow the Washington "standard" and purchase additional grapes from those vineyards that lie east of the mountains. While not strictly "island" wineries, McCrea Cellars – a major quality player in Rhône-style wines – and Andrake Cellars – a high-quality red wine producer – both technically lie within the Puget Sound appellation; they aren't located close enough to Seattle to be grouped with those producers who, like McCrea and Andrake, source fruit from top eastern Washington vineyards. Instead, these two wineries are located near Olympia, in an area without many wineries.

Bob Andrake penned a wine column for the Olympia newspaper in the early 1990s and got hooked on the "why" and "how" questions of winemaking. He left his restaurant consulting business in 1996 to begin producing his own wines. He also gave up the wine column so there could be no conflict of interest.

His first two vintages were produced in his own home garage. Today, Andrake is no longer a "garagiste" as he now revels in the luxury of a newly built winery, designed as a modern gravity-fed operation. Andrake is exclusively interested in producing red wines – Merlot, Cabernet Sauvignon, Sangiovese, Malbec, Syrah, and a Bordeaux-blend reserve wine.

The cellar is Andrake's passion. Andrake sources grapes from top notch vineyards in eastern Washington – Ciel de Cheval and Artz on Red Mountain, Seven Hills, and Pepper Bridge in Walla Walla, as well as Alder Creek along the Columbia River – but he prefers leaves the farming entirely to the vineyard managers and, contrary to the trend these days, focuses exclusively on the cellar when crafting his wines.

Andrake tinkers with a different combination of yeasts and fermentation temperatures each vintage, attempting to build the colour, aromatics, and high glycerine content of his wines. Andrake has extremely strong opinions about winemaking, believing in the advantages of commercial yeasts and cold soaking the grapes to a particular colour he identifies, and then inoculating the must. He doesn't carry out post-fermentation maceration, or micro-oxygenation.

Andrake uses only free-run juice in his eponymous wines; the pressed wine is used in his second label "Hurricane Ridge". The focus manifests itself: Andrake wines are concentrated and packed with a trademark silky richness.

Doug McCrea arrived in the Washington wine world in the mid-1980s and only began to look seriously at wine when he encountered Alex Golitzen of Quilceda Creek. The first wine McCrea produced was a Chardonnay, in 1988. But Rhône varieties were always on his mind. In 1989 McCrea discovered Grenache in a vineyard in Dallesport, Oregon in the Columbia Valley (Grenache that wine grape researcher Dr Walter Clore had helped plant), and the vines were already twenty years old. The quality of the resultant wine was very high, but the vines froze in the record 1996 winter freeze, and never made a recovery.

In 1990, Doug McCrea came up with the idea of planting Syrah in a number of Yakima Valley vineyards, using cuttings from McDowell Winery in Sonoma, and Phelps Winery in Napa, in just the same way as David Lake MW and Mike Sauer had previously done at Red Willow Vineyard in the Yakima Valley. In 1994, McCrea made available its first big commercial release of Syrah, which received enormous critical acclaim (see page 141). McCrea also became the region's first producer of Viognier in 1997 – another Rhône variety.

What better symbol of warm summer than beautiful sunflowers?

In 1994, McCrea made its first big commercial release of Syrah, which received critical acclaim.

Notable producers

Andrake Cellars

☎ 360-943-3746 ☏ 360-493-0427
6315 Boston Harbor Road NE, Olympia,
Washington 98506
Production capacity 5,000 cases
2000 production 2,200 cases
Established 1996
First wines released 1997 vintage
Andrake sources fruit from some of the best
spots: a number of Red Mountain vineyards,
plus Champoux, Seven Hills, and Alder Ridge.

Bainbridge Island Vineyards & Winery

☎ 206-842-9463
✉ gbentryn@seanet.com
682 State Highway 305, Bainbridge
Island, Washington 98110
Acreage in production 0.4ha (1 acre) Pinot
Noir, 0.4ha (1 acre) Pinot Gris, 0.8ha (2 acres)
Madeleine Angevine, 1.2ha (3 acres) Müller-
Thurgau, 0.4ha (1 acre) Siegerrebe
Production capacity 2,000 cases
2000 production 2,000 cases
Established 1977
First wines released 1981 vintage
Gerard and JoAnn Bentryn make good quality,
fruity wines meant for earlier consumption.

Camaraderie Cellars

☎ 360-452-4964 F 360-452-2015
✉ corson4@tenforward.net
335 Benson Road, Port Angeles,
Washington 98362
Production capacity 1,500 cases
2000 production 1,300 cases
Established 1992
First wines released 1994 vintage
Olympic Peninsula-based producer, crafting
small quantities of very good Cabernet
Sauvignon and Sauvignon Blanc from well-
known vineyards in eastern Washington.

FairWinds Winery

☎ 360-385-6899
✉ cavett@waypt.com
1924 Hastings Avenue West, Port
Townsend, Washington 98368
Production capacity 5,000 cases
2000 production 975 cases
Established 1993
First wines released 1996 vintage
FairWinds wines – Cabernet Sauvignon,
Lemberger, Aligoté, Gewürztraminer, white
Lemberger, Merlot and a Port-style wine – can
be a bit rustic. By 2002, the winery will be
planting Madeleine Angevine and Sieggerrebe.

Greenbank Cellars, Ltd.

☎ 360-678-3964
✉ rayle@whidbey.com
ⓦ www.Whidbey.com/wine
3112 Day Road, Greenback,
Washington 98253
Acreage in production 1.2ha (3 acres) total
Müller-Thurgau, Siegerrebe, and Madeleine
Angevine
Production capacity 1500 cases
2000 production 500 cases
Established 1998
First wines released 1998 vintage
Itty bitty producer, making a number of
varietals: Sauvignon Blanc, dry Riesling,
Cabernet Franc, and Cabernet Sauvignon.

Hoodsport Winery, Inc

☎ 360-877-9894 ☏ 260-877-9508
✉ hoodsport@hctc.com
ⓦ www.hoodsport.com
N 23501 Highway 101, Hoodsport,
Washington 98548

Hoodsport II

☎ 253-396-9463 F 253-383-8080
1948 Pacific Avenue, Tacoma,
Washington 98402
Acreage in production 3 acres Island Belle
Production capacity 21,000 cases
2000 production 6,000 cases
Established 1978
First wines released 1980 vintage
This producer makes a wide range of good-
value wines that have a fruity style.

Lopez Island Vineyards

☎ 360-468-3644
✉ winery@lopezislandvineyards.com
ⓦ www.lopezislandvineyards.com
724 Fisherman Bay Road, Lopez Island,
Washington 98261
Acreage in production 1.2ha (3 acres)
Madeleine Angevine, 1.2ha (3 acres) Siegerrebe
Production capacity 1,500 cases
2000 production 1,200 cases
Established 1987
First wines released 1990 vintage
The grapes grown at this small, family-run
winery are all certified organic. Chardonnay,
Merlot, and Cabernet Sauvignon fruit come
from eastern Washington.

Lost Mountain Winery

☎ 360-683-5229 ☏ 360-683-7572
✉ wine@lostmountain.com
ⓦ www.lostmountain.com
3174 Lost Mountain Road, Sequim,
Washington 98382
Production capacity 2,000 cases
2000 production 1,200 cases
Established 1981
First wines released 1983 vintage
A family operation producing hearty, rustic
wines. Merlot, Cabernet Sauvignon, Cabernet
Franc, Syrah, and Madeleine Angevine grapes
are purchased mostly from eastern
Washington. Lost Mountain Red (table wine),
Lost Mountain White (dry Muscat), and
Zinfandel are made with California grapes.

McCrea Cellars

☎ 360-458-9463 F 360-458-8559
✉ dougmccrea@aol.com or
mccreawine@aol.com
13443 118th Avenue SE, Rainier,
Washington 98576
Production capacity 6,000 cases
2000 production 2,500 cases
Winery **established** in 1988
First wines released January 1990
Washington's first Rhône ranger, committed to
top-quality Syrah and other classic Rhône
varieties. Varietal character is excellent.

Olympic Cellars Winery

☎ 360-452-0160 F 360-452-3782
✉ wines@olympiccellars.com
🌐 www.olympiccellars.com
255410 Highway 101, Port Angeles,
Washington 98362
Acreage in production Less than 0.4ha (1
acre) – experimental only
Production capacity 7,000 cases
2000 production 5,400 cases
Established 1979
First wines released 1979 vintage
Produces a wide range of wines, with an
emphasis on white wines, from Riesling to
white Lemberger, and lighter styled reds.

San Juan Vineyards

☎ 360-378-9463 F 360-378-3411
✉ sjvineyards@rockisland.com
W www.sanjuanvineyards.com
3136 Roche Harbor Road, Friday
Harbor, Washington 98250
Acreage in production 1.6ha (4 acres)
Madeleine Angevine, 1.2ha (3 acres)
Siegerrebe, 0.8ha (2 acres) Pinot Noir
2000 production 3,500 cases
First wines released 1998 vintage
Winemaker Michael Carr was hired in 1999 and
has improved the quality of a number of white
varietals and Cabernet Sauvignon, made from
purchased grapes. The estate vineyards have
just begun to bear fruit.

Sorensen Cellars

☎ 360-379-6416 F 360-379-4907
✉ sorensenclrs@olympus.net
PO Box 2011, Port Townsend,
Washington 98368
Acreage in production None
Production capacity 3,000 cases
2000 production 1,200 cases
Established 1998
First wines released 1998 vintage
New small producer purchasing grapes from
premium eastern Washington vineyards.

Doug McCrea of McCrea Cellars

Vashon Winery

☎ 206-463-2990
✉ vashonwinery@yahoo.com
12629 SW Cemetery Road, Vashon
Island, Washington 98070
Production capacity 1,500 cases
2000 production 600 cases
Established 1984
First wines released 1987 vintage
Pleasant, well-made Merlot, Cabernet
Sauvignon, Chardonnay, a red blend, and a
crisp, pleasant Sémillon, all made with grapes
sourced from Yakima vineyards.

Whidbey Island Vineyards & Winery

☎ 360-221-2040
✉ winery@whidbeyisland.com
🌐 www.whidbeyislandwinery.com
5237 S. Langley Road, Langley,
Washington 98260
Acreage in production 0.8ha (2 acres)
Madeleine Sylvaner,0.8ha (2 acres) Madeleine
Angevine, 1.2ha (3 acres) Siegerrebe, 0.2ha (0.5
acres) Pinot Noir
Production capacity 4,000 cases
2000 production 2,500 cases
Established 1991
First wines released 1991 vintage
The vineyards were planted in 1986; most of
the estate vineyards produce slightly sweet
white wines. Most of its other wine is produced
from eastern Washington-grown grapes.

Yakima Valley

The **Yakima Valley** was Washington's first American Viticultural Area (AVA), and was formally designated as a winegrowing appellation in 1983; the name Yakima Valley has been used as a wine-region name, however, since the late 1960s. The Yakima Valley appellation is wholly contained within the larger Columbia Valley AVA, running along the Yakima River and stretching from the community of Yakima east almost to the river's confluence with the Columbia River at Tri-Cities, and measuring 97km (60 miles) east to west by 32km (20 miles) north to south.

Grapes (table, juice, and wine) have been grown in the region since the very early years of the 1900s, when irrigation transformed this desert-like valley into a **major agricultural oasis**. By 2001, Yakima Valley has developed into the fifth largest producer of fruits and vegetables in the United States. Crops besides grapes include apples, pears, cherries, peaches, corn, and asparagus, so abundantly planted that the Zillah-area wineries have called their wine touring circuit the "Zillah Fruit Loop."

The black dashed lines represent the county borders.

The Yakima Valley AVA also boasts the greatest concentration of vineyards and wineries in the state, with about 4,455 hectares (11,000 acres) of wine grapes (out of 12,150 hectares/30,000 acres in the state) and thirty of the state's 160 wineries located here. Most of the region's vineyards are planted north of the Yakima River, up the south slope of the Rattlesnake Hills that form the northern boundary of the appellation.

The soils are primarily composed of volcanic and alluvial sand with varying degrees of loess (wind-deposited fine clay and silt particles) content, all well-drained material atop a base of basalt rock. Vineyards in the AVA higher than 305 metres (1,000ft) can have a heavier, more clay-based soil, with less sand.

The **weather** in the Yakima Valley is usually a little cooler than its neighbouring viticultural areas, with temperatures −15 to −12°C (5 to 10°F) below those of the Columbia Basin. Generally, red grape varieties reach maturity easily, bringing dense colour, high tannins, and

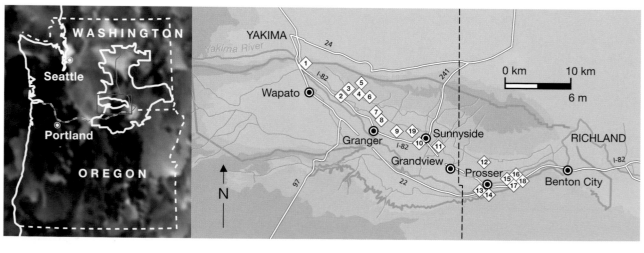

wineries

1 Sagelands
2 Bonair
3 Hyatt Vineyards
4 Covey Run
5 Wineglass
6 Portteus
7 Horizon's Edge
8 Eaton Hill
9 Tefft Cellars
10 Washington Hills Cellars (Apex and Bridgman)
11 Tucker
12 Pontin del Roza
13 Yakima River
14 Hinzerling
15 Hogue
16 Thurstonwolfe
17 Chinook
18 Kestrel
20 Paul Thomas

key to map

0 – 1500 ft
0 – 456 m

1500 – 2000 ft
456 – 608 m

2000 ft +
608 m +

Approved Viticultural Area Boundary (Yakima Valley).

black fruit flavours to the wines. Nights cool significantly, enough to create the firm acidity which characterizes Washington wines. And of course, winter temperatures can dip dangerously low for the survival of the more tender varieties of vines such as Grenache, and even occasionally Merlot, which was severely damaged in the freeze of 1996.

Hinzerling Vineyards – now known as Hinzerling Winery since it sold its vineyards (first planted in 1972) to Kestrel Winery in 1989 – was established here in 1976. The only other **producers** in the state at that time were Chateau Ste Michelle, Associated Vintners, Preston Premium Wines, Salishan Vineyards, and two or three other small wineries that no longer exist. Many of the currently most significant vineyards in the Yakima Valley were planted around the same time.

In Associated Vintners' (AV) early years, the winery developed relationships with growers in the Yakima Valley, and still maintains those relationships. AV is now called Columbia Winery, and winemaker David Lake MW has been working in collaboration with a number of Yakima area vineyards since his affiliation with AV/Columbia in 1979, designating them on Columbia's reserve-level bottle labels.

The 30-hectare (75-acre) Otis Vineyard, one of the oldest in the region, is located just north of Grandview and is still producing high-quality grapes for Columbia. The vineyard contains Cabernet Sauvignon planted in 1957, with other plantings from 1970 to 1997. The oldest Cabernet Sauvignon vineyard is spaced 3 x 3 metres (10 x 10ft); more recent plantings are narrower and more tightly spaced at 1.8 x 2.7 metres (6 x 9ft) or even 1.2 x 2.7 metres (4 x 9ft). The trellising varies – there is a preponderance of fanned, multiple-trunk vines, but there is also double or single cordon trellising that requires leaf-stripping and hedging. Otis is a late ripening vineyard, with harvest for Cabernet Sauvignon often delayed until the end of October or early November. Columbia controls most of its fruit, and crops it at 42–63 hectolitres per hectare (3–4.5 tons per 1 acre) for Cabernet and the Dijon clones of

Chardonnay, with slightly higher yields for its Merlot, Pinot Gris, and non-Dijon Chardonnay.

Columbia's most significant **grape supplier** is Mike Sauer's Red Willow Vineyard near Wapato, in a far western and warmer corner of the Yakima Valley. Mike Sauer oversees the 891-hectare (2,200 acre) Latham Creek Ranch belonging to his wife's family. Most of the farm is planted with wheat and alfalfa, with about 71 hectares (175 acres) of grapes: 30.4 hectares (75 acres) of Concord, and about 41 hectares (100 acres) of wine grapes at Red Willow Vineyard. Wine grapes have become Sauer's passion since he planted his first vineyard on the farm in 1973 at the request of Washington-State-College research horticulturist Dr Walter Clore. Sauer's first vines came from Harrison

Columbia's most significant grape supplier is Mike Sauer's Red Willow Vineyard near Wapato, in a far western ... corner of the Yakima Valley.

The rise of Syrah

In the mid-1990s, you could count on one hand the number of Syrahs produced in Washington. By the turn of the century, Syrah was being made by a majority of the state's most respected producers, as well as by a few "new kids" passionately committed to the grape.

The move to Syrah in Washington was initiated in 1984 by David Lake MW of Columbia Winery and Mike Sauer, owner of Red Willow Vineyard. Columbia's first Syrah varietal was made in 1988. By 1994, McCrea Cellars had its initial large commercial release of Syrah, which received terrific scores and a great response. That year, McCrea talked Jim Holmes, the owner of Ciel de Cheval Vineyard on Red Mountain, and Dick Boushey of the eponymous vineyard in the Yakima Valley into planting Syrah. By 1994, Columbia Crest had produced its first Syrah from grapes planted in 1992. And by 1993, Berle "Rusty" Figgins, then vineyard manager at Pepper Bridge vineyards in Walla Walla, convinced owner Norm McKibben to plant one block of Syrah.

The watershed year for Syrah was 1996, the year of the big freeze. Syrah survived the harshest winter in years where other varieties didn't. Since then, Syrah plantings have taken off to almost 1,013 hectares (2,500 acres) by 2001. Rusty Figgins developed his own label, Glen Fiona, and his Syrahs are real beauties. Cayuse Vineyards' lovely Syrah debuted in 1997. (Both are from Walla Walla.)

There is a bright future for Syrah. The vines survive the winter well and produce a good crop. Washington has had to learn how to grow it; it needs both water and canopy management. Coming on the market soon are Washington Syrahs priced in the $11–14 range, as well as a number of top-end bottlings such as DeLille's rich Doyenne. Syrah could be the future for Washington. The quality is there, and the prices are good. These wines could give the state a better defined identity and status all of its own.

Red Willow Vineyard's chapel sits at the crest of the hill, in obvious homage to the La Chappelle Hermitage vineyard in the northern Rhône valley.

Hill, from cuttings from the first block planted in 1963 by Associated Vintners (at pioneer W B Bridgman's vineyard).

That first **Red Willow Vineyard** was planted on a gravely south-facing hillside that warms up easily and retains the heat. Red Willow didn't gain fame until Lloyd Woodburne of AV discovered it and arranged to buy all the fruit from its first commercial harvest in 1978. David Lake MW entered the scene in 1979; from that point the growth and increasing success of Red Willow and Columbia Winery have been parallel, and in very many ways intertwined.

There has been a gradual evolution of the Red Willow Vineyard, with many small blocks now planted on differing *terroirs*. Today, Columbia separately vinifies and ages five Cabernet Sauvignon, five Merlot, three Cabernet Franc, eight Syrah, three Sangiovese, and two Viognier slopes.

Red Willow is widely spaced, declining from the original 3 x 3 metres (10 x 10ft grid) to 1.8 x 2.7 metres (6 x 9ft) spacing in the 1990s. Trellising is mostly bilateral cordon managed to permit light and air penetration. A five-year exploration of Smart-Dyson training on Merlot, Syrah, Cabernet Sauvignon, and Cabernet Franc has given mixed results. It did well in cool years, such as 1997 or 2000, but it allowed too much light penetration in hot years, such as 1998.

Red Willow soil is complex because much of it is above 335 metres (1,100ft). On the south and west slopes, the soil is sandy loam with volcanic ash and pumice, including some gravel bars from an oldbed ancient the Columbia River. Clay and heavier soils are found on the eastern slopes. Most of Red Willow's vineyards lie on far steeper slopes (up to 35 per cent slope) than other Yakima Valley vineyards. This, in conjunction with dropping un-coloured fruit at *veraison* and

relatively modest yields (between 28–70 hectolitres per hectare/2–5 tons per acre), depending on the variety; smaller yields of Merlot and Cabernet Franc usually give too much tannin content.

The climate at Red Willow is fairly warm, 1,510–1,593 degree days Centigrade (2,750–2,900 Fahrenheit) versus Prosser in the cool mid-valley region, which averages 1,304 degree days Centigrade (2,380 Fahrenheit). Eastern and southern slopes usually ripen earlier than western slopes, as the latter become too warm in the afternoon sun for optimal ripening conditions.

Columbia takes 90 per cent of Red Willow's fruit, selling limited quantities to other wineries: the Nebbiolo goes to Cavatappi, Lemberger to Hogue, and a small quantity of Sangiovese to Facelli. Modest quantities of Bordeaux red varieties go to Sagelands. With the exception of Cavatappi, Columbia has sole rights to use the Red Willow name on its labels. Other older vineyards of note include W B Bridgman's early vineyards that were first planted 1914–1918, and are now owned by the Newhouse family. These are the Upland Vineyard – now the Upland Farms – on Snipes Mountain near Sunnyside, and Harrison Hill in Sunnyside, replanted and owned by Columbia in 1963, and later sold to the Newhouses. Upland's fruit mostly goes to Chateau Ste Michelle, while Harrison Hill Vineyard is now a 2 hectare (5 acre) site of premier Cabernet Sauvignon, Merlot, and Cabernet Franc fruit farmed exclusively for DeLille Cellars.

Other modern vineyards of importance include Boushey Farms near Grandview, owned and farmed by Dick Boushey who works closely with each of the wineries for whom he grows fruit. He planted his vineyard twenty years ago; today, Boushey

Other ... vineyards of note include W B Bridgman's early vineyards that were first planted 1914–1918, and are now owned by the Newhouse family.

Farms possesses 10 hectares (25 acres) bearing Cabernet Sauvignon, Cabernet Franc, and Merlot, and another with 5.7 hectares (14 acres) of Syrah and 2.8 hectares (7 acres) of Sangiovese. The best sites within the vineyard – like other top Yakima-area vineyards – offer south-facing slopes; the slopes help boost heat by reflecting warmth in the spring and autumn, and by draining cold air when frost might be a problem on the valley floor.

Chinook Winery in Prosser purchases grapes from three different Boushey locations: half of Chinook's total needs for Cabernet Franc and Cabernet Sauvignon come from one site, while two other Boushey vineyards supply Merlot. Doug McCrea of McCrea Cellars worked with Dick Boushey to select a 1.6-hectare (4-acre) parcel at Boushey Farms to plant Syrah. The vines are trellised in an experimental combination: 1.2 hectares (3 acres) planted 1.8 x 2.7 metres (6 x 9ft) and trained in Vertical Shoot Positioning and 0.4 of a hectare (1 acre) spaced at 1.2 x 2.7 metres (4 x 9ft) and trained in a Scott Henry trellis to help control Syrah's tendency for aggressive growth.

While Chinook produces a range of well-balanced wines, it is its Cabernet Franc that calls out for attention: an aromatic Chinon-like wine.

Another young vineyard to follow is Snipes Canyon Vineyard, owned and operated by Keith Klingele, who purchased the ranch in 1990 from former Washington State Senator, Max Benitz, who had planted some of the vineyards in the late 1970s and early 1980s. With a total of 111 plantable hectares (275 acres), vineyards account for approximately half of the Snipes Canyon agriculture, with apples, pears, and cherries being the other fruit crops.

Elevations are significant at Snipes Canyon, all in the range of 274 metres (900ft) to over 305 metres (1,000ft), with steep, south-facing vineyards. The Malbec and Cabernet Sauvignon grown here show great depth.

Other vineyard names to recognize in the Yakima Valley are Elerding Vineyard and DuBrul Vineyard, each of which grows high-quality fruit for a large number of wineries, and are usually vineyard-designated on labels.

The winery that once anchored the Yakima Valley is **Chateau Ste Michelle** (CSM), whose facility at Grandview was previously used to produce the brand's red wines. CSM red wines are now produced at the River Ridge Winery at Canoe Ridge, south of the Yakima Valley near the Columbia River. Today, the Grandview facility makes wines destined for Columbia Crest. While CSM is Washington's largest producer, it has no production in the Yakima Valley, nor any vineyards. However, it does purchase fruit from a few high-quality growers here, including Bill denHoed's Rattlesnake Acres and Steve Newhouse's Upland Farms. CSM vineyards – that include what it owns as well as purchases – lie outside the appellation in the Columbia Valley, both north and south of the Yakima Valley.

Former CSM enologist and winemaker Kay Simon left her position at Ste Michelle in 1983 to open Chinook Wines in Prosser with her partner (now husband) Clay Mackey. Simon handles winemaking and Mackey oversees the viticulture, having developed a successful career as a vineyard manager in the Napa Valley.

While Chinook produces a range of well-balanced wines, it is its Cabernet Franc that calls out for attention: an aromatic Chinon-like wine with bright, ripe fruit and minimal oak presence. Chinook has become a leader with the varietal, showing off its strength as an independent wine in contrast to Cabernet Franc's more usual role in Washington as part of a blend.

At Chinook Simon and Mackey handle everything themselves from the selection and monitoring of the grapes they purchase to staffing the tasting room and distributing their wine. In contrast, its neighbour **Hogue Cellars** seems particularly large. Since the 1950s, the Hogue family has been growing apples, hops, mint, and other crops in eastern Washington's Columbia and Yakima Valleys. Mike Hogue planted the family's first wine grapes in 1974, and by 1982 he and his brother Gary were producing their own wine. Annual production – under the able direction of Dr Wade Wolfe – has now grown to almost half a million cases. While a large commercial operation, the Hogue name has come to represent quality and value.

The Hogue family farms almost 162 hectares (400 acres) of grapes in the Columbia Valley. Most of the vinyards are planted with white wine varieties, though more red acreage has been planted in the last ten years than white, reflecting the general trend in the Yakima Valley. Most red varieties are planted on sites with above-average heat during the growing season and mild winter temperatures to avoid winter damage, while most white varieties are planted in cooler areas to retain firm acidity.

Hogue's vineyard yields tend to be high, not surprisingly for such a commercial winery: approximately 56 hectolitres per hectare (4 tons per acre) for red varietals and approximately 84 hectolitres per hectare (6 tons per acre) for whites. Its vineyards are planted with 1,730–1,980 vines per hectare (700–800 vines per acre) on average.

Washington Hills in Sunnyside is one of the Valley's larger wineries, producing 65,000 cases of wine annually under three separate brands: basic Washington Hills, select Bridgman (named in honour of W B Bridgman) and Apex, its ultra-premium label. The winery is a partnership between Seattle-area former retailer and distributor Harry Alhadeff and noted winemaker Brain Carter.

At 396 metres (1,300ft), Washington Hills' Outlook Vineyard – its primary grape supply – is one of Washington's highest vineyards, with good protection from winter cold injury. In freezes, valley floors usually suffer the most. Soils are well-drained and quite shallow, without a great deal of water-holding capacity, which allows the winery to control vigour by limiting water application.

Yields vary from year to year and from variety to variety, but 56–70 tons per hectare (4–5 tons per acre) is typical here as in many other large operations. Riesling does well at the higher end of this range but Cabernet Sauvignon usually comes in at or below 56 hectolitres (4 tons) in most years. Carter is still experimenting with some varieties to

determine the ideal cropping level: in 2000, he cropped one Syrah block at 84 hectolitres (6 tons) and one at 24 hectarolitres per hectare (2 tons per acre). The latter block produced a rich, concentrated wine, destined for the Apex label.

Washington Hills' Outlook Vineyard supplies about 30 per cent of its grapes for all three brands. Most of the rest is purchased from other growers. The winery has learned that generally yields of 28–42 hectolitres per hectare (2–3 tons per acre) on low vigour vines at a good site can be rewarding. For this type of yield to be economically viable for a contracted grower, per acre contracts are becoming much more common than tonnage contracts, and so has become the trend for Washington Hills and others in the Yakima Valley.

Beware the driverless tractor...

Notable producers

Apex Cellars

☎ 425-889-9463 ☏ 425-889-4581
✉ info@washingtonhills.com
🌐 www.Washingtonhills.com
111 E Lincoln Avenue, Sunnyside,
Washington 98944
Acreage in production 4.5ha (11 acres)
total Merlot, Chardonnay, Gewürztraminer,
Cabernet Sauvignon, and Syrah
Production capacity 90,000 cases (three
related wineries)
2000 production 6,000 cases
Established 1988
First wines released 1988 vintage
The ultra-premium brand of Washington Hills
Cellar; talented winemaker Brian Carter's best
wine. Only made when the quality of grapes is
exceptional.

Bonair Winery

☎ 509-829-6027 ☏ 509-829-6410
✉ winemaker@bonairwine.com
🌐 www.bonairwine.com
500 S Bonair Road, Zillah, Washington
98953
Acreage in production 1ha (2.5 acres)
Chardonnay, 0.2ha (0.5 acres) Cabernet
Sauvignon
New plantings 1.2ha (3 acres) Cabernet
Sauvignon, 1.2ha (3 acres) combined Touriga
Nacional/Tinta Cao/Tinta Madeira, 0.2ha (5
acres) White Riesling, 1.2ha (3 acres) Cabernet
Franc, 1.2ha (3 acres) Merlot
Production capacity 10,000 cases
2000 production 5,000 cases
Established 1985
First wines released 1985 vintage
A producer of a range of styles and wines, from
dry varietals to fruity meads. A frequent local
fair competition entrant, and medal winner.

Bridgman Cellars

☎ 425-889-9463 ☏ 425-889-4581
✉ info@washingtonhills.com
🌐 www.Washingtonhills.com
111 E Lincoln Avenue, Sunnyside,
Washington 98944
Acreage in production 6.9ha (17 acres)
total Merlot, Chardonnay, Viognier, Cabernet
Sauvignon, and Syrah
Production capacity 90,000 cases
2000 production 10,000 cases
Established 1988
First wines released 1993 vintage
The mid-level of Washington Hills' three
brands, this one with more oak influence than
the basic *cuvées*, and presenting a varietal
range that includes Syrah and a good Viognier.
Not as concentrated or complex wines as
Apex, but very pleasant and good value.

Chinook Wines

☎ 509-786-2725 ☏ 509-786-2777
PO Box 387, Corner of Wittkopf Loop &
Wine Country Road, Prosser,
Washington 99350
Acreage in production 0.8ha (2 acres)
Cabernet Franc
Production capacity 3,000 cases
2000 production 3,000
Established 1985
First wines released 1983 vintage
One of the Yakima Valley's top producers, with
a real commitment to a personal approach. The
fruity Cabernet Franc is well-executed example
and the Merlot and a lovely crisp Sémillon are
also worth seeking out.

Brian Carter of Washington Hills Cellars, Apex Cellars, and Bridgman Cellars

Covey Run Vintners

☎ 509-829-6235 ☏ 509-829-6895

✉ coveyrun@corusbrands.com

W www.coveyrun.com

1500 Vintage Road, Zillah, Washington 98953

Acreage in production 179ha (194 acres) Chardonnay, 26.3ha (65 acres) Fumé Blanc, 2.8ha (74 acres) Riesling, 8ha (20 acres) Gewürztraminer, 6ha (15 acres) Semillon, 6ha (15 acres) Chenin Blanc, 2.8ha (7 acres) Morio-Muskat, 40ha (100 acres) Merlot, 39.3ha (97 acres) Cabernet Sauvignon, 1.6ha (4 acres) Syrah, 7.3ha (18 acres) Lemberger

Production capacity 330,000 cases

2000 production 220,000 cases

Established 1982

First wines released 1982 vintage

A part of the former Corus Brands (Columbia Winery's parent company). Now, like Columbia, owned by Canandaigua Wines, this brand makes value-priced, quality wines, always good examples of the grape variety.

Eaton Hill Winery

☎ 509-854-2220 ☏ 509-854-2508

530 Gurley Road, Granger, Washington 98932

Acreage in production Less than 0.4ha (1 acre) Cabernet Sauvignon

Production capacity 2,100 cases

2000 production 1,900 cases

Established 1988

First wines released 1989 vintage

This former fruit and vegetable cannery still grows pears, apples and cherries, and crafts a few fruit-blended wines as well as other – not particularly well-focused – varietal wines.

Hinzerling Winery

☎ 509-786-2163 ☏ 509-786-2163

✉ info@hinzerling.com

W www.Hinzerling.com

1520 Sheridan Avenue, Prosser, Washington 99350

2000 production 1,000 cases

Established 1976

First wines released 1976 vintage

Hinzerling wines were made with fruit from its own vineyards (planted in 1972) until 1989, when the winery changed hands and the vineyards were sold to Kestrel. Original owner Mike Wallace and his family regained control of

the winery in 1990. Wines produced from purchased grapes include a long list of varietals, all well made but lacking finesse.

Hogue Cellars

☎ 509-786-4557 ☏ 509-786-1166

✉ info@hogue-cellars.com

W www.hoguecellars.com

2800 Lee Road, Prosser, Washington 99350

Acreage in production 40ha (100 acres) Merlot, 52.7ha (130 acres) Chardonnay, 28.4 (70 acres) Riesling, 26.3ha (65 acres) Cabernet Sauvignon, 5ha (12 acres) Sauvignon Blanc, 4ha (10 acres) Syrah

Production capacity 500,000 cases

2000 production 450,000 cases

Winery established 1982

First wines released 1982 vintage

The Hogue family are longtime Columbia Valley farmers who first planted grapes in 1974. One of the largest producers in Washington, with a well-deserved reputation for quality and value pricing. The other Hogue farm products (pickled green beans and asparagus in particular) are well-known and delicious.

Hyatt Vineyards

☎ 509-829-6333 ☏ 509-829-6433

✉ hyattvineyards@nwinfo.com

W www.hyattvineyards.com

2020 Gilbert Road, Zillah, Washington 98953

Acreage in production 48.6ha (120 acres) total Cabernet Sauvignon, Merlot, Syrah, Riesling, Cabernet Franc, and Chardonnay

New plantings 1.2ha (3 acres) Sémillon

Production capacity 30,000 cases

2000 production 28,000 cases

Established 1983

First wines released 1987 vintage

Hyatt has always made solid, good-value wines; a number of Yakima Valley's best-known winemakers started their careers here.

Kestrel Vintners

☎ 509-786-2675 or 888-343-2675

☏ 509-786-2679

✉ kestrelwines@quicktel.com

W www.kestrelwines.com

2890 Lee Road, Prosser, Washington 99350

Acreage in production 4ha (10 acre) Syrah, 4ha (10 acres) Chardonnay, 8.6ha (21 acres) Cabernet Sauvignon, 8ha (20 acres) Merlot, 0.8ha (2 acres) Malbec, 2.8ha (7 acres) Pinot Gris, 2.8ha (7 acres) Viognier, 2.4ha (6 acres) Cabernet Franc

New plantings 2.8ha (7 acres) Merlot, 4ha (10 acres) Chardonnay, 2.8ha (7 acres) Sangiovese, 2.4ha (6 acres) Syrah, 4ha (10 acres) Cabernet Sauvignon

Production capacity 12,000 cases

2000 production 10,000 cases

Established 1995

First wines released 1995 vintage

Ray Sandidge, a former Hyatt winemaker, creates well-focused, elegant smooth wines.

Paul Thomas Winery

☎ 509-837-5605 ☏ 509-837-5612

✉ paulthomas@corusbrands.com

W www.paulthomaswinery.com

2310 Holmason Road, Sunnyside, Washington 998944

Acreage in production 20.3 ha (50 acres) Chardonnay, 13ha (32 acres) Riesling, 11ha (27 acres) Merlot, 11ha (27 acres) Cabernet Sauvignon

Production capacity 77,000 cases

2000 production 60,000

Established 1979

First wines released 1979 vintage

Owned by Columbia Winery's parent company, now Canandaigua Brands, the winery was constructed in 1995 on the site of the original Phil Church (Associated Vintners) vineyard. A very good value brand for bright, lighter styled varietal wines, as well as fruit wines.

Pheasant Canyon Vineyards

☎ 509-829-5753 📠 509-829-5753
📧 crsandidgewines@hotmail.com
🌐 www.crsandidgewines.com
**2890 Lee Road, Prosser,
Washington 99350**
Production capacity 2,000 cases
2000 production 1,200 cases
Established 2000
First wines released 2000 vintage
A second, premium brand produced by Ray
Sandidge at his Kestrel Winery.

Pontin del Roza

☎ 509-786-4449 📠 509-786-4449
📧 pontindelroza@aol.com
**35502 Hinzerling Road, Prosser,
Washington 99350**
Acreage in production 5.3ha (13 acres)
Merlot, 5.1ha (12.5 acres) Cabernet Sauvignon,
3.6ha (9 acres) White Riesling, 1.6ha (4 acres)
Pinot Gris, 1.4ha (3.5 acres) Sangiovese
New plantings 2ha (5 acres) Syrah, 1ha (2.5
acres) Dolcetto, 1ha (2.5 acres) Malbec
Production capacity 4,500 cases
2000 production 3,000 cases
Established 1984

First wines released 1984 vintage
Commercial quality wines made from grapes
grown only from "the Roza", an area of south-
facing slopes along the north side of the
Yakima Valley.

Kay Simon of Chinook Wines

Portteus Vineyards

☎ 509-829-6970 ℻ 509-829-5683

✉ port4you@aol.com

5201 Highland Drive, Zillah,
Washington 98953

Acreage in production 8.6ha (21 acres)
Cabernet Sauvignon, 4.5ha (11 acres) Merlot,
2ha (5 acres) Syrah, 0.5ha (1.3 acres)
Chardonnay, 1.2ha (3 acres) Zinfandel, 0.4ha (1
acre) Cabernet Franc.

New plantings 0.4ha (1 acre) Malbec, 0.5ha
(1.2 acres) Sangiovese, 1.2ha (3 acres) Petite
Sirah, 1.2ha (3 acres) Cabernet Franc

Production capacity 4,300 cases

2000 production 3,500 cases

Established 1981

First wines released 1986 vintage
Solid producer of good quality wines,
especially Zinfandel and Cabernet Sauvignon.
Sadly, Portteus' first vintages (1984 and 1985)
were lost in a fire.

Sagelands Vineyard

☎ 509-877-2112 ℻ 509-877-3377

✉ redwine@sagelandsvineyard.com

71 Gangl Road, Wapato,
Washington 9895

Acreage in production 41ha (101 acres)
Merlot, 38.5ha (95 acres) Cabernet Sauvignon,
4ha (10 acres) Chardonnay, 3.2ha (8 acres)
Cabernet Franc, 2.4ha (6 acres) Sémillon, 2ha
(5 acres) Malbec

Production capacity 35,000 cases

2000 production 25,000 cases

Established 1985

First Sageland wines released 2000 vintage
Formerly known as Staton Hills Winery, the
Chalone Group of California – which also owns
Canoe Ridge Vineyard Winery in Walla Walla –
purchased this property in 2000. Red wines are
the focus, with Cabernet Sauvignon and Merlot
showing particularly well.

Tefft Cellars Winery

☎ 509-837-7651 ℻ 509-839-7337

✉ info@tefftcellars.com

🌐 www.tefftcellars.com

1320 Independence Road, Outlook,
Washington 98938

Acreage in production 4ha (10 acres) total
Sangiovese, Syrah, Nebbiolo, Viognier,
Cabernet Sauvignon

Production capacity 21,000 cases

2000 production 19, 600 cases

First wines released 1989 vintage
Well-made wines, with a few unusual offerings,
including a sparkling Cabernet Sauvignon and
a sweet Nebbiolo.

Tucker Cellars Winery

☎ 509-837-8701 ℻ 509-837-8701

✉ wineman@televar.com

🌐 www.tuckercellars.com

70 Ray Road, Sunnyside,
Washington 98944

Acreage in production 2.8 (7 acres)
Cabernet Sauvignon, 2.8ha (7 acres) Merlot,
2.4ha (6 acres) Chardonnay, 1.6ha (4 acres)
Muscat Canelli, 0.8ha (2 acres) Chenin Blanc,
3.2ha (8 acres) Riesling, 3.2ha (8 acres)
Gewürztraminer, 3.2ha (8 acres) Pinot Noir, 4ha
(10 acres) other varieties

Production capacity 12,500 cases

2000 production 8,300 cases

Established 1981

First wines released 1981 vintage
Well established fruit and produce growers,
crafting solid wines.

Washington Hills Cellars

☎ 425-889-9463 ℻ 425-889-4581

✉ info@washingtonhills.com

🌐 www.washingtonhills.com

111 E Lincoln Avenue, Sunnyside,
Washington 98944

Acreage in production 44.6ha (110 acres)
total Merlot, Chardonnay, Sémillon, Cabernet
Sauvignon, Riesling, Gewürztraminer, Syrah,
and Viognier

Production capacity 90,000 cases

2000 production 65,000 cases

Established 1988

First wines released 1988 vintage
Sibling label to Apex and Bridgman, this one
representing the most commercial wines. Good
value wine, and very well made.

Wineglass Cellars

☎ 509-829-3011 ℻ 509-829-6666

✉ wgcllrs@attglobal.net

🌐 www.wineglasscellars.com

260 N Bonair Road, Zillah, Washington
98953

Production capacity 5,000 cases

2000 production 3,500 cases

Established 1994

First wines released 1994 vintage
Well-crafted, nicely structured wines –
Chardonnay, Merlot, Cabernet Sauvignon, and
Zinfandel – made from fruit purchased from
local vineyards.

Yakima River Winery

☎ 509-786-2805 ℻ 509-786-3203

✉ redwine@yakimariverwinery.com

🌐 www.yakimariverwinery.com

143302 W North River Road, Prosser,
Washington 99350

Acreage in production 1ha (2.5 acres) Petit
Verdot

Production capacity 38,130 cases

2000 production 6,000 cases

Established 1978

First wines released 1979 vintage
Most wines here – all red, with grapes
purchased from local vineyards – are fruity and
bright, except for the reserve Cabernet
Sauvignon and Merlot wines, which age in
French barrels for 36 months.

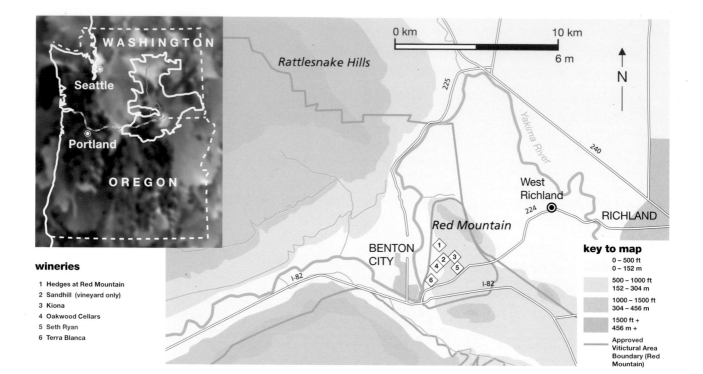

wineries

1 Hedges at Red Mountain
2 Sandhill (vineyard only)
3 Kiona
4 Oakwood Cellars
5 Seth Ryan
6 Terra Blanca

Red Mountain

Red Mountain – Washington's (and the Pacific Northwest's) newest appellation – is located just north of the community of Benton City. Wholly enclosed within the larger Yakima Valley appellation, Red Mountain sits on a southwest-facing slope east of the Yakima River, where the river turns from its east–west path to arch north before joining the Columbia River near the Tri-Cities of Richland, Pasco, and Kennewick.

The name Red Mountain can be misleading: the soil – unlike the Red Hills of Dundee in Oregon – bears no red hue. The name instead refers to a native grass that sports a red blossom each spring, tinting the hillside a scarlet colour for a few months of the year. "Mountain" may also be a slight misstatement; elevations on Red Mountain range from 152–457 metres (500–1,500ft), very well sloped and broad, more a plateau than a mountain. In the flatter Yakima Valley, however, this singular rise of the terrain stands out.

The nearby Yakima River helps moderate any temperature extremes, but even so, Red Mountain is the warmest sub-region of the Yakima Valley, with temperatures as much as 4.5–5.5°C (8–10°F) higher than those at in western Yakima Valley. On Red Mountain itself, temperatures can vary by 1°C (3–4°F), top to bottom. Ripening is never an issue; most vineyards struggle to keep alcohol levels under 14 per cent, certainly not the typical concern in other Washington growing regions.

In the mountains to the north of Red Mountain, there is a gap that allows cooler air to flow down from Canada. Red Mountain heats up early in the day, but cools off each evening as the wind picks up and the cooler air descends, creating a contrast between very warm daytime temperatures and significantly cooler night-time levels, allowing good natural acidity to develop. Rainfall, like most of Yakima Valley, reaches only 15cm (6in) per year, and irrigation is necessary.

The **soils** on Red Mountain are all high pH. They tend to be light sandy loam, windblown earth atop ancient lake bedrock, with calcareous patches and differing levels of particle matter, as well as streaks of volcanic ash. Topsoils vary in depth (and they can be up to 6 metres/20ft deep), studded with various rock outcroppings, which tend to reduce yields and produce more interesting, concentrated berries. The soils lack most nutrients, and water; vigour in a vine is controlled by fertilization, irrigation, and canopy management.

Red Mountain covers 1,360 hectares (3,400 acres): only 280 hectares (700 acres) of vineyards are established now, but 400 more hectares (1,000 more acres) of plantable land exists. The major grape varieties planted include Cabernet Sauvignon, Merlot, and Cabernet Franc as well as smaller amounts of Syrah, Sangiovese, Lemberger, Sémillon, and Sauvignon Blanc.

While there are a handful of wineries in the appellation – Hedges Cellars (which spearheaded the AVA designation process), Blackwood Canyon, Kiona Vineyards Winery, Oakwood Cellars, Seth Ryan Winery, Taptiel Winery, and Terra Blanca Vintners – it is the vineyards that have given Red Mountain its reputation as the premier winegrowing region in Washington, bearing firmly structured, ripe, lush fruit, with Merlot at times masquerading as Cabernet Sauvignon, wearing the same big tannins and full-bodied persona.

Jim Holmes and John Williams together were Red Mountain's Christopher Columbus, jointly purchasing 32 hectares (80 acres) in 1972. But Red Mountain then did not resemble the verdant Red Mountain of today; instead, it looked like the frontier, with few roads, fewer people, and dusty sagebrush. But the chalky soil intrigued Holmes. In 1975, the first 4 hectares (10 acres) of grapes were planted on what would become Kiona Vineyards, the joint Williams/Holmes venture; they planted one-third each of Riesling, Cabernet Sauvignon, and Chardonnay.

Holmes and other partners purchased another 32 hectares (80 acres) soon after. Holmes and Williams ultimately parted company in 1994. The Williams family kept the original Kiona Vineyards and the winery; Holmes got the bulk of the other vineyard land that has now become one of the premier vineyards in Washington, **Ciel de Cheval** (a Frenchified homage to the Horse Heaven Hills to the south of Red Mountain).

Holmes now controls 64 hectares (160 acres), the largest vineyard on Red Mountain. The soils here are shallower than most other areas of the appellation, 0.6 metres (2ft) of soil over cobbled river rock. The first two plantings of Ciel – in 1975 and 1982 – were spaced at 2 x 3 metres (7 x 10ft) and trained in classic double Guyot trellising, vertical shoot positioning. In 1994, Homes added the most recent 12 hectares (30 acres) of vines (Syrah, Viognier, Sangiovese, Cabernet Franc, and Merlot), and chose instead to train the vines on a fan system, a more open framework of growth without a single horizontal fruiting zone, and with better sun exposure for the fruit. With this system, it is harder to train the plant, and more expensive. But Holmes is convinced that the resulting fruit quality is better, fuller-bodied wine, with richer flavour and complexity.

Yields for Ciel vary according to the purchasing producer's economic and stylistic goals, from as

Scott Williams of Kiona Vineyards Winery.

Yes, there really is a Red Mountain (well, hills) seen here behind the Hedges' vineyard and production facility.

low as 28 hectolitres per hectare (2 tons per acre) to the more standard 56–70 hectolitres per hectare (4–5 tons per acre). The Merlot on Red Mountain is able to handle the higher crop loads; if the crop loads are much lower, the tannins become too aggressive, as Red Mountain Merlot in general tends to be bigger and more muscular than Merlot grown anywhere else in Washington. Ciel may be a particularly fine vineyard, much sought after by Washington's top

wineries, but Klipsun is no less important or in demand.

Just north of Red Mountain lies the Hanford Site (the US Department of Energy nuclear facility, where essential components for World War II's Manhattan Project were assembled). Materials scientist Dave Gelles and his British-born wife Tricia joined a wine tasting group with Jim Holmes and John Williams and spent time working in the vineyard with them. By

purchase was as close to Kiona's vineyard as they could get. André Tchelistcheff had selected Kiona Cabernet Sauvignon as the best Cabernet Sauvignon in Washington for his nephew, Alex Golitzin, to use for the Quilceda Creek wines.

The vineyard they purchased was named **Klipsun,** a Chinook Indian term for the end of day. It was essentially flat land, desirable to the Gelleses because they thought that the flatness could more effectively ward off frost and be farmed more easily. They weren't necessarily right, as the 1996 winter freeze caused considerable damage. Wind machines now keep air circulating throughout the vineyard to prevent frost. In fact, most vineyards on Red Mountain sport wind machines; Jim Holmes says that each time he plants a vineyard, he plants a wind machine, as well.

Wind machines now keep air circulating throughout the vineyard to prevent frost. In fact, most vineyards on Red Mountain sport wind machines.

The Gelleses planted varieties they liked to drink, just in case no one wanted the grapes and they had make wine for home consumption: Cabernet Sauvignon, Chardonnay, Sauvignon Blanc, Sémillon, and Nebbiolo. But the Klipsun fruit was popular from the very beginning. Merlot was planted at Klipsun in 1991, and today the vineyard contains around 48 hectares (120 acres). Vines are planted at 1,137 per hectare (760 per acre), at 1.8 x 3 metres (6 x 10ft) spacing.

Fred Artz manages Klipsun and has had an unusual compensation agreement with the Gelles; in addition to a salary, the Gelles have given Artz 0.4 of a hectare (1 acre) of Red Mountain land per year, for the first eleven years of his employment. Artz has purchased additional land and now has a 16-hectare (40-acre) fruit-bearing vineyard of his own, known as Artz Vineyard, selling quality fruit since 1997. Artz also manages Hedges Vineyard, affiliated with one of the best wineries – Hedges Vineyard – on Red Mountain. Artz and Tom Hedges were school classmates.

Tom and Anne-Marie Hedges exported specially-made Washington red wines to Europe, and made a decison to plant their own vineyards. After asking a number of winemakers – Mike

1981 (and armed with money to invest), they learned that the Kennewick Irrigation District was in need of money and was willing to sell land on Red Mountain that the District had obtained for non-payment of taxes during the Depression. The Gelleses signed the papers for 32 hectares (80 acres) in 1982, but it took an extra year to plant because they didn't drill a well until 1983. Close to 16 hectares (40 acres) were planted in 1984–1985. The land they chose to

Januik, Brian Carter, and others – where the best red grapes in the state were grown, and hearing the name Red Mountain most often, the Hedges purchased their vineyard site in 1989, 14.4 hectares (36 acres) at 182–305 metres (600–1,000ft) of elevation. The Hedges planted only the classics – Cabernet Sauvignon, Cabernet Franc, and Merlot – because that is what they were exporting at the time, and with Anne-Marie's French heritage, it of course made sense to them. The vines were spaced at 1.2 x 3 metres (4 x 10ft).

Tom Hedges has since discovered that both Scott Henry and/or Lyre trellising may be preferable to the Guyot system to which he originally trained the vines, needing to mitigate vigour in his warm vineyard with its particularly deep soils. Yields average around 52.2 hectolitres per hectare (3.75 tons per acre), with yields slightly higher for Merlot, and lower for Cabernet Sauvignon.

Red Mountain grapes are different: bigger, more tannic, and richer. Red Mountain vineyards sell their fruit to the state's most celebrated wineries.

The newest vineyards on Red Mountain are joint projects initiated in 2001 between **DeLille Cellars** and **Ciel de Cheval** (the Grand Ciel Vineyard), and Quilceda Creek Vintners and Ciel de Cheval (the Golitzin Vineyard), each co-developing 8-hectare (20-acre) parcels on the borders of the Ciel de Cheval Vineyards.

Before planting their Grand Ciel Vineyard, DeLille commissioned a satellite profile of the vineyard, to discover the land's specific properties: there is a higher pH in the southern part of the vineyard where Cabernet Sauvignon is going in, and a volcanic ash streak where DeLille has started to plant Syrah. DeLille has oriented the rows of vines north-east to south-west in order to give the vines 60 per cent morning sun and 40 per cent of the hotter afternoon sun, seeking to balance the ripening of both sides of the vine better. In the more typical north–south-running rows, the afternoon side of the rows tends to get the more intense, late-in-the-day heat and can produce riper fruit, with potentially more "sunburn." East–west rows get the sun to go over the rows as opposed to across them, thus distributing the sun more evenly. But in Washington – where the sun travels in more of an arc due to its more northerly location – DeLille hopes to better balance the vines with angled-row planting, as well as slowing the grapes' ripening to give the fruit more time to hang.

DeLille is also planting at a moderately high density. It has chosen 0.9 x 2.1 metres (3 x 7ft) spacing, about 4,942 vines per hectare (2,000 per acre), with double Guyot trellising. And like the classic Bordeaux vineyard, the vine canes will be only 46cm (18in) off the ground. DeLille emulates Bordeaux even down to the names it gives its wines: the Chaleur Estate, and the D2, DeLille's second wine, is a nod to the route that runs through the Médoc wine communities.

Alex Golitzin is planting his Golitzin vineyard on Red Mountain in 2001 as well, but only the first 6.8 hectares (17 acres). He is planting at an extremely high density, 5,930 vines per hectare (2,400 per acre). Golitzin intends to sell all his young fruit, not using it for his Quilceda Creek wines until the vines are at least six or seven years old. He will taste the first crop of grapes (Cabernet Sauvignon and Merlot) before deciding what crop load would be best in the future. And he says he will consider putting in Cabernet Franc later.

The advantage of the new Red Mountain appellation is the ability now to formally recognize the **status** that the name already carries, the distinction the fruit has been carrying for dozens of years. Red Mountain grapes are distinctly different: bigger, more tannic, and richer. Red Mountain vineyards sell their fruit to the state's most celebrated wineries, who almost always proudly display the vineyard from which their grapes were sourced on the label: Andrew Will Cellars, Betz Family Winery, Bernard Griffin Winery, Bookwalter Winery, Canoe Ridge Vineyard, DeLille Cellars, Januik Wine Cellars, L'Ecole No. 41, Matthews Cellars, McCrea Cellars, Owen Sullivan Winery, Quilceda Creek Vintners, Seven Hills Winery, Soos Creek Cellars, Woodward Canyon Winery, Wilridge Winery, Tamarack Cellars, Washington Hills Cellars (particularly the Apex brand), and Waterbrook. Now, with this new AVA designation, the proud appellation name can still be proclaimed, even for wines blended from more than one vineyard.

Notable producers

Hedges Cellars

☎ 509-588-3155 📠 509-588-5323
📧 rdmountn@nwlink.com
🌐 www.hedgescellars.com
**53511 N Sunset Road, Benton City,
Washington 99320**
Acreage in production Hedges Estate
Vineyard – 7.3ha (18 acres) Merlot, 6.5ha (16
acres) Cabernet Sauvignon, 0.4ha (1 acre)
Cabernet Franc, 0.2ha (0.7 acre) combined
Tinta Cao/Touriga/Souzao
Bel' Villa Vineyard – 15.7ha (4 acres) Cabernet
Sauvignon, 2ha (5 acres) Syrah, 3.2ha (8 acres)
Merlot, 1.2ha (3 acres) Cabernet Franc
Production capacity 55,000 cases
2000 production 53,000 cases
Established 1986
First wines released 1987 vintage
Fine quality wine showing off the big bones of
rich Red Mountain fruit in its Red Mountain
reserve; a Three Vineyards blend is also deeply
concentrated and smooth.

Kiona Vineyards Winery

☎ 509-588-6716 📠 509-588-3219
📧 kiona1wine@aol.com
**44612 N Sunset NE, Benton City,
Washington 99320**
Acreage in production 1.6ha (4 acres)
Chardonnay, 1.6ha (4 acres) White Riesling,
3.2ha (8 acres) Chenin Blanc, 2.4ha (6 acres)
Sémillon, 10ha (25 acres) Cabernet Sauvignon,
5ha (12 acres) Merlot, 2.8ha (7 acres)
Lemberger
New plantings 2.8ha (7 acres) Lemberger,
0.8ha (2 acres) Sangiovese, 0.8ha (2 acres)
Merlot
Production capacity 40,000 cases
2000 production 34,000 cases
Established 1972
First wines released 1980 vintage
Red Mountain's first winery, and the first
vineyard that helped establish Red Mountain's
reputation for high-quality grapes, even before
any winery was built there. Lemberger is a
particular specialty, and its rich Cabernet
Sauvignon shows all the classic big-boned Red
Mountain hallmarks.

Trish Gelles of Klipsun Vineyard

Seth Ryan Winery

☎ 509-588-6780 📠 509-588-6780
📧 ronandjo@televar.com
🌐 www.sethryan.com
**35306 Sunset Road, Benton City,
Washington 99320**
Acreage in production 1.6ha (4 acres)
Merlot, 0.8ha (2 acres) Cabernet Sauvignon,
0.8ha (2 acres) Cabernet Franc, 0.4ha (1 acre)
Chardonnay
Production capacity 5,000 cases
2000 production 2,200 cases
Established 1983
First wines released 1985 vintage
The Red Mountain vineyard is managed by
Fred Artz (of Klipsun and his own eponymous
vineyard); Seth Ryan also owns a second
vineyard nearby. Quality is solid, but does not
display the power that so often typifies Red
Mountain fruit.

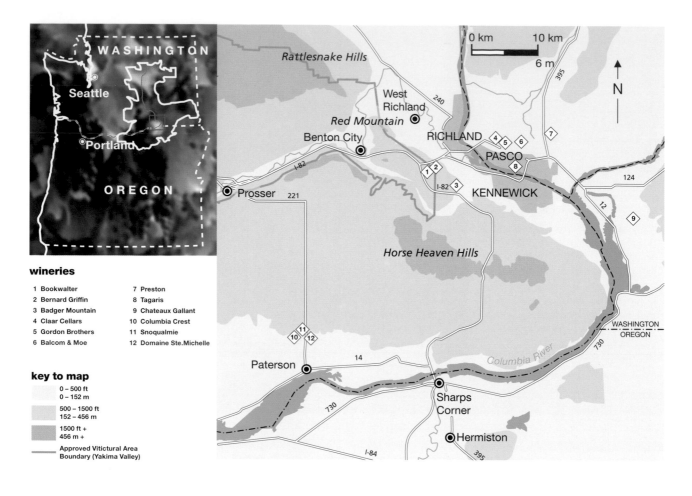

wineries

1 Bookwalter	7 Preston
2 Bernard Griffin	8 Tagaris
3 Badger Mountain	9 Chateaux Gallant
4 Claar Cellars	10 Columbia Crest
5 Gordon Brothers	11 Snoqualmie
6 Balcom & Moe	12 Domaine Ste.Michelle

key to map

0 – 500 ft
0 – 152 m

500 – 1500 ft
152 – 456 m

1500 ft +
456 m +

—— Approved Viticultural Area
Boundary (Yakima Valley)

Tri-Cities

The black dotted-and-dashed line represents the state border.

The so-called **Tri-Cities of Washington** consists of the small neighbouring communities of Richland, Kennewick, and Pasco. They lie at the confluence of the Columbia, Snake, and Yakima Rivers. Although Tri-Cities is not a formal appellation, this chapter focuses on the Tri-Cities as an extended geographic area lying at the western edge of the Yakima Valley (just beyond the boundary of the AVA), northwest of the Walla Walla appellation, and within the broad Columbia Valley AVA.

The Tri-Cities are also located under the shadow of the Hanford Nuclear Reservation. The region was defined almost overnight as a result of the famous Manhattan Project of World War II, which provided the nuclear material used for the bombs that destroyed Hiroshima and Nagasaki, Japan and ended World War II. Plutonium production continued until the 1980s;

it's end triggered a long recession for the area. In the 1990s, the US government poured billions of dollars into cleaning up Hanford wastes. (None of the wastes affect the surrounding agricultural land.) But the vibrant economic strength that once empowered the area has been diminished forever.

Farming has always been important in the Tri-Cities area – like the Yakima Valley – producing an extremely broad bounty of goods such as wheat, fruit, and vegetables and, since 1972, wine grapes. Over the last ten years, tourism and wine have become increasingly important, helping to create a renewed identity in the area. Wine has played a large part in that effort (see page 157)

Like the weather in the Yakima Valley, the summers in the Tri-Cities area can get very hot; parched hills dominate the landscape, and violent dust storms are frequent. The warmth is similar to the Red Mountain's climate.

Family-owned vineyards and wineries played a large part in this area's early grape history. The Preston family planted the first grapes in 1972 near Pasco. Bill and Joanne Preston planted 20.3 hectares (50 acres) with eight different varieties, and built a winery near their vineyards in 1976. The Preston Estate Vineyards – all on relatively flat land – now total 81 hectares (180 acres) and are planted with Cabernet Sauvignon, Merlot, Cabernet Franc, Syrah, Chardonnay, Sauvignon Blanc, and Gamay Noir.

In 1978, brothers Bill and Jeff Gordon purchased a sagebrush-covered slope overlooking the Snake River, 21km (12 miles) northeast of Pasco. The two asked research horticulturist Dr Walter Clore for help in assessing the site, and Clore was impressed with the potential of the area for viticulture. Today, Gordon Brothers has 38.5 hectares (95 acres) of grapes: Chardonnay, Sauvignon Blanc, Gewürztraminer, Cabernet Sauvignon, Merlot, and Syrah.

All of the vineyards are planted with 1.8 x 3 metres (6 x 10ft) spacing, trellised on a bilateral cordon; most are oriented in a north–south direction. The vineyards rise to between 191–209 metres (625–687ft) of elevation, offering good slopes for ripening and frost protection. The site also offers excellent air drainage, and the Snake River below provides a moderating influence on temperatures, with growing season daytime highs of 36.7 °C (95° F) dropping to 12.8°C (55°F) at night. As a result, the grapes tend to boast a fruit-dominant flavour high in both acids and sugar, with soft tannic structure.

Soils in this area are a sandy loam; well drained, but heavy enough to have adequate moisture-holding capacity. Crop loads vary from less than 42 hectolitres per hectare (3 tons per acre) to 56 hectolitres (4 tons) for Cabernet Sauvignon, and higher levels for Merlot, depending on the growing conditions.

The Gordon Brothers wines have witnessed increasingly high quality grapes since 1996. Prior to that, the Gordon Brothers sold a large part of their crop to other quality wineries; their own wines were produced at Hogue Cellars. The combination of establishing their own production facility near the vineyards, using more of their own grapes, and hiring their first winemaker in 1997 has since allowed the Gordons to pay better attention to the details and produce less-commercial, more focused wines.

Winemaker Marie-Eve Gilla lifted the Gordon Brothers wines to a new level, before she was lured away to Fougeron, a new Walla Walla winery, in mid-2001. A former winemaker at Hogue, Gilla was trained at the University of Dijon in Burgundy and has worked at top Burgundian domaines as well as at Argyle in Dundee, Oregon, and Covey Run in the Yakima Valley. Gilla produced beautifully understated, well-defined wines.

Bookwalter Winery is another Tri-Cities winery which is on the rise – in this case because of an infusion of excellence from the younger generation. Jerry Bookwalter opened the winery in 1983, armed with a degree from the University of California at Davis and more than twenty years of experience as General Manager at the

The two asked research horticulturist Dr Walter Clore to help assess the site, and Clore was impressed with the potential of the area for viticulture.

The wine and tourism partnership

The Washington Wine Tourism Task Force is made up of five wine professionals and five tourism professionals. Among the Task Force's current projects is a state-wide directional signage programme for wineries and other wine-related tourism destinations throughout the state.

The Washington State Department of Tourism and the Wine Country Convention and Visitors Bureaus have also become involved in wine events as a result of the Task Force. Local and statewide tourism information is now available at all programmes the Washington Wine Commission sponsors: the World Vinifera Conference, the Taste Washington (held in locations around North America nad in London), and all barrel tastings and promotional events in eastern Washington. All State Tourism media packets now include Washington Wine Touring Brochures and all media packets that are distributed from the Washington Wine Commission contain Washington State Tourism materials.

Washington's approach to tourism is pro-active, different from the historically more reactive Napa, California. Washington markets itself more for travel organisers and business travellers, not the individual wine tourist. The success of Washington's wine tourism will depend on presenting a different wine experience from Napa and Sonoma, gaining cooperation from a critical mass of wineries for tourists to visit, and of course, providing consistent, quality wine from year to year.

successful Sagemoor, Bacchus, and Dionysus Vineyards near Pasco.

Bookwalter has made good enough wines over the years from purchased grapes, focusing mainly on sweet white wines made from Riesling, Chenin, and Muscat, with a lesser emphasis on Chardonnay, Cabernet Sauvignon, and Merlot. The wines were sold exclusively through the winery. In 1997, son John Bookwalter returned to the family winery, bringing with him a marketing degree and more than ten years of beverage sales and marketing experience. Now John Bookwalter is focused on red wine production, sales and marketing while his father manages the vineyards.

Bookwalter's 4 estate acres (1 acre Cabernet Sauvignon, 2 acres Merlot, and 1 acre Cabernet Franc) are densely planted, based on 1.2 x 1.8 metre (4 x 6ft) rows. Yields range from 14–42 hectolitres per hectare (1–3 tons per acre). Area soils are fairly poor and the plants are young, so the vines cannot support much crop.

The young Bookwalter has increased quality tremendously, paying particular attention to Cabernet Sauvignon. All vineyard contracts are on a per acre rather than tonnage basis with well-established, important vineyards such as Ciel de Cheval on Red Mountain. Bookwalter also hired noted California winemaker Zelma Long as consultant winemaker.

The young Bookwalter has increased quality tremendously, paying particular attention to Cabernet Sauvignon.

Just about every aspect of how fruit is handled has changed, from a new state-of-the-art destemmer-crusher to reworking all fermentation, temperature, and pressing strategies. Bookwalter now uses French *barriques*. Wines prior to the new regime were good; but now, they are much more focused and complex.

South and west of the Tri-Cities lies a broad **expanse of land**, due south of the Yakima Valley and the Horse Heaven Hills, stretching down to the Columbia River. While not technically a part of the Tri-Cities, this region of the Columbia Valley is important enough to include with the more "populated" area of nearby Tri-Cities. A number of important vineyards lie in this southern stretch of the Columbia Valley appellation, as well as one enormously significant

winery near the town of Paterson: Columbia Crest. Owned by the Stimson Lane organization, Columbia Crest is Washington's largest single winery, with an annual production of a staggering 1.3 million cases of wine. Nevertheless, some of the most delicious wines in Washington are made at Columbia Crest, where undoubtedly value always reigns.

Columbia Crest purchases more grapes than it grows. Winemaker Doug Gore says he can't possibly grow all the good grapes in the Columbia Valley, making the point that virtually all grapes in the Columbia Valley are premium. The estate vineyard has a drip irrigation system in order to create a drier canopy with less disease, and to help reduce the risk of frost as well. The estate vineyard produces well-balanced fruit with floral and fruity characteristics, as well as tannin and acid. The purchased fruit comes from established quality vineyards in the Horse Heaven Hills, Mattawa, Cold Creek, and the Yakima Valley areas.

Gore has created a winery within a winery, literally cordoning off a section of the winery to create a smaller area devoted just to production of

the reserve wines. For his very fine reserve wines – easily among the best in the state – he undertakes a more rigorous selection in the vineyard than usual, down to a block-to-block, row-to-row *triage*. He sets plant yields for all his wines at between 28–56 hectolitres per hectare (2–4 tons per acre).

Nearby, the vineyards of the **Alderdale** area lie on a ridge that runs along the north side of Columbia River, 24km (15 miles) to either side of Paterson, boasting elevations between 183–304 metres (600–1,000ft). Heat units are variable, but generally warm, with around 1,538 degree days Centigrade (2,800 Fahrenheit). Soils tend to be sandy and variable in depth.

The well-regarded Champoux Vineyard here, originally planted by Don Mercer and nowadays managed by Paul Champoux, is still referred to as the Mercer Ranch. The 60.8-hectare (150-acre) vineyard is now a partnership between Champoux and a number of top wineries, each of which owns blocks of the vineyard: Quilceda Creek, Woodward Canyon, Andrew Will, and Powers Winery. Hogue Cellars, Soos Creek,

Hedges Cellars, Bernard-Griffin, and a few other small wineries purchase grapes as well. The vineyard is known for its generous Cabernet Sauvignon.

The Mercer family is now involved with another fine vineyard in the same area, the 92-hectare (226-acre) Destiny Ridge. The Syrah, Viognier, and Grenache established here should create very interesting, top-quality fruit. McCrea Cellars (among others) is involved, co-managing 5.3 hectares (13 acres) of the fruit that it purchases.

Alder Ridge, with most of its fruit going to Columbia Winery, and the new Zephyr Ridge, with most of its fruit going to Hogue, frame the Canoe Ridge along the Columbia River. Canoe Ridge lends its name to two top vineyards that can be very easily confused: the Canoe Ridge Vineyard (whose winery is located in Walla Walla) owned by the California-based Chalone Group; and the 284-hectare (700-acre) Canoe Ridge Estate, which is owned by Stimson Lane. Stimson Lane also owns the very fine Horse Heaven Vineyard, adjacent to the Columbia Crest Estate vineyard.

Notable producers

Badger Mountain Vineyard

☎ 509-627-4986 📠 509-627-2071
📧 winery@badgermtnvineyard.com
🌐 www.BadgerMtnVineyard.com
1106 S Jurupa Street, Kennewick, Washington 99338
Acreage in production 9.8ha (24 acres) Chardonnay, 4.8ha (12 acres) Cabernet Sauvignon, 3.8ha (9 acres) Riesling, 2.7ha (7 acres) Merlot, 2.4ha (6 acres) Cabernet Franc, 1.7ha (4 acres) Chenin Blanc, 1ha (2.4 acres) Sémillon
New plantings 2.4ha (6 acres) Syrah
Production capacity 40,000 cases
2000 production 40,000 cases
Established 1982
First wines released 1988 vintage
Father and son, Bill and Greg Powers established Badger Mountain Vineyard in 1982. In 1983 they were joined by a partner, Tim DeCook, and began producing wine at their 32-ha (80-acre) estate winery. The vineyard is organic and situated on a south-facing slope of Badger Mountain in the Columbia Valley west of Kennewick. A few sulphite-free wines are produced, but lack distinction as well as ageing potential. The estate wines are generally very pleasant and good buys. See Powers Winery.

Balcom & Moe Wines

☎ 509-547-7307 📠 509-547-7307
📧 balcom@owt.com
🌐 www.balcomandmoewines.com
2520 Commercial Avenue, Pasco, Washington 99301
Acreage in production 27.5ha (68 acres) Riesling, 5.5ha (13.5 acres) Sauvignon Blanc, 13ha (32 acres) Chardonnay, 5ha (12 acres) Cabernet Sauvignon, 5.7ha (14 acres) Merlot, 2ha (5 acres) Sangiovese, 4ha (10 acres) Pinot Noir
Production capacity 15,000 cases
2000 production 15,000 cases
Established 1985
First wines released 1986 vintage
Former potato farmer Maury Balcom planted grapes in 1971. He sold most of his fruit to area wineries before launching Quarry Lake Vintners, later changing the name to reflect his 1,215-ha (3,000-acre) Balcom & Moe Farm, planted with cherries, apples, onions, corn, Concord grapes for juice, and vinifera. The wines are well made, but a bit commercial.

Bernard Griffin Winery

☎ 509-627-0266 📠 509-627-7776
📧 BarnardGriffin@aol.com
🌐 www.BernardGriffin.com
878 Tulip Lane, Richland, Washington 99336
Production capacity 40,000 cases
2000 production 35,000 cases
Established 1983
First wines released 1984 vintage
Talented former Hogue General Manager Rob Griffin and partner Deborah Barnard craft well-focused, lovely wines from purchased fruit, especially the reserve bottlings. Fumé Blanc and Merlot are the standout varietals.

Bookwalter Winery

☎ 509-627-5000; toll-free:
1-887-667-8300 📠 509-627-5010
📧 info@bookwalterwines.com
🌐 www.bookwalterwines.com
894 Tulip Lane, Richland, Washington 99352
Acreage in production 0.4ha (1 acre) Cabernet Sauvignon, 0.4ha (1 acre) Cabernet

Franc, 0.8ha (2 acres) Merlot.
Production capacity 15,000 cases
2000 production 12,000 cases
Established 1983
First wines released 1983 vintage
The quality keeps rising at Bookwalter, with wines that show depth and character.

Claar Cellars

☎ 509-266-4449 📠 509-266-4473
📧 claar@claarcellars.com
🌐 www.claarcellars.com
1081 Glenwood Road, Pasco, Washington 99301
Acreage in production 7.3ha (18 acres) Merlot, 7.3ha (18 acres) Cabernet Sauvignon, 1.2ha (3 acres) Sangiovese, 1.2ha (3 acres) Cabernet Franc, 2.4ha (6 acres) Chardonnay, 5.7ha (14 acres) Riesling, 1.2ha (3 acres) Sauvignon Blanc
New plantings 5.3ha (13 acres) Syrah
Production capacity 25,000 cases
2000 production 6,000 cases
Established 1996
First wines released 1996 vintage

Doug Gore of Columbia Crest Winery

The Claar family first planted grapes in 1980 in a vineyard above the Columbia River near Pasco, not far from Sagemoor Vineyard. They sold their fruit to other wineries until 1996. The family owns a total of 121.4ha (300 acres) planted with wine grapes, apples and asparagus. The Claar botrytized Riesling ice wine is a winner.

Columbia Crest Winery

☎ 509-875-2061 ℻ 509-875-2080
✉ info@Columbia-crest.com
ⓦ www.Columbia-crest.com
Highway 221, Columbia Crest Drive, Paterson, Washington 99345
Acreage in production 150ha (370 acres) Chardonnay, 54ha (133 acres) Chenin Blanc, 17.4ha (43 acres) Gewürztraminer, 8.4ha (21 acres) Muscat Canelli, 84.4ha (208 acres) Sauvignon Blanc, 110.6ha (273 acres) Sémillon,192ha (475 acres) white Riesling, 2ha (5 acres) Cabernet Franc, 175ha (432 acres) Cabernet Sauvignon, 31 acres Grenache, 320 acres Merlot, 1.2ha (3 acres) Malbec, 73ha (179 acres) Syrah
2000 production 1,302,000 cases
Established 1982
First wines released 1985 vintage
The largest producer in Washington, but the wines never seem entirely commercial. Value is the driving force, with quality of almost equal importance. The reserve wines can be terrific, and Chardonnay in particular can show what Washington is able to produce.

Domaine Ste Michelle Sparkling Wine

☎ 509-875-2061 ℻ 509-875-2568
✉ info@domainestemichelle.com
ⓦ www.domainestemichelle.com
Highway 221, Columbia Crest Drive, Paterson, Washington 99345
Acreage in production 18.2ha (45 acres) Chenin Blanc, 15.4ha (38 acres) Sémillon, 0.5ha (1.3 acres) Pinot Noir
Production capacity 600,000 cases
2000 production 242,000 cases
Established 1978
First wines released 1978 vintage
The sparkling label of the Stimson Lane empire, easily confused with sibling winery Chateau Ste Michelle. Credible *méthode traditionelle* wines, more commercial than fine, but very well priced.

Gordon Brothers Cellars

☎ 509-547-6331 ℻ 509-547-6305
✉ info@gordonwines.com
ⓦ www.gordonwines.com
5960 Burden Boulevard, Pasco, Washington 99301
Acreage in production 8ha (20 acres) Merlot, 10ha (25 acres) Chardonnay, 8ha (20 acres) Cabernet Sauvignon, 6ha (15 acres) Syrah, 5.7ha (14 acres) Sauvignon Blanc, 0.4ha (1 acre) Gewürztraminer,
New plantings 0.4ha (1 acre) Petite Syrah
Production capacity 10,000 cases
2000 production 10,000 cases
Established 1983
First wines released 1983 vintage
Winemaker Marie-Eve Gilla raised the standard here with understated but elegant wines. Her departure in 2001 for a new Walla Walla winery leaves big shoes to fill at Gordon Brothers.

Powers Winery

☎ 800-643-9463 ℻ 509-627-2071
✉ winery@badgermtnvineyard.com
ⓦ www.PowersWinery.com
1106 S Jurupa Street, Kennewick, Washington 99338
Production capacity 40,000 cases
2000 production 40,000 cases
Established 1982
First wines released 1992 vintage
The higher end label of Badger Mountain Vineyard, rich and seemless, nicely concentrated wines with clear varietal character. Especially good are the Mercer Ranch-labelled wines, with fruit from the fine vineyard now called Champoux, where the Powers family is a co-owner.

Preston Premium Wines

☎ 509-545-1990 ℻ 509-545-1098
ⓦ www.prestonwines.com
502 E Vineyard Drive, Pasco, Washington 99301
Acreage in production 16ha (41 acres) Chardonnay, 7ha (17 acres) Sauvignon Blanc, 2.4ha (6 acres) Gewürztraminer, 11.4ha (28 acres) white Riesling, 3.2ha (8 acres) Gamay Beaujolais, 10.6ha (26 acres) Merlot, 15ha (37 acres) Cabernet Sauvignon, 1.4ha (3.5 acres) Cabernet Franc,2.5ha (6 acres) Pinot Noir, 1 ha (3 acres) Syrah, 1.5ha (4 acres) Royalty
Production capacity Over 100,000 cases

2000 production 19,000 cases
Established 1976
First wines released 1976 vintage
Former tractor salesman Bill Preston first planted grapes in 1972 on his 81-ha 200-acre) farm. The wines are good commercial quality, well-made and pleasant.

Snoqualmie Vineyards

☎ 425-415-3703 ℻ 425-415-3657
✉ info@Snoqualmie.com
ⓦ www.Snoqualmie.com
PO Box 247, Paterson, Washington 99345
Acreage in production 97ha (240 acres) among vineyards in the Wahluke Slope, Horse Heaven Hills, and Yakima Valley
2000 production 53,000 cases
Established 1983
First wines released 1983 vintage
Another brand of the Stimson Lane group, and produced at Columbia Crest by Joy Anderson. Good quality varietal wines, and well priced.

Tagaris Winery

☎ 509-547-3590 or 877-862-7999
℻ 509-547-8264
✉ tagaris@3-cities.com
ⓦ www.tagariswines.com
1625 W A Street, Pasco, Washington 99301
Acreage in production 19ha (47 acres) Chardonnay, 6.5ha (16 acres) Cabernet Sauvignon, 3.6ha (9 acres) Chenin Blanc, 3.6ha (9 acres) Merlot, 3.2ha (8 acres) Pinot Noir, 6ha (15 acres) Riesling, 7.3ha (18 acres) Sauvignon Blanc, 0.8ha (2 acres) Sémillon, 4ha (10 acres) Gewürztraminer, 2ha (5 acres) Müller-Thurgau
Production capacity 50,000 cases
2000 production 5,000 cases
Established 1987
First wines released 1987 vintage
The Taggares family owns this winery in Pasco, using the original (Greek) spelling of the family name. Their 100 per cent organic vineyard is located on the east end of the Saddle Mountains near Othello, in the northern Columbia Valley AVA. At an elevation of 4,265 metres (1,300 ft), the site is notably cooler than other Washington vineyards, but produces ripe grapes of good quality. The family also has a long history of Concord grape farming in the Yakima Valley.

Spokane Area

Spokane is the second largest city in Washington, located near the state's western border with Idaho and at the same latitude as Seattle. In 2001, the Spokane metropolitan area boasts a population of 405,000, making Spokane the largest city between Seattle and Minneapolis, Minnesota.

The Spokane River snakes through downtown, tumbling over one of the largest urban waterfalls in the United States to become the focal point of Riverfront Park. The park – a former Indian fishing area – was the site of the 1974 World's Fair. Spokane is often described as a big small town, and the community has received a number of awards for being a good place to raise a family. It is also a recreational paradise, with mountain biking, riding, skiing, white water rafting, camping, hiking, fishing, canoeing, and kayaking all easily accessible to the city.

Sitting outside any formal appellation, Spokane – like Seattle – sees very little viticulture, in part because of a cool climate so far north, with peak summer temperatures only reaching about 27° C (82° F). Much of urban Spokane lies along the Spokane River at an elevation of approximately 610 metres (2,000ft) above sea level. This is extremely marginal for ripening any grape variety, especially as winter freezes can also damage vines. Also like Seattle, most wineries tend to be located near the city as a lifestyle choice for the owners, who purchase their grapes from the relatively distant Columbia Valley. But as Spokane is not the successful mecca Seattle is, there are fewer wineries in the Spokane area.

The first winery to open in the Spokane area was **Worden's Washington Winery** in 1980, always producing a wide range of wines. That name no longer exists; in 2000, Worden Winery became Wyvern Cellars and moved its location from a log cabin to a better production facility.

Latah Creek Wine Cellars opened in 1982 as a joint project between Mike Conway and Hogue Cellars of Prosser. Mike Conway began his wine career as a microbiology technician at E & J Gallo, followed by work at Franzia brothers in California. In 1977, Conway became an assistant winemaker with the Parducci winery in Northern California, where he stayed for three years before coming up to Washington to open Latah Creek. In 1984, Conway became the sole owner of Latah Creek. But Hogue and Latah Creek still remain close – nearly 50 per cent of Latah Creek's grapes come from Hogue vineyards. The remaining grapes are sourced from other Yakima-area vineyards as well as vineyards on the Wahluke Slope in the Northern Columbia Valley.

Mountain Dome Winery was another early producer in the area, established as a sparkling wine house in 1984. Dr Michael Manz crafts a very fine *méthode traditionelle* bubbly. Around the same time, Arbor Crest Wine Cellars opened. This is a name to follow not only in the Spokane area, but also in Washington State.

Arbor Crest Wine Cellars was started by brothers David and Harold Mielke and Harold's

Most Washington wineries are visitor-friendly; even the elite producers will welcome guests who make appointments in advance.

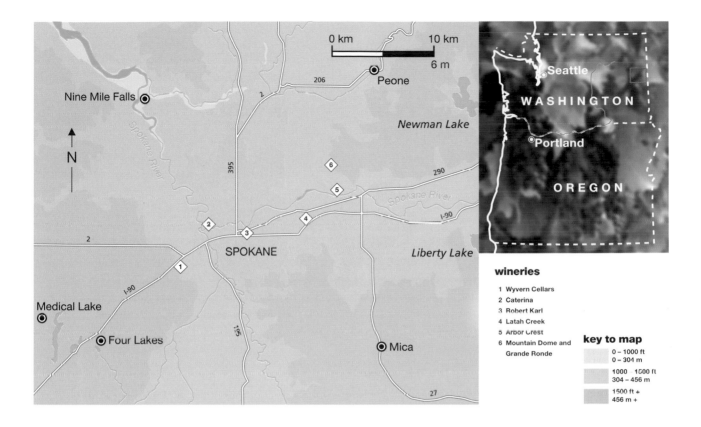

wife Marcia in 1982. The Mielkes were in the farming business and grew many different types of fruit, including cherries: they even made cherry pie filling for Hostess fruit pies until 1972. The winery's production facility is in fact now where the cherry-processing plant was located.

The Mielkes realized that Spokane was not the right climate for growing ultra-premium quality wine grapes. They decided to start a winery instead and purchase their grapes from the better sited Columbia Valley. In 1984, they bought the Riblet Mansion, a 30.4-hectare (75-acre) historically-designated building. It is now known as the Arbor Crest Cliff House.

The estate vineyard was planted with the three most common **sparkling wine varieties**: Chardonnay, Pinot Noir and Pinot Meunier, with the addition of a little Pinot Gris. The vineyard was primarily planted for aesthetic reasons; however, they do sell the grapes to sparkling wine producers and they themselves make a small amount of sparkling that is sold only in the tasting room.

Arbor Crest's wines have always been very good quality. But a grand renaissance is underway here, due chiefly to the infusion of expertise and enthusiasm by its new owners and operators, Harold and Marcia Mielke's daughter and son-in-law, Christina and Jim van Loben Sels.

After graduating from the University of California at Davis in 1993, Christina went to work for Ferrari-Carano Vineyards and Winery in Sonoma, as an enologist. She later became responsible for Ferrari-Carano's Experimental Winery, where she made red wines from a small experimental vineyard that mixed and matched clones with different rootstocks. In 1997, she was promoted to associate winemaker at Ferrari-Carano.

When her uncle David Mielke decided to retire in 1999, her family asked the van Loben Sels if they were interested in moving to Spokane to take over the family business. The young couple accepted, pleased they could rely on local resources for the majority of their production needs: barrels, corks, and bottles are sourced outside Washington, but the remaining supplies can be purchased locally. The van Loben Sels' experience with the vinifera

Eventually the van Loben Sels want to take fruit from each of the distinctive viticultural regions of Washington.

grapes struggle is that although winter temperatures may periodically cause vine damage and force replanting, ripening can be achieved with proper thinning and fruit exposure and by keeping yields in the 28–42 hectolitre per hectare (2–3-tons per acre) range. For sparkling wine, they always source their fruit from the Columbia Valley, where growing conditions are better.

Arbor Crest fruit now comes from the Central section of the Columbia Valley, from several vineyards in the areas of Mattawa, Othello, and Pasco. Eventually, the van Loben Sels want to take fruit from each of the distinctive viticultural regions of Washington, which will ultimately add to the complexity and layers of their wines.

Jim van Loben Sels, armed with invaluable good vineyard management experience picked up in Napa, California, took over the management of all their fruit and oversees the vineyard contracts, working directly with growers to explore new ways for the grapes to achieve the higher quality that the van Loben Sels now demand.

Jim has changed from traditional tonnage contracts to acreage contracts to better control yields and quality, and has been experimentally changing trellising at a number of vineyards to see if he can improve fruit quality further.

Christina has also started implementing a variety of changes that have increased the quality of her wines. She also realized that she needed to focus her wine programme on only four main varieties – Chardonnay, Sauvignon Blanc, Merlot, and Cabernet Sauvignon. She also plans to produce very small quantities of limited edition wines, such as Pinot Gris, Syrah, Cabernet Franc and Sangiovese if a particular lot "speaks" to her.

Arbor Crest primarily produced white wines in the past. However, since the van Loben Sels' vision is to be a part of the Washington wave of fine red wines, they have modified their production facility to be able to accommodate red varietals too. Even the Arbor Crest label has changed to reflect the new regime. The van Loben Sels bring a wealth of experience and expertise to Arbor Crest, and the quality of the wines from the 1999 vintage forward seem to prove that.

Cristina van Loben Sels of Arbor Crest Wine Cellars.

Notable producers

Arbor Crest Wine Cellars

☎ 509-927-9463 ℻ 509-927-0574

✉ info@arborcrest.com

🌐 www.arborcrest.com

4705 North Fruithill Road, Spokane, Washington 99217

Acreage in production 0.4ha (1 acre) Pinot Gris, 0.4ha (1 acre) Pinot Noir, 0.8ha (2 acres) Chardonnay

Production capacity 40,000 cases

2000 production 22,000 cases

Established 1982

First wines released 1984 vintage

New life was breathed in here when the daughter of the founders (and her husband) took command of Arbor Crest in 1999. Christina van Loben Sels is a former Ferrari-Carano (California) winemaker with tremendous talent; Jim van Loben Sels focuses on the vineyards (of contracted fruit) and their combined efforts are terrific, with wines that show it.

Caterina Winery

☎ 509-328-5069 ℻ 509-328-9694

✉ mscott@caterina.com

🌐 www.caterina.com

905 North Washington Street, Spokane, Washington 99201

Production capacity 10,000 cases

2000 production 6,000 cases

Established 1993

First wines released 1993 vintage

First established as the Steven Thomas Livingstone label, the name changed to Caterina after a threatened lawsuit from Gallo over the name Livingstone. Mike Scott crafts very supple, rich wines from purchased fruit from the Wahluke Slope.

China Bend Vineyards

☎ 800-700-6123 ℻ 509-732-1401

✉ bart@chinabend.com

🌐 www.chinabend.com

3596 Northport-Flat Creek Road, Kettle Falls, Washington 99141

Acreage in production 0.2ha (0.5 acres) Chardonnay, 0.2ha (0.5 acres) Lemberger, 0.8ha (2 acres) Marechal Foch, 0.1ha (0.3 acres) Baco Noir, 0.2ha (0.5 acres) Lucy Kuhlman, 0.2ha (0.5 acres) Siegerrebe

New plantings 0.3ha (0.8 acres) Leon Millot, 0.2ha (0.5 acres) Aurora

Production capacity 1,500 cases

2000 production 1,500 cases

Established 1993

First wines released 1993 vintage

One of Washington's most northern wineries, about 145km (90 miles) northwest of Spokane on the banks of the Columbia River's Lake Roosevelt, about 64km (40 miles) from the Canadian border. The winery grows cool-climate organic grapes, and produces light, sulphite-free wines.

Grande Ronde Cellars

☎ 509-928-2788 ℻ 509-922-8078

✉ manz@mountaindome.com

🌐 www.granderondecellars.com

16315 E Temple Road, Spokane, Washington 99217

2000 production 1,000 cases

Established 1997

First wines released 1999 vintage

The second project of child psychiatrist Michael Manz M.D. and his family (see Mountain Dome), this one dedicated to Merlot and Cabernet Sauvignon sourced from the Seven Hills Vineyard in the Walla Walla appellation.

Latah Creek Wine Cellers

☎ 509-926-0164 ℻ 509-926-0710

✉ mconway@latahcreek.com

🌐 www.latahcreek.com

13030 E Indiana Avenue, Spokane, Washington 99216

Production capacity 30,000 cases

2000 production 12,000 cases

Established 1982

First wines released 1982 vintage

Modestly priced, well-crafted wines, including a juicy, very good Lemberger.

Mountain Dome Winery

☎ 509-928-2788 ℻ 509-922-8078

✉ manz@mountaindome.com

🌐 www.mountaindome.com

16315 E Temple Road, Spokane, Washington 99217

2000 production 5,000 cases

Established 1984

First wines released 1992 vintage

A focus on very creamy, slightly toastier-styled *méthode traditionelle* wines. Pinot Noir is also produced as a varietal wine. From 1987 to 1990 David Ramey, fresh from Matanzas Creek Winery in Sonoma, California was consultant. Raphael Brisbois, the former sparkling winemaker at Iron Horse and most recently at Piper Sonoma. (both California wineries), now consults.

Robert Karl Cellars

☎ 509-363-1352 ℻ 509-363-1353

✉ info@robertkarl.com

115 W Pacific Avenue, Spokane, Washington 99201

Production capacity 50,000 cases

2000 production 20,000 cases

Established 1980

First wines released 1980 vintage

Anaesthesiologist Joseph Gunsleman and his wife Rebecca converted an old fire station into a functional winery. Only Cabernet Sauvignon is produced, with fruit sourced in the Yakima Valley. Their first wines will not be released in June 2002.

Wyvern Cellars

☎ 509-455-7835 ℻ 509-838-4723

✉ wordenwine@aol.com

7217 W Wbow, Spokane, Washington 99224

Production capacity 50,000 cases

2000 production 20,000 cases

Established 1980

First wines released 1980 vintage

The Northwest's largest custom label facility, producing wines for over 850 clients including Costco, Hilton Hotels, and Amtrack Trains. The Wyvern label is its supermarket brand, made from Prosser and Walla Walla area fruit. Plans include producing a premium wine under the Chateaubriand label, but not until 2002.

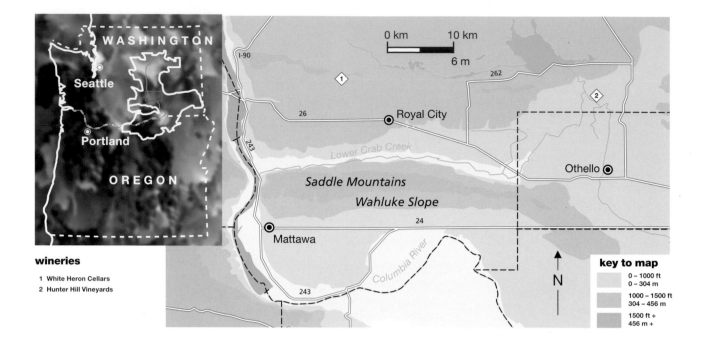

wineries

1 White Heron Cellars
2 Hunter Hill Vineyards

Northern Columbia Valley

The black dashed lines represent the county borders.

The **Columbia Valley** appellation is enormous – one-third of Washington's total land mass – shaped somewhat like a wide-rooted tree rising from its broad base to a thick truck sprouting fat branches. The wide base of the AVA surrounds the stretch of the mighty Columbia River that separates Washington and Oregon; this is where the greatest concentration of prime vineyard land lies, and indeed represents the geographic regions previously discussed (and includes Walla Walla following this chapter).

Viticulture is not limited to the more southern reaches of the appellation. North of the Yakima Valley and its defining Rattlesnake Hills, the Columbia River flows from its source in the north, continuing its southerly route, flattening out to a west–east flow and rounding the top edges of the Hanford Nuclear Reservation (whose facilities extend down to the Tri-Cities), before the river turns south again on its way to its long, straight stretch as Washington's southern boundary. It is here on either side of the more northern Columbia River, where is twists and turns – to the east, north and west of Hanford – that viticulture returns to the landscape.

This northern subregion of the AVA is a desert-like, sagebrush-covered area, that is home to only a handful of wineries. Those that have attempted to operate here have not done well. Most visitors glimpse the region from a speeding car, travelling to or from the more eastern city of Spokane. Few small towns, and a limited infrastructure keep the area underpopulated and somewhat isolated.

However, the many vineyards in the north Columbia Valley – Chateau Ste Michelle's superb Cold Creek and Indian Wells Vineyards, and those in the Wahluke Slope, Mattawa and Othello areas – produce high-quality grapes, with fruit going to many of the state's well-respected producers.

Chateau Ste Michelle has had faith in the region since the early 1970s when it planted its Cold Creek Vineyard, the jewel in its grapevine crown. Located just north of the Yakima Valley on an extended high plateau (and in a very warm mesoclimate), the nearby Columbia River provides little temperature moderation. The 267-hectare (660-acre) vineyard sits on a south-facing slope, on soil that is low in organic matter. Heat spikes in the summer months help to make Cold Creek a very early ripening vineyard.

The wines Chateau Ste Michelle produces from this site are among its best, especially a superb, fat Chardonnay, always Cold Creek Vineyard-designated. Chardonnay doesn't typically command respect in Washington, but this wine always shows the variety off very well. Riesling also excels at Cold Creek; it is from here that the grapes for Eroica are grown, the wonderful Riesling made in collaboration with Weingut Dr Loosen of the Mosel in Germany. The red wines made from grapes grown at Cold Creek Vineyard are typically deeply coloured and concentrated, with firm structure offering good ageability.

Chateau Ste Michelle's **Indian Wells Vineyard** is located across the Columbia River and north of Cold Creek on the Wahluke Slope, planted on a west-facing slope to capture the afternoon heat. The fine, sandy soils prove ideal for Merlot, and some of Chateau Ste Michelle's top Merlots are from this Indian Wells Vineyard. The Wahluke Slope itself is a long, broad plateau on the west

and north side of the Columbia River as the river zigzags east towards the town of Othello. The Mattawa area at the west end of the Wahluke Slope has a particularly warm climate. Sun and lean soils combine to produce small berries that can result in wines of great concentration.

On the valley floor near Mattawa (from which this subregion takes its name), very sandy soils with river rock and gravel prevail in the lower sections of the slope, especially the closer you move towards the River. Cabernet Sauvignon, Merlot, and Syrah perform well in this area, achieving full ripeness and varietal expression.

Moving up the slope to 305 metres (1,000ft) of elevation, the soils become well-drained sandy-loam, and can be quite shallow – generally very fine conditions for producing good quality, more complex grapes.

Arbor Crest Wine Cellars has entered a partnership with a Mattawa-area vineyard to plant different clones of Cabernet Sauvignon, Malbec, Syrah, Merlot, and Sangiovese here; Hogue, Latah Creek, and Bookwalter each own or

Irrigation turned the eastern Washington desert into a verdant garden basket, growing everything from wheat to apples, and increasingly grapes.

manage vineyards in the Mattawa area of the Wahluke Slope, and focus on the same red varieties, but Hogue has some Cabernet Franc and Sémillon as well. Spacing in these vineyards is fairly consistent, at 1.8 x 3 metres (6 x 10ft), double cordon trained, with vertical shoot positioning. Yields, like in most other vineyards in Washington, vary from 28–56 hectolitres per hectare (2–4 tons per acre), depending on the variety and the vintage.

At the other end of the Wahluke Slope, close to Othello, the Conner Lee Vineyard is located on extremely sandy, very deep soil. This site is much cooler compared to Mattawa; it ripens about two weeks behind Pasco-area vineyards and one week behind Mattawa vineyards.

Arbor Crest has contracted by the acre at this site and crops its Chardonnay, Cabernet Sauvignon, Cabernet Franc, and Merlot within a range of 35–56 hectolitres per hectare (2.5–4 tons per acre), depending on the variety. Despite the cooler growing conditions, the grapes still achieve good colour development by means of canopy management, irrigation control, and fruit thinning. The Chardonnay produced by Arbor Crest in 1999 was so concentrated and fruity that the van Loben Sels gave the wine a vineyard designation.

Bookwalter Winery also contracts for 4 hectares (10 acres) in the same Conner Lee Vineyard. Planted in 1988 and spaced at 1.2 x 3 metres (4 x 10ft), the vineyard is at an extremely cool site, at 396 metres (1,300ft) elevation on a slight southerly slope with very sandy soils. Bookwalter's vines employ a hybrid arrangement using a cane pruned, fan-trained system. Because this site is so cool, efforts have to be focused on maximum fruit exposure, and the employment of a moveable catch wire helps to achieve that. Yields typically range from 28–42 hectolitres per hectare (2–3 tons per acre), depending on the year. Of all the vineyards where Bookwalter's fruit is grown, this vineyard produces some of the most structured and concentrated of wines.

The above vineyards, which together are labelled the **Northern Columbia Valley** – may not be in the most northern reaches of the appellation anymore. They are northern relative to the dense Yakima and Walla Walla Valleys, but the Columbia Valley AVA extends further north still. Until recently there was no grape growing further north, other than the limited amount of vineyard on the Royal Slope, just above the Wahluke Slope. However, this may be changing.

As of 2000, there is very new viticultural activity in the Lake Chelan region, north of the Royal Slope by approximately 120km (75 miles). What has been called the Northern Columbia Valley may soon need to be renamed as the Central Columbia Valley, if the not-yet-producing Lake Chelan vineyards and wineries are successful. Agriculture and tourism have been the mainstays of this northern Washington recreational area.

Only about 14.2 hectares (35 acres) of grapes are now planted in the region, although the new Lake Chelan Grape Growers Association can claim sixty due-paying members. A few acres of vines planted a century ago by Italian immigrants are still alive, growing at 610 metres (2,000ft) of elevation. Pinot Noir was also discovered in the hills above Lake Chelan. Lake Chelan Winery intends to plant Pinot Noir and Pinot Gris. The biggest challenge to these growers will be the cold weather and market forces. The risks of growing grapes in such a cold northerly climate are crop losses and inconsistent yields. However, the Lake might provide a moderating influence, and winter snow could insulate the vines from wind and freezing damage. Lake Chelan Winery had its first crush in 2000, with grapes purchased from Oregon and elsewhere in Washington. About 800 cases of Chardonnay, Cabernet Franc, Syrah, and Cabernet Sauvignon have been produced.

Another tiny winery – La Toscana Vineyard and Cellar, near Leavenworth – debuted in 2000, with a distinctive solution to dealing with its limited resources: lacking a crusher-destemmer or a press, old-fashioned foot stomping was used instead.

Without many vines, and lacking any recorded harvest data, it is too early to predict whether the Lake Chelan pioneers will succeed, or whether the Royal and Wahluke Slope areas' distinction as the Northern Columbia Valley will last.

Because the site is so cool, efforts are exposed on maximum fruit exposure, and using a moveable catch wire helps to achieve that.

Columbia Gorge

The large **Columbia Valley AVA** reaches down from central Washington and crosses the Columbia River into Oregon, spanning the Columbia River Gorge, a spectacular river canyon cutting the only commercially navigable route through the Cascade Mountain Range. The Gorge stretches 129km (80 miles) long and is up to 1,219 metres (4,000ft) deep, with its northern walls in Washington and its southern walls in Oregon.

The Gorge itself is protected as a federally designated Columbia River Gorge National Scenic Area, which restricts and controls development and promotes responsible land stewardship. The Gorge's development took millions of years.

In the Miocene age, twelve to seventeen million years ago, unusual volcanoes, called basalt floods, erupted in eastern Washington and Oregon. These eruptions were enormous cracks in the earth's crust, several miles long,

The black dashed lines represent the county borders.

which poured out floods of molten rock. As that lava cooled it formed smooth, dark grey basalt rock.

Less than two million years ago, in the Pleistocene age, hundreds of smaller volcanoes erupted in the Cascade Mountain Range. These dormant volcanoes are now familiar mountains: Mount Adams in Washington and Mount Hood in Oregon. During this same period, the Cascade Mountains began to rise. As the mountains rose, the Columbia River carved out a deep gorge through the uplifted crust. And then the Missoula floods 16,000–14,000 years ago (still in the Pleistocene age) further defined the dramatic area as we know it today.

During the last ice age, ice sheets covered much of Canada. One lobe of ice grew southward, blocking the Clark Fork Valley in Idaho. This 600 metres (2,000ft) high ice dam blocked the river, creating a lake that stretched

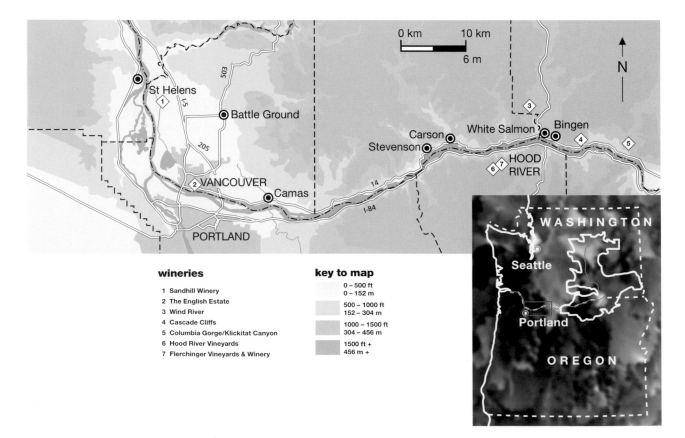

wineries

1 Sandhill Winery
2 The English Estate
3 Wind River
4 Cascade Cliffs
5 Columbia Gorge/Klickitat Canyon
6 Hood River Vineyards
7 Flerchinger Vineyards & Winery

key to map

	0 – 500 ft / 0 – 152 m
	500 – 1000 ft / 152 – 304 m
	1000 – 1500 ft / 304 – 456 m
	1500 ft + / 456 m +

for hundreds of miles. When the lake was full, it contained 2,500 cubic km (600 cubic miles) of water. Eventually, water travelled under the ice dam. It is believed the water drained out of the lake in only two or three days, with the result of flooding eastern Washington. This flood, moving up to 100kph (60mph), scooped out hundreds of miles of canyons, called coulees, and created the largest waterfall ever to exist, leaving 90 metre (300ft) high gravel bars throughout the region. During a period of 2,500 years, as many as one hundred of these floods scoured the Gorge in succession, further defining its spectacular and dramatic beauty.

Today, the **Columbia River Gorge** and surrounding communities offer a wide diversity of recreational opportunities. Fishing, windsurfing, boating, and hiking are leading activities. Also within this area, not far from a fine vineyard and one winery, lies a remarkable Museum – the Maryhill Museum – and a scale replica of Stonehenge.

In 1907, wealthy Washington entrepreneur Sam Hill purchased 2,430 hectares (6,000 acres) of land overlooking the Columbia River with the intention of establishing a Quaker agricultural community. He chose the bluff that Maryhill Museum now occupies as the site for his own home.

Among Hill's many personal friends were three influential women. Loie Fuller, an acclaimed *Folies Bergere* pioneer of modern dance, conceived the idea of creating a museum of art in Sam Hill's mansion. Through Loie's friendships within Parisian art circles, Hill acquired an extensive collection of original Auguste Rodin sculptures. In 1926, Queen Marie of Romania dedicated his still unfinished museum. After Hill's death in 1931, a third friend, Alma Spreckels, assumed responsibility for completing the museum. Together with her husband, Adolph Spreckels, she had already established the Palace of the Legion of Honor in San

This bridge spans the mighty Columbia River, reaching from Oregon (foreground) across to Washington (background) near the Columbia Gorge. Beware of windsurfers speeding along the river.

During a period of 2,500 years, as many as 100 of these floods scoured the Gorge in succession, further defining its spectacular beauty.

171

Francisco. Alma Spreckels became Maryhill's principal benefactor and donated much of her own art collection to the museum. Under her guidance, the museum opened to the public on Sam Hill's birthdate, 13 May 1940.

Maryhill's **Stonehenge** replica was built by Sam Hill as a tribute to the soldiers of local Klickitat County who lost their lives; it became the first monument in the United States to honour the dead of World War I. The structure is a full-scale replica of England's famous neolithic Stonehenge. A Quaker pacifist, Hill was mistakenly informed that the original Stonehenge had been used as a sacrificial site, and thus constructed the replica to remind us that "humanity is still being sacrificed to the god of war."

Maryhill and Stonehenge rise up on the Washington side of the Gorge near Goldendale, about 97km (60 miles) from the vineyard-rich Alderdale area and the town of Paterson. But Cascade Cliffs Winery, one of the lone wineries in the Gorge, lies close to Maryhill.

Cascade Cliff's 9.3-hectare (23-acre) vineyard and winery are situated on a bench one hundred feet above the Columbia River, backed by 122-metre (400-ft) tall, dramatic basalt cliffs formed by the region's geologic forces described above. Planted primarily with red grape varieties, its protected mesoclimate provides a very long growing season, allowing Nebbiolo in particular to ripen well; in most years, it is harvested as late as early November. Wines from Cascade Cliffs show strong clean varietal flavours, with the quality improving each year.

This area of the Columbia Valley is sparsely populated with producers, but there is a movement afoot (see page 98) to bring about the creation an independent Gorge appellation. Cascade Cliffs – one of the few wineries on either side of the Gorge – wants no part of it, preferring instead to stay aligned with the broad and well-respected Columbia Valley appellation.

The Washington side of the AVA is not as rich with vineyards as the Oregon side,

This area of the Columbia Valley is sparsely populated with producers, but there is a movement to create an independent Gorge appellation.

save one. And an impressive one at that. Rick and Jody Ensminger own Celilo Vineyard, although their primary business is cultivating pear orchards. Located on Underwood Mountain, Celilo Vineyard rises to an elevation of 335 metres (1,100ft) on a ridge above the Columbia River near White Salmon, Washington and opposite Hood River, Oregon. The vineyard takes its name from the still-legendary prime Indian fishing area and waterfall on the Columbia River known as Celilo Falls. The Falls were a major, historic site that ceased to exist when the Dalles Dam was opened in 1957 and covered them with water.

Celilo Vineyard has achieved an almost legendary status itself, supplying a number of top Oregon and Washington wineries with high-quality fruit. The first 14 hectares (35 acres) of Celilo were planted with a vast cornucopia of grape varieties in 1972, from table grapes to Pinot Noir and everything in between. The Pinot has a very tough time ripening, but the Gewürztraminer does particularly well and is made into a good wine by Covey Run Vintners in the Yakima Valley. Chardonnay doesn't always show its best expression in this vineyard, but in warm years, it can be delicious, with firm, crisp acidity. Panther Creek Cellars in Oregon purchases Chardonnay from this vineyard, and also buys Chardonnay from a more recently planted, better ripening block on a lower slope of the vineyard.

The next block to be planted at Celilo was a vineyard which stood 46 metres (150ft) lower than the initial vineyard. 3.2 hectares (8 acres) of Chardonnay was established in 1983–1984, and the grapes today go only to Ken Wright Cellars and Cristom Vineyards in Oregon and Covey Run and Woodward Canyon Winery in Walla Walla, Washington. Celilo-designated Chardonnays from these producers tend to be very attractive, ripe, almost rich, balanced wines, with a good acid backbone.

Until Ken Wright "discovered" the vineyard in 1992, Celilo had trouble selling its grapes and had to resort to a California-based broker to do it. Steve Doerner and Paul Gerrie from Cristom tasted Wright's 1992 Chardonnay in barrel and liked it so much they approached Celilo's owners to purchase their fruit. After that, Celilo had little difficulty with sales: another block was planted: 4.9 hectares (12 acres) of Chardonnay and Merlot, this time on a lower slope.

The most recent planting was done in 1997 at Wright's insistence; 0.8 hectares (2 acres) of a Dijon Chardonnay clone were also planted at the lower elevations. At these lower elevations (below 305 metres/1,000ft), the soils at Celilo are deep and gravely, riddled with pellet-like volcanic material that creates a well-drained soil. Grapes tend to ripen well here. At the upper levels of the vineyard, the weather is cooler, and the soils are more clay based and compact, explaining the difficulties with ripening. Wind is a huge issue everywhere in the Gorge (as there are strong east–west flows through this gap in the Cascade Range), and many trees have been planted as a windbreak. But the wind also helps to cool the lower vineyards, supplying relief from the warmth of the sun on the rocky cliffs; the fruit maintains better acidity as a result.

As a whole, the site is very vigorous, too vigorous to maintain classic simple cane trellising once the vines have reached several years of age. All vines used to be trained in what is commonly called California sprawl, a hanging, floppy trellis. In 1990, the vineyard was switched to a Scott Henry system to mitigate the vigour. The new plantings, since 1991, are still on a vertical shoot positioning system, but will be changed over to Scott Henry soon.

With the success of the Celilo Vineyard, the Ensmingers keep replacing pear trees with more vinifera. That trend is likely to continue, as this vineyard becomes better known.

Notable producers

Cascade Cliffs Vineyard & Winery

☎ 509-767-1100
✉ cascadecliffs@gorge.net
🌐 www.cascadecliffs.com
8866 Highway 14, Wishram, Washington 98673
Acreage in production 1.2ha (3 acres) Merlot, 1.2ha (3 acres) Cabernet Sauvignon, 1.2ha (3 acres) Syrah, 1ha (2.5 acres) Nebbiolo, 1ha (2.5 acres) Petite Syrah, 1ha (2.5) acres Barbera, 0.6ha (1.5 acres) Symphony
New plantings 1.2ha (3 acres) Barbera, 1.2ha (3 acres) Petite Syrah
Production capacity 6,000 cases
2000 production 2,500 cases
Established 1985
First wines released 1991 vintage
The best producer in the Columbia Gorge area, with a pleasant, bright Barbera and varietally-strong Nebbiolo among its wines.

Columbia Gorge Winery & Klickitat Canyon Winery

☎ & 🖷 509-365-2900
✉ cgw@columbiagorgewinery.com
🌐 www.columbiagorgewinery.com &

www.klickitatcanyonwinery.com
6 Lyle-Snowden Road, Lyle, Washington 98635
Acreage in production 1.2ha (3 acres) Syrah
Production capacity 600 cases.
2000 production 600 cases (including both labels)
Established 1994
First wines released 1994 vintage
Credible wines from an intentionally tiny producer, using grapes purchased from the fine Celilo Vineyard. The Klickitat Canyon Winery – a less expensive brands – also bottled by the same management in the same facilities.

Sandhill Winery

☎ 360-887-5629 🖷 360-887-5629
✉ sandhillwinery@aol.com
2830 S Cornett Drive, Ridgefield, Washington 98642
Acreage in production 10ha (24 acres) Cabernet Sauvignon, 5.2ha (13 acres) Merlot, 0.8ha (2 acres) Cabernet Franc, 0.4ha (1 acre) Pinot Gris
Production capacity 10,000 cases
2000 production 1,300 cases

Established 1988
First wines released 1997 vintage
This winery is not technically in the Columbia Gorge, nor even the Columbia Valley appellation; the production facility is located just north of urban Vancouver, Washington. Sandhill Winery owns the Red Mountain Vineyard of the same-named mountain and appellation, selling most of its grapes, but also using them more recently for its own label.

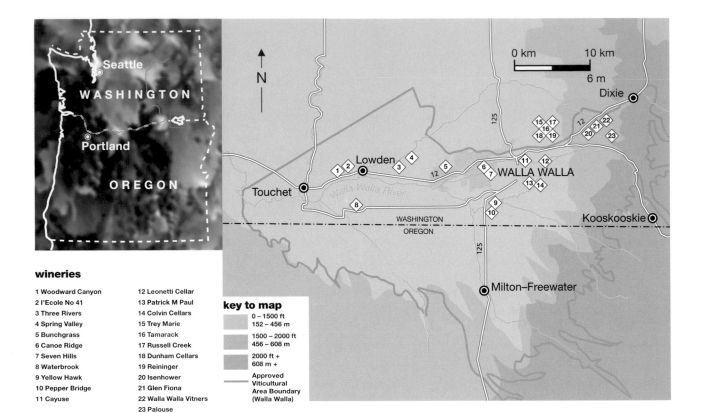

wineries

1 Woodward Canyon	12 Leonetti Cellar
2 l'Ecole No 41	13 Patrick M Paul
3 Three Rivers	14 Colvin Cellars
4 Spring Valley	15 Trey Marie
5 Bunchgrass	16 Tamarack
6 Canoe Ridge	17 Russell Creek
7 Seven Hills	18 Dunham Cellars
8 Waterbrook	19 Reininger
9 Yellow Hawk	20 Isenhower
10 Pepper Bridge	21 Glen Fiona
11 Cayuse	22 Walla Walla Vitners
	23 Palouse

key to map

0 – 1500 ft
152 – 456 m

1500 – 2000 ft
456 – 608 m

2000 ft +
608 m +

Approved
Viticultural
Area Boundary
(Walla Walla)

Walla Walla Valley

The black dashed lines represent the county borders.

The boom in Washington in both vineyard land and the number of wineries has been felt all over the state, but nowhere more noticeably than in Walla Walla, the region that has been generating the most excitement over the last few years.

The **Walla Walla appellation** can be described as a large 853 square kilometres (530 square miles) belt of agricultural land, made possible by irrigation, lying south of the Touchet River which meanders from the easterly defining Blue Mountains, flowing west and then south to join the Walla Walla River before it flows into the Columbia River just south of the Tri-Cities. The appellation crosses south into Oregon, near the city of Milton-Freewater, and close to the Umatilla Indian Reservation and the southern extension of the Blue Mountains. Like Washington's other eastern Washington appellations, Walla Walla is contained within the Columbia Valley AVA.

Geographic names in the area lend themselves to winery names: there really is a

Woodward Canyon, Spring Valley, Yellow Hawk Creek, Russell Creek, Mill Creek, Titus Creek, Patit Creek, the Palouse, and, of course, a Walla Walla River, all within the greater Walla Walla Basin and appellation.

The above names primarily represent new wineries (although not Woodward Canyon which was founded in 1981), which are all part of the tremendous growth this region has seen in the last five years. Of the thirty-five wineries scheduled to crush in the fall of 2001, nine of them will be commercially producing wine for the first time; seven of them began operations in 1999, and six more released their first wines in 2000. That's more or less a total of twenty-two new wineries in three years, which represents an increase of more than 50 per cent in the number of producers in Walla Walla over that time period.

Vineyard land has increased quickly as well, jumping from 180 hectares (450 acres) in 1999 to 485 hectares (1,200 acres) in 2001, and still growing. The varieties planted in Walla Walla include Cabernet Sauvignon, Merlot, Syrah, Cabernet Franc, Sangiovese, Grenache, Mourvèdre, Cinsault, Petit Verdot, Carmenère, and a small amount (36 hectares/90 acres total) of Chardonnay, Gewürztraminer, Viognier, and Muscat. Red varieties are overwhelmingly preferred, both in terms of vineyard acreage and production.

Walla Walla is one of the warmer agricultural areas of the state, with degree days in the 1,659 Centigrade (3,000 Fahrenheit) range. Average annual rainfall is about 48cm (19in), a bit higher than in other eastern Washington regions due to Walla Walla's proximity to the Blue Mountains on its eastern and southern flanks. And winter freeze is an issue here, too, especially as there isn't any large body of water like the Columbia River to mitigate the cold.

Farming has always played a very important role. As a group, Walla Walla County's farms are the oldest in the state. Wheat, peas, strawberries, alfalfa hay, and deservedly famous Walla Walla sweet onions grow in the region's rich volcanic soil. But with each year, vineyards are replacing other crops, now making grape growing the largest agricultural activity in the area.

Positioned at the eastern edge of the **geological events** that created the Columbia Gorge (see pages 170–1), the geography in the Walla Walla Basin was formed under the same dramatic conditions. Enormous basaltic lava flows established the foundation of the Columbia Plateau (which includes the Walla Walla Plateau).

Beginning about 15,000 years ago, periodic melting of ice dams to the east caused giant "glacier outbursts" approximately every 50 years. Enormous volumes of water burst through the dams, scouring out channels in the landscape where water speeds were fastest. When the floodwaters retreated, lakes were left behind, and fine-grained sediments were deposited.

Basically, the two types of soils found in the Walla Walla region are a direct result of those ancient geological events. On elevations below 366 metres (1,200ft) within the region, the soils are shallow silty loam, over caliche – small coarse gravel-like particles. Beneath that is an impervious rocky layer that remains from the ancient lakebed. Above 366metres (1,200ft) the soil's origins are windblown, with more blocky, angular particles, and better draining.

The first vineyard of modern times was planted by **Gary Figgins** of Leonetti Cellar in 1974, on the same, vineyard site that his two Leonetti uncles (Leonetti is the maiden name of Figgins' mother) had cultivated until the freeze of 1956 destroyed all the vines. The uncles' original vineyard sat on a hillside of only 183 metres (600ft) in elevation and was planted with Black Price, a variety resistant to powdery mildew, which produced a light red wine and is alleged to be another name for Cinsault.

But with each year, vineyards are replacing other crops, now making grape growing the largest agricultural activity in the area.

Water issues threaten Walla Walla farmers

The raging salmon, water, and power crisis that is plaguing the Northwest in 2001 has reached grape growing in Walla Walla. Steelhead salmon have become a major concern since the fish was listed as a threatened species in March 1999. Serious water and fish protection issues have converged on the entire Walla Walla basin, including the booming Walla Walla AVA. Players include the National Marine Fisheries Service and the US Fish and Wildlife Department, together with the Confederated Tribes of the Umatilla Indian Reservation, and several environmental groups led by the Center for Environmental Law and Policy in Seattle.

On the "other side" are Umatilla County (Oregon) and Columbia and Walla Walla Counties (Washington), as well as local farmers, irrigation districts, and other government groups. And grape growers have emerged as the largest farming group.

The political threat on the table is that the Endangered Species Act will take precedence over long established state water rights. The potential outcome could be to limit or even forbid irrigation of vineyards, potentially a death knell in dry eastern Washington.

The issues are complex. The source of the Walla Walla water problems is a 1934 Supreme Court case that divided the Columbia River water between Oregon and Washington, resulting in an over-appropriation of water by users in both states.

A negotiating group of all concerned parties continues to meet every few months to set up a one-year plan, and by 2002 there should be a consensus on exactly what needs to happen next. But one thing is for sure, irrigation will be more regulated. And while Walla Walla is certainly the current focus of concern, the pressure will not stop with a Walla Walla solution. The Walla Walla controversy and proposed solutions set an example that the environmentalists and water regulators hope will influence other water users in Washington and even other states: you could be next, so pay attention to how you treat the earth.

Figgins replanted the vineyard in 1974 with white Riesling and Cabernet Sauvignon. He placed the vines in 2.4 x 3 metres (8 x 10ft) spacing, trained in bilateral cordon, with catch wires for the floppy shoots. It was a dry-farmed vineyard, and provided many of the grapes Figgins used when he bonded his winery in 1977, making Leonetti Cellar the first wine producer in the Walla Walla Valley. It is now one of Washington's few cult producers whose fine wines are hotly sought as trophy wines. Figgins is best known for his well-structured, complex red wines. He also produced a Riesling from his vineyard until 1983, when the vineyard was sold and converted to other uses.

In 1977, Figgins planted 0.6 hectares (1.5 acres) of Merlot next to his Walla Walla home and winery. Spaced at 2.4 x 2.8 metres (8 x 9.5ft), the vines were initially trellised in a bilateral cordon, but later switched to Smart-Dyson to control vigour better. In 1993, Figgins bought another 1.2 hectares (3 acres) next to his property, and planted Syrah, Sangiovese, and Cabernet Franc, and has trained those vines in bilateral cordon and vertical shoot positioning.

Figgins' newest vineyard, planted in 2001, is a dry-farmed 6.3-hectare (15.5-acre) parcel called Mill Creek Upland, newly planted with Cabernet Sauvignon, Merlot, Sangiovese, and Petit Verdot. While he crops his other vineyards at about 35 hectolitres per hectare (2.5 tons per acre), he plans to reduce the Mill Creek Upland crop levels to under 14 hectolitres per hectare (1 ton per acre), intended for his reserve label wines.

Figgins does not grow all the grapes he needs. All his Cabernet Sauvignon wine is made from Walla Walla appellation fruit from his vineyards as well as contracted fruit. For his Merlot, he has long-term contracts with two very respected vineyards: Connor Lee on the Wahluke Slope and Sagemoor, north of Pasco.

Typically, most **Walla Walla producers**, like the majority of Washington's wineries, still use purchased grapes to make their wines, but they are now starting to look to Walla Walla for fruit as well. The region originally gained prominence because a number of top-flight wineries were based in the region, even though they bought fruit elsewhere. But Walla Walla is now becoming a region known for its vineyards.

People such as Norm McKibben, however, always saw the vineyard potential. His Seven Hills Vineyard (co-owned with Leonetti's Gary Figgins and L'Ecole's Marty Clubb, among others) and Pepper Bridge Vineyards have sold fruit to the state's top producers for years.

The first block of the Seven Hills Vineyard, located on the Oregon side of the appellation, was originally owned and planted by the McClellan and Hendricks families. The Seven Hills Vineyards were planted in 1980 in a fairly sloppy manner, with inconsistent spacing. The trellising was different as well, with a double cordon upward sprawl system of sorts.

The vineyard and neighbouring orchard were sold in 1994 to a group of wine producers including **Norm McKibben**, who manages the property. At the Seven Hills Vineyard, McKibben has interplanted vines to even the spacing, and has changed the trellising to a Smart-Dyson split canopy to help control the vigour. The vineyard sits on a slope between 869–360 metres (950–1180ft) of elevation, with very pebbly soils, a loam that is both free-draining and water-retaining. These now-planted 81 hectares (200 acres) at Seven Hills make up the appellation's largest vineyard.

Nearby, but just within the Washington border, McKibben planted another vineyard he called Pepper Bridge. A 4-hectares (10-acre) block was planted in 1991; a total of 75 hectares (185 acres) was planted by 1998, making Pepper Bridge the second largest vineyard in the Walla Walla appellation. This vineyard sits at 260 metres (850ft) of elevation, and was originally trellised on a Scott Henry system; in 1996 the vines were retrained on a Smart-Dyson method for better light control and canopy management. But when Dr Richard Smart came to look at the vineyards in 1997, he suggested that one 2-hectare (5-acre) block be kept on Scott-Henry to be able to track the differences.

Cabernet Sauvignon, Merlot, Syrah, Sangiovese, Cabernet Franc, and Malbec have been planted. A number of top wineries contract

by the acre for fruit, and most fruit is cropped under 56 hectolitres per hectare (4 tons per acre). Wineries such as Andrew Will, Cayuse, Dunham, Glen Fiona, Leonetti, Pepper Bridge, and Woodward Canyon buy from this vineyard.

28 hectares (70 acres) of McKibben's newest vineyard have just been planted. Les Collines is a 121-hectare (300-acre) site located 6.4km (4 miles) east of Walla Walla, with elevations up to 421 metres (1,380ft). Soils tend to be the wind-blown, high-mountain type. He has planted Syrah, Cabernet Sauvignon, and Merlot, and has not yet decided how to train the plants.

McKibben is also one of the newer Walla Walla producers. His **Pepper Bridge Winery** was

vineyards, the Cayuse Vineyards, stand out. The French-born Baron is passionate about the Rhône region of France and about Syrah in particular; he worked for a number of years as a "flying winemaker" in Australia, focusing on Shiraz. Baron marvelled at the rocky, cobblestoned land he found on the Oregon side of the appellation. His 25-hectare (10-acre) Cailloux Vineyard – planted with Syrah and Viognier in 1997 sits at 260 metres (850ft) of elevation on ancient riverbed soil: 30–46cm (12–18in) of silty loam on top of large, smooth rocks. The vines are planted in spacing of 1.2 x 3 metres (4 x 10ft), and trained in double cordon, vertical shoot positioning; the vines are only 30–46cm (12–18in) off the ground,

Among the other significant vineyards in the region, Christopher Baron's four organic vineyards, the Cayuse Vineyards, stand out.

capturing all the warmth of the cobblestones beneath them. Wine from this site, despite being made from very young fruit, shows a definite mineral quality.

The 1.6-hectare (4-acre) Coccinelle Vineyard, planted in 1998, sits closer to the foothills of the Blue Mountains at 287 metres (940ft). Its soil is not as rocky as the Cailloux Vineyard (there is more silty loam topsoil instead). The vines are planted and trained as those in the Cailloux Vineyard, but the wines are more minerally.

The En Cerise Vineyard's (3.6 hectares/9 acres), also planted in 1998, resemble Cailloux more, with very rocky soil covered by more sand-like, lighter topsoil. The wine from this vineyard is brighter, with strong berry fruit. To be fair, the fruit is still very young and needs more time to establish a taste of place, which can be said for all of Baron's wines from his own vineyards.

In 2000, Baron planted another (3.2 hectares/8 acres) nearby, at the En Chamberlin Vineyard. The soil here is pebbly silty loam, with two patches of cobblestones. Departing from the Rhône focus, Baron has planted Cabernet Sauvignon, Syrah, and Tempranillo (with cuttings from Earl Jones of Abacela in Oregon).

But Baron's latest vineyard is certainly his most ambitious. In 2001, he obtained 8 hectares (20 acres) of land near the Cailloux Vineyard and planted Grenache, Syrah, and Mourvèdre, hoping to ultimately make a Châteauneuf-du-

constructed in 2000. While he has always been vineyard focused, McKibben wants to prove to himself that the grapes he grows are indeed good. He also wants a legacy for his grandchildren, leaving them a quality brand of wine

Among the other **significant vineyards** in the region, Christopher Baron's four organic

Pape-style blend. The Grenache will be a challenge to keep alive in winter freezes, but Baron plans to bury the canes. He has planted all vines in a tight, with a massive 5,227 vines per hectare (2,178 vines per acre). He will aim for a crop load of about 28 hectolitres per hectare (2 tons per acre).

Baron's Cayuse Vineyards certainly produce very fine wine, but the winery stands in very good company in the Walla Walla appellation. Its high percentage of outstanding producers strongly competes with the greater Seattle area for the highest quality in the state. The "old guard" of wineries in Walla Walla includes Woodward Canyon, L'Ecole No 41, Leonetti, Seven Hills,

This is a glass of Viognier – can't you tell?

Waterbrook, and Canoe Ridge, the producers who established Walla Walla's enviable reputation for excellence.

The **"new kids"** include Cayuse, Dunham Cellars, Reininger Glen Fiona (owned by Gary Figgins' brother Berle "Rusty" Figgins, a major Rhône Ranger, the only exclusively Syrah producer in the state), Three Rivers Winery, Tamarack Cellars, Isenhower Cellars, Yellow Hawk, Palouse Cellars, and Walla Walla Vintners. Even Stimson Lane is starting to get into the Walla Walla act, with the construction of a new facility in downtown Walla Walla in 2001 for it's ultra-premium Merlot brand Northstar, which is currently produced in the Yakima Valley.

It's hard to keep up with the wineries in Walla Walla. The following producers have just set up shop, not even registering on anyone's radar screen yet, but may be names to watch: Buty Winery, Fort Walla Walla Cellars, Forgeron Cellars, Mill Creek Cellars, Morrison Lane Winery, Patit Creek Cellars, Rulo Winery, Titus Creek Winery, and Whitman Cellars.

This growth in the Walla Walla appellation is to be expected. Walla Walla itself is an ever-improving small town, with a fine undergraduate college. Quality restaurants and hotels have been opening steadily. Tourism is definitely rising. The Walla Walla appellation has always had a high reputation for quality and its success with focused, boutique-style wine production.

The winegrowers and winemakers of Walla Walla have established, in 2001, the Walla Walla Valley Wine Alliance, a non-profit association created to promote quality and excellence along with awareness of the Walla Walla Valley wine region. The Alliance will soon become an organized and unified marketing organization that will develop programmes and activities to enhance Walla Walla's reputation as a premier wine region.

Previously, members of the local industry organized informally and worked together on a volunteer basis. But with the phenomenal growth of the valley's wine industry, a more formal structure was deemed necessary. Impressively, virtually all wineries and vineyards participated in the creation of the Alliance.

Notable producers

Bunchgrass Winery

☎ 509-525-1492 📠 509-525-1492
📧 rocher@bmi.net
**151 Bunchgrass Lane, Walla Walla,
Washington 99362**
Acreage in production 0.4ha (1 acre)
Cabernet Sauvignon, 2.8ha (7 acres) Cabernet
Franc,0.1ha (0.3 acres) Merlot
Production capacity 350 cases
2000 production 350 cases
Established 1997
First wines released 1997 vintage
Retired educator Roger Cockerline planted
Merlot on the family farm in the early 1980s and
returned to the farm to locate a winery in the
former dairy barn. His two red wines (one a
Cabernet Sauvignon, the other a Merlot-Syrah
blend aged in American oak) show promise.

Canoe Ridge Vineyard

☎ 509-527-0885 📠 509-527-0886
📧 info@canoeridgevineyard.com
**1102 West Cherry Street, Walla Walla,
Washington 99362**
Acreage in production 30ha (75 acres)
Merlot, 19.4ha (48 acres) Cabernet Sauvignon,
5.3ha (13 acres) Chardonnay, 2ha (5 acres)
Cabernet Franc, 0.2ha (0.5 acres) Syrah
New plantings 8ha (20 acres) Merlot
Production capacity 45,000 cases
2000 production 38,000 cases
Established 1989
First wines released 1993 vintage
Owned by the Chalone Wine Group in
California and managed by talented winemaker
John Abbott, who was formerly the winemaker
at Acacia Winery in California (a property also
owned by Chalone). Most fruit comes from its
eponymous vineyard, located along the
Columbia River near Paterson. Merlot is the
standout wine, particularly the new reserve
bottlings.

Cayuse Vineyards

☎ 509-526-0686 📠 509-526-4686
📧 info@cayusevineyards.com
🌐 www.cayusevineyards.com
**17 E Main Street, Walla Walla,
Washington 99362**
Acreage in production 4.8ha (12 acres)
Syrah, 2ha (5 acres) Cabernet Sauvignon,
0.6ha (1.5 acres) Merlot, 0.4ha (1 acre)
Cabernet Franc

New plantings 1.2ha (3 acres) Syrah, 0.8ha
(2 acres) Cabernet Sauvignon, 1.2ha (3 acres)
Tempranillo, 1.2ha (3 acres) Grenache, 0.8ha
(1.5 acres) Syrah, 0.8ha (1.5 acres) Mourvèdre
Production capacity 2500 cases
2000 production 1800 cases
Established 1997
First wines released 1997 vintage
A former Australia-based "flying winemaker"
originally from the Champagne region of
France, Christophe Baron crafts particularly
good Syrahs and Viognier, which show definite
terroir variations. New Tempranillo, cropped at
28 hectolitres per hectare (2 tons per acre),
should be interesting to watch.

Colvin Cellars

☎ 509-525-7802 📠 509-525-7802
📧 colvinmj@bmi.net
🌐 www.colvinvineyards.com
**4130 Powerline Road, Walla Walla,
Washington 99362**
Acreage in production 4.8ha (12 acres)
Merlot, 3.2ha (8 acres) Cabernet Sauvignon,
1.6ha (4 acres) Cabernet Franc, 0.8ha (2 acres)

Carmenère, 1.2ha (3 acres) Syrah
New plantings 3.2ha (8 acres) Cabernet
Sauvignon
Production capacity 8,000 cases
2000 production 2,300 cases
Established 1999
First wines released 1999 vintage
New producer first releasing wines (a Merlot
and a Syrah) in the summer of 2001, from a
combination of purchased fruit and estate fruit
from vineyards planted by Mark Colvin in 1994.

Dunham Cellars

☎ 509-529-4685 📠 509-529-0201
📧 wine@dunhamcellars.com
🌐 www.dunhamcellars.com
**150 E Boeing Avenue, Walla Walla,
Washington 99362**
New plantings 0.4ha (1 acre) Syrah, 0.4ha (1
acre) Cabernet Sauvignon
Production capacity 5,000 cases
2000 production 3,650 cases
Established 1995
First wines released 1995 vintage
The former assistant winemaker at L'Ecole No

John Abbot of Canoe Ridge Vineyard

Gary Figgins of Leonetti Cellar

41, Eric Dunham now devotes his talents to his own brand (and also makes the wine for Trey Marie, see page 184). Dunham wines are big, oaky, concentrated wines, made for the long haul. The wines are produced at a temporary facility at the old Walla Walla airport until Eric's own winery is completed, located near Lowden on the Dunham family's old farm.

Glen Fiona

☎ 509-522-2566 ⓕ 509-526-5299
ⓔ syrah@glenfiona.com
ⓦ www.glenfiona.com
PO Box 2024, Walla Walla, Washington 99362
Acreage in production None
Production capacity 6,000 cases
2000 production 4,600 cases
Established 1995
First wines released 1995 vintage
Berle "Rusty" Figgins – brother of cult winemaker Gary Figgins of Leonetti Cellars – has championed varietally true, Syrah-based wines aged in neutral puncheons. The name Glen Fiona pays homage to the Figgins' family's Scottish-Irish heritage (in contrast to Gary Figgins' Italian – Leonetti – family reference).

Isenhower Cellars

☎ 509-386-6504 ⓕ 603-375-4669
ⓔ isenhowe@bmi.net
ⓦ www.isenhowercellers.com
2014 Mill Creek Road, Walla Walla, Washington 99362
New plantings 0.8ha (2 acres) Roussanne
Production capacity 8,000 cases
2000 production 2,600 cases
Established 1999
First wines released 1999 vintage
Originally known as Wildflower Winery, a trademark conflict with J Lohr Winery in California forced a name change. Brett Isenhower previously worked with the Canoe Ridge and Glen Fiona wineries. Isenhower's first wines – a Merlot and a Syrah made from grapes purchased through per acre contracts – were released in 2001. Isenhower's goal, ultimately, is to emphasize Syrah, Merlot, Primitivo, and Roussanne, as well as small amounts of Cabernet Sauvignon, Cinsault, Counoise, Grenache, Marsanne, and Sangiovese for blending purposes. A new winery is under construction.

L'Ecole No 41

☎ 509-525-0940 ⓕ 509-525-2775
ⓔ winery@lecole.com
ⓦ www.lecole.com
PO Box 111, 41 Lowden School Road, Lowden, Washingon 99360
Acreage in production 1.2 (3 acres) Sémillon, 1.6ha (4 acres) Syrah, 0.4ha (1 acre) Carmenère, 0.8ha (2 acres) Cabernet Franc, 3.2ha (8 acres) Merlot, 3.2ha (8 acres) Cabernet Sauvignon
Production capacity 25,000 cases
2000 production 20,000 cases
Established 1983
First wines released 1985 vintage
Founded by Jean and Baker Ferguson, the winery is now owned and operated by their daughter and son-in-law Megan and Martin Clubb. The original focus had been Merlot and barrel-fermented Sémillon, but small quantities of Cabernet Sauvignon, Chardonnay, and Chenin Blanc are also being produced. Most of the fruit has been sourced from the region's top vineyards. Wines show traditional, hands-off style, tightly focused and oak influenced.

Leonetti Cellar

☎ 509-525-1428 ⓕ 509-525-4006
ⓦ www.leonetticellar.com
1875 Foothills Lane, Walla Walla, Washington 99362
Acreage in production 4.5ha (11 acres) Cabernet Sauvignon, 1.6ha (4 acres) Merlot, 0.2ha (0.5 acres) Syrah, 0.6ha (1.5 acres) Sangiovese, 0.4ha (1 acre) Petit Verdot, 0.4ha (1 acre) Cabernet Franc. 58.2ha (144 acres), owned in partnership with Seven Hills Vineyard, mixed red varietals.
New plantings 5ha (12 acres) Cabernet Sauvignon, 3.2ha (8 acres) Merlot, 2ha (5 acres) Petit Verdot, 0.8ha (2 acres) Syrah, 0.4ha (1 acre) Sangiovese
Production capacity 20,000 cases
2000 production 5,500 cases
Established 1977
First wines released 1978 vintage
Gary Figgins has developed a national reputation; his big, mouth-filling (and age-worthy) wines always make it to the "top 100" lists of most publications. Figgins – using both his own vineyards and purchased fruit – blends single varietals from many different vineyards, believing in the sum of parts to build the most complexity; his Sangiovese, though, is blended

with Syrah. The oak regime is varied, with a range of American, French, Hungarian, Oregon, and Russian barrels in regular use. These wines are hard to find, sold primarily through a waiting list; to be placed on it, there is another waiting list!

Palouse Vineyards

☎ 509-529-8572

2014 Mill Creek Road, Walla Walla, Washington 99362

Acreage in production 1.2ha (3 acres) Cabernet Sauvignon, 1.4ha (3.5 acres) Syrah, 0.4ha (1 acre) Viognier

Production capacity 7,000 cases

2000 production 400 cases

Established 2000

First wines released 2000 vintage

Former Oregon utility executive (and wine collector) Ken Harrison and his wife Ginger purchased the Mill Creek Inn and established a winery on the premises. (Glen Fiona formerly used the barn for ageing his wines). Consulting winemaker Ron Coleman of Tamarack Cellars produced the first vintage of (estate) Cabernet Sauvignon and a Bordeaux-style blend. The wines will not be released until 2003.

Patrick M Paul Vineyards

☎ 509-526-0676 📠 509-526-0676

📧 paulte@wwics.com

1554 School Avenue, Walla Walla, Washington 99362

Acreage in production 1.2 (3 acres) Cabernet Franc planted in 1984

Production capacity 2,000 cases

2000 production 500 cases

Established 1988

First wines released 1990 vintage

Established producer especially noted for full-bodied, somewhat tannic Cabernet Franc, aged in American oak. Sales are primarily by mailing list.

Pepper Bridge Winery

☎ 509-525-6502 📠 509-525-9227

📧 info@pepperbridge.com

🌐 www.pepperbridge.com

1704 J B George Road, Walla Walla, Washington 99362

Acreage in production 22.2ha (55 acres) Cabernet Sauvignon, 5.6ha (14 acres) Merlot, 2.8ha (7 acres) Syrah

New plantings 32.3ha (80 acres) of Cabernet Sauvignon, 32.8ha (80 acres) Merlot, 16.2ha (40 acres) Syrah and a small amount of Sangiovese, Cabernet Franc, and Malbec

Production capacity 10,000 cases

2000 production 4,000 cases

Established 1999

First wines released 1998 vintage

Vineyard owner and manager Norm McKibben – also the long-time chairman of the Washington Wine Commission – hired former Heitz (Napa, California) winemaker Jean-François Pellet to be winemaker.

Reininger

☎ 509-522-1994 📠 509-522-3530

📧 email@reiningerwinery.com

🌐 www.reiningerwinery.com

PO Box 1576, 720 C Street, Walla Walla Regional Airport, Walla Walla, Washington 99362

New plantings 3.6ha (9 acres) Merlot, 3.2ha (8 acres) Cabernet Sauvignon

Production capacity 2,500 cases

2000 production 2,400 cases

Established 1997

First wines released 1997 vintage

Chuck Reininger purchased a 115 hectare (285-acre), irrigated site in 1999 and now produces wine at a facility at the old airport, next door to Tamarack Cellars. He makes stunning Cabernet Sauvignon, among the best in the state.

Berle "Rusty" Figgins of Glen Fiona

Norm McKibbin of Pepper Bridge Winery

Russell Creek Winery

☎ 509-386-4401 ☏ 509-522-6515

✉ krivoslg@wwics.com

🌐 rusellcreek-winery.com

1836 Brevor Drive, Walla Walla, Washington 99362

Production capacity 1,500 cases

2000 production 1,100 cases

Established: 1998

First wines released 1998 vintage

Larry Krivoshein has been an amateur winemaker since 1988; he began a small commercial operation in 1998, producing only a limited quantity of Cabernet Sauvignon and Merlot.

Seven Hills Winery

☎ 509-529-7198 ☏ 509-529-7733

✉ info@sevenhillswinery.com

🌐 www.sevenhillswinery.com

212 N Third Avenue, Walla Walla, Washington 99362

Production capacity 9,000 cases

2000 production 8,500 cases

Established 1988

First wines released 1988 vintage

Casey and Vicky McClellan joined the founders of Seven Hills Vineyard in 1988 to form Seven Hills Winery. Originally located near Milton-Freewater in Oregon (and then the only winery on the Oregon side of the appellation), the McClellans moved the winery to be nearer their Walla Walla colleagues. Casey received a Master's degree in enology from UC Davis and then spent time in Oporto making Port before returning to Walla Walla. Wines in production include pleasant single vineyard-designated Cabernet Sauvignon, Merlot, and Syrah, as well as Riesling, and Pinot Gris from Oregon.

Spring Valley Vineyard

☎ 800-210-4194 ☏ 509-337-6685

✉ info@springvalleyvineyard.com

🌐 www.springvalleyvineyard.com

1682 Corkrum Road, Walla Walla, Washington 99362

Acreage in production 7.3ha (18 acres) Merlot, 1.6ha (4 acres) Cabernet Franc, 0.8ha (2 acres) Petit Verdot, 0.6ha (1.5 acres) Syrah

New plantings 2.8ha (7 acres) Cabernet Sauvignon, 1.6ha (4 acres) Cabernet Franc, 0.8ha (2 acres) Syrah, 0.4ha (1 acre) Petit Verdot

Production capacity 5,000 cases

2000 production 1,000 cases

Established 1999

First wines released 1999 vintage

Shari and Dean Derby began to convert their family wheat farm to grapes in 1992 and a new winery was ready for the 1999 crush, their first. Walla Walla Vintners winemakers Myles Anderson and Gordon Venneri are Spring Valley's consulting winemakers.

Tamarack Cellars

☎ 509-526-3533 ☏ 509-526-4662

✉ ron@tamarackcellars.com

🌐 tamarackcellars.com

700 Central Street, Walla Walla Regional Airport, Walla Walla, Washington 99362

Production capacity 6,000 cases

2000 production 4,200 cases

Established 1998

First wines released 1998 vintage

Ron Coleman crafts lovely Merlot, Cabernet Sauvignon, and Syrah from top vineyards in Walla Walla, Red Mountain, and the Yakima Valley.

Three Rivers Winery

☎ 509-526-9463 ☏ 509-529-3436

✉ info@threeriverswinery.com

🌐 www.threeriverswinery.com

5641 W Highway 12, Walla Walla, Washington 99362

Acreage in production 4.5ha (11 acres) Cabernet Sauvignon, 0.4ha (1 acre) Syrah, 2.4ha (6 acres) Gewürztraminer, 0.4ha (1 acre) Cabernet Franc

Production capacity 15,000 cases

2000 production 12,000 cases

Established 1999

First wines released 1999 vintage

Partners Steve Ahler, Duane Wollmuth, and Bud Stocking hired winemaker Charlie Hoppes, the former head red winemaker at Chateau Ste Michelle's Canoe Ridge facility, to produce a range of delicious wines, with an emphasis on red varieties.

Trey Marie Winery

☎ 509-529-1371 📠 509-529-0201
✉ wine@treymarie.com
🌐 www.treymarie.com
150 E Boeing Avenue, Walla Walla,
Washington 99362
New plantings 0.4ha (1 acre) Cabernet
Franc, 1.6ha (4 acres) Syrah, 1.6ha (4 acres)
Cabernet Sauvignon
2000 production 7,000 cases
Established 1998
First wines released 1998 vintage
A joint project between the Dunham and Syre
families, Eric Dunham crafts a blended wine
called Trutina, designed to be a different blend
of grapes each vintage, in contrast to his single
varietal focus as winemaker at Dunham Cellars.

Walla Walla Vintners

☎ 509-525-4724 📠 509-525-4134
✉ mjanders@bmi.net
🌐 www.wallawallavintners.com
PO Box 1551, 225 Vineyard Lane & Mill

Creek Road, Walla Walla, Washington
99362
Production capacity 2,500 cases
2000 production 2,500 cases
Established 1995
First wines released 1995 vintage
Myles Anderson and partner Gordon Venneri
produce handcrafted, high quality red wines –
Cabernet Franc, Cabernet Sauvignon, and
Merlot – aged in a combination of American
and French oaks. The two winemakers
produced hom- crafted wines for 10 years
before making commercial wines.

Waterbrook Winery

☎ 509-522-1262 📠 509-529-4770
✉ waterbrook.com
🌐 www.waterbrook.com
31 E Main, Walla Walla,
Washington 99362
Acreage in production 5.3ha (13 acres)
Chardonnay
Production capacity 40,000 cases
2000 production 25,000 cases

Established 1984
First wines released 1984 vintage
Eric and Janet Rindal operate Walla Walla's
largest winery, producing solid barrel-
fermented Chardonnay, Sauvignon Blanc,
Merlot, Cabernet Sauvignon, Viognier, and two
red blends, made with fruit primarily from Red
Mountain vineyard sites.

Woodward Canyon Winery

☎ 509-525-4129 📠 509-522-0927
✉ info@woodwardcanyon.com
🌐 www.woodwardcanyon.com
11920 W Highway 12, Lowden,
Washington 99360
Acreage in production 3ha (7.4 acres)
Merlot, 1ha (2.5 acres) Chardonnay, 2.5ha (6.5
acres) Cabernet Sauvignon, 2.2ha (5.5 acres)
Cabernet Franc, 0.9ha (2.3 acres) Barbera
New plantings 0.2ha (0.5 acres) Sauvignon
Blanc, 0.5ha (1.2 acres) Dolcetto
Production capacity 20,000 cases
2000 production 15,000 cases
Established 1981
First wines released 1981 vintage
Walla Walla pioneer Rick Small has developed
a strong following for his small production. lots
of barrel-fermented Chardonnay, toasty
Cabernet Sauvignon, and rich Merlot wines.
Wines in the past perhaps showed too much
new oak influence, but in the more recent
vintages, oak seems more judiciously used and
better integrated.

Yellow Hawk Cellar

☎ 509-529-1714 📠 509-526-4201
✉ hetrick@bmi.net
395 Yellow Hawk Street, Walla Walla,
Washington 99362
Production capacity 600 cases
2000 production 540 cases
Established 1998
First wines released 1998 vintage
Tim Sampson worked at Canoe Ridge
Vineyards through 1999. In 1998, he made a
small lot of good Sangiovese, purchasing
grapes from Seven Hills Vineyard. He also
makes a pleasant off-dry Muscat Cannelli.

Rick Small of Woodward Canyon Winery

Vintages

The primary growing areas of Washington all lie east of the mountains in a desert-like landscape, transformed into an agricultural wonderland through irrigation. Weather varies little across the region; water is controlled and rain isn't a real threat. As a result, like many regions of California, there is little vintage variation in Washington. The bigger threat to a successful harvest is a cold winter freeze that can devastate grapevines and lower the yields of the harvest that follows.

Some vintages are indeed a bit better than others. But there really have neither been terrible years, nor terrible grapes. The wines get better and better because the vines mature and the farmers learn more about growing grapes. That's exactly what makes Washington such a dependably good wine-producing state.

2000 Across all of the growing regions, this was a wonderfully long growing season and marvellous vintage. There was an extended period for the grapes to hang on the vine, allowing flavour maturity (phenolics) to catch up with the sugar ripeness. The result was a particularly large crop, which produced dark, concentrated red wines and fresh, balanced whites. This was the first year that more red varieties were harvested than white. Most wines offer immediate pleasure; most also have the ability to age.

1999 An extended ripening period during a very warm and dry September delivered a crop with perfectly balanced levels of natural acidity and rich, ripe flavours. The overall yield was down due to green harvesting during the long, cool summer in anticipation of an equally cool autumn and the possibility of unripe grapes (fortunately, an unrealized threat). The fruitier, lighter wines should be consumed soon, but most of the big reds need a little more time in the bottle and will age well.

1998 This year's yield and quantity topped the charts: full, even ripening yielded balanced sugars and acids, while increased acreage bumped up the total harvest. The wines are very big and delicious. Drink most now, but the top bottles will hold nicely.

1997 Growers were delighted with this year's rebound with twice the tonnage of the previous year. Mild temperatures meant even ripening. Although this was not a blockbuster year, it has produced pleasant, easy-to-drink wines ready for consumption.

1996 An unusually harsh, freezing winter severely reduced the crop by roughly half of what was expected. Red varieties – Merlot in particular – were affected most, but a mild spring and a hot summer nurtured good-quality grapes. What wine was produced shows deep concentration and richness; the reds will continue to age nicely.

1995 Moderate weather extended the growing season and resulted in a good harvest of excellent quality. Both reds and whites are drinking well now and will last until 2005, and beyond for the better structured wines.

1994 A cool spring followed by a hot mid-summer led to an early harvest and lower crop levels than the previous year. The warmth produced small grapes and clusters with intensified flavours. The wines boast super concentration and big varietal character, but most lack a firm structure and finesse. Drink most wines soon for the best pleasure.

1993 A warm finish to an unusually cool summer allowed fruit to reach ripeness. Mild winters the previous years and the maturing of several new vineyards combined to yield a record crop. Red wines are softly pleasant; white varietals approach the benchmark quality of 1983 and 1989.

1992 The crop averaged just over 56 hectolitres per hectare (4 tons per acre) and the grapes hung heavy and ripe in the early autumn, with excellent colour and low to moderate tannins thanks to the gentle winter, mild spring, and hot summer. Most wines are approaching term, with enough structure to last only another few years.

1991 A severely icy winter freeze gave way to a cool, wet spring. A dry summer and warm harvest season saved the vintage. The result was dramatically reduced vineyard yields, and one of the state's best years for white wines with solid acid levels and full flavours.

1990 A fairly classic, by-the-book growing season, except for cool weather at flowering that reduced the crop. Washington whites drinking well now, but the reds still have enough oomph to keep going.

Other notable vintages: 1989, 1988, 1987, 1985, and 1983

Acknowledgements

It has taken me years to understand and fully appreciate the wines of this beautiful region, my Pacific Northwest.

Along the way, far too many people to name offered me good advice, explained the whys and hows, and made me privy to the trials and errors of grape growing and wine making in a dynamic developing region.

Many people have provided personal insights as well as data; wines to enjoy and wines to analyze. Even more have been willing to argue with me, challenge my conclusions, and make me thoroughly learn concepts that, without their help with practical experience and exposure, would have only had hollow meaning for me.

I could not have come to understand Oregon without David Adelsheim and Dick Erath as my guides. Additionally, Alan Campbell, Bill Hatcher, David Lett, Harry Peterson-Nedry, Dick Ponzi, Myron Redford, Doug Tunnell, and Ken Wright provided support, details, and loads of invaluable perspectives. I am additionally indebted to the many Oregon wine producers who have always welcomed me to their wineries and opened their doors and bottles for my research.

In Washington, Steve Burns and his attentive staff at The Washington Wine Commission made my work far easier than it would have been, cheerfully and efficiently providing drop-everything access to anyone and every detail. Additionally, Bob Betz MW, David Lake MW, Keith Love, Doug McCrea, Norm McKibben, and Kay Simon provided insight and advice above and beyond anything that I requested. There isn't a producer in the state who refused me information, helping me to better understand the vast range and depth of what Washington has to offer.

I owe many thanks to Cyril Penn, my editor at Wine Business Monthly and the weekly Wine Business Insider, who has allowed me to write extensively about the Pacific Northwest over the past several years, and who has been patient while I have been distracted writing this book. My gratitude also goes to Jancis Robinson MW for her on-going encouragement.

But most of my indebtedness is saved for Kirk, my long-suffering other half, without whom this book could not have been written. Years ago, he begged me to pay more attention to the wine regions in my backyard, and he strongly encouraged me to write this book. He believed in me, and still does. Always the questioning voice in my head, my most-demanding editor and critic, Kirk is my muse, and simply, my best friend.

Bibliography

Cass, Bruce, Editor, The Oxford Companion to the Wines of North America (Oxford University Press, 2000)

Casteel, Ted, Editor, Oregon Winegrape Grower's Guide (Oregon Winegrowers' Association, Fourth Edition, 1992)

Clark, Corbet, American Wines of the Northwest (William Morrow, 1989)

Gregutt, Paul, Prather, Jeff, and McCarthy, Dan Northwest Wines (Sasquatch Books, 1996)

Hill, Chuck, The Gourmet's Guide to Northwest Wines & Wineries (Speed Graphics, 1998)

Irvine, Ron and Clore, Walter J, The Wine Project (Sketch Publications, 1997)

Johnson, Hugh and Robinson, Jancis, The World Atlas of Wine (Mitchell Beazley, 2001)

Peterson-Nedry, Judy and Reynolds, Robert M, Oregon Wine Country (Graphic Arts Center Publishing Company, 1998)

Peterson-Nedry, Judy and Reynolds, Robert M, Washington Wine Country (Graphic Arts Center Publishing Company, 2000)

Pintarich, Paul, The Boys Up North (The Wyatt Group, 1997)

Purser, J Elizabeth and Allen, Lawrence J, The Winemakers of the Pacific Northwest (Harbor House, 1977)

Robinson, Jancis, Guide to Wine Grapes (Oxford University Press, 1996)

Robinson, Jancis, Vines, Grapes and Wines (Mitchell Beazley, 1986, reprinted 1996)

Robinson, Jancis, Editor, The Oxford Companion to Wine (Oxford University Press, second edition, 1999)

Reports

Economic Impact of the Washington State Wine and Wine Grape Industries (Motto, Kryla & Fisher LLP, 2001)

The Grape in Western Oregon (Oregon Agricultural Experiment Station, Oregon Agricultural College Printing Office, 1901)

Oregon Agriculture and Fisheries Statistics (Oregon Department of Agriculture, 2001)

Oregon Winery Report (Oregon Agricultural Statistics Services, 2000)

Index

Picture Credits

All photographs are by Reuben Paris apart from the following:

10-1 RootStock/Hendrik Holler; **31, 42-3** John A. Rizzo; **52-3** Cephas/Mick Rock; **55** courtesy Cooper Mountain Vineyard, photo Kathryn Allenby Brock; **66-7** Steven Morris Photography; **69** courtesy Willamette Valley Vineyard, photo Robert M. Reynolds; **71** John A. Rizzo; **72-3** Steven Morris Photography; **76** Cephas/R & K Muschenetz; **80** courtesy of Oregon Wine Report; **81** courtesy King Estate, photo John A. Rizzo; **89, 91** Cephas/Mick Rock; **93** courtesy Foris Vineyards Winery, photo Richard Gross; **96** Cephas/Mick Rock; **99** courtesy The Academy Vineyard; **101, 103** courtesy Hood River Vineyards, photo Anne Lerch; **138** courtesy McCrea Cellars, photo Robert M. Reynolds/Wulf Design Inc; **146** courtesy Chinook Wines, photo Susan Marionneaux; **148** courtesy Washington Hills Cellars; **149** Cephas/R & K Muschenetz; **152-3** Cephas/Mick Rock; **158-9** Steven Morris Photography; **165** courtesy Brightworks Communications, photo Don Hamilton; **167, 171, 180** Cephas/Mick Rock.